CW00819668

GODFATHER
OF THE
REVOLUTION

**By the same author
and published by Peter Owen**

Hitler's Loss:
What Britain and America Gained
from Europe's Cultural Exiles

GODFATHER
OF THE
REVOLUTION
THE LIFE OF PHILIPPE ÉGALITÉ, DUC D'ORLÉANS

TOM AMBROSE

PETER OWEN PUBLISHERS
LONDON AND CHESTER SPRINGS, PA, USA

PETER OWEN PUBLISHERS
73 Kenway Road, London SW5 0RE

Peter Owen books are distributed in the USA by
Dufour Editions Inc., Chester Springs, PA 19425-0007

First published in Great Britain 2008 by
Peter Owen Publishers

© Tom Ambrose 2008

All rights reserved. No part of this publication may be
reproduced in any form or by any means without the written
permission of the publishers.

ISBN 978-0-7206-1301-8

Printed and bound in Great Britain by
Windsor Print Production Ltd, Tonbridge

Every effort has been made to contact owners of copyright
material. The author and publishers regret if there are missing
acknowledgements; if copyright holders contact the publishers
with these they will be included in future editions.

Picture acknowledgements on plates: Musée Condé, Chantilly
(pages 2, 7); Château de Versailles, Versailles (pages 3 top and bottom, 10 top);
Private Collections (pages 4 bottom, 6); Houghton Library, Harvard University
(page 5 top); Musée Carnavalet, Paris (pages 5 bottom, 12 top); Archives
Nationales, Paris (pages 8, 10 top, 16); Bibliothèque Nationale, Paris
(pages 11 top, 15 top); Collection Roger-Viollet (page 14)

For Gabriel,
born on 14 July

PREFACE

O F THE MILLIONS of tourists who visit the Louvre every year few venture a hundred metres beyond to the great house and gardens of the Palais-Royal. Yet in the last two decades of the eighteenth century this Paris seat of the Orléans family was the most politically significant building in all Europe. Here the ideas of radical political change were distilled into action and revolution, and from the gardens of the Palais-Royal the Paris mob marched out to demolish the Bastille and begin the process that saw the overthrow of the monarchy and the birth of democratic government in France.

Their actions had been promoted and funded by one of the most extraordinary figures in European history, Louis Philippe Joseph, fifth Duc d'Orléans, prince and revolutionary. This man, later to be given the name Philippe Égalité, was born to almost unimaginable wealth and splendour as the Bourbon First Prince of the Blood. A cousin of the French King Louis XVI, he married the richest heiress in Europe, becoming the owner of one-tenth of all France.

Why then did he abandon this life of luxury and debauchery to become the promoter, paymaster and first figurehead of the French Revolution? What is certain is that after the monarchy was overthrown he could have become the leader of the new, democratic France. The second mystery of his life is why he decided to vote in the new National Convention for the conviction and execution of the King, so losing popular favour and becoming the most despised figure in France and a pariah to the aristocracy of Europe.

This book attempts to explain why he acted as he did and to show that he was not the unprincipled maverick driven purely by personal hatred of the court at Versailles that many of his contemporaries thought him. When scrutinized in the light of subsequent events, Philippe Égalité can now be seen as a key figure in understanding the discontent and agitation that led inevitably to the French Revolution. Certainly, without the backing of his vast wealth the campaign against the despotism of Versailles could not have been so well organized and promoted. That the man who urged the mob to action on 14 July 1789 was Camille Desmoulins, a beneficiary of Philippe Égalité, is no surprise; for many of the leading radical figures who would later play important roles in the revolution were in his pay or employed by him at the Palais-Royal. One of the most important was his secretary, the enigmatic political activist Pierre Choderlos de Laclos, author of one the most celebrated novels in literary history, *Les Liaisons dangereuses*. Alongside Laclos worked dozens of other highly talented journalists, political schemers and agitators determined to change fundamentally French society. Surrounded by the splendour and luxury of inherited privilege, great paintings, liveried servants and elaborate manners, they exchanged ideas and plotted to make their patron the first democratic king of France with a constitution based on concepts of freedom derived from the works of Voltaire, Rousseau and the *encyclopédistes*. From Paris these revolutionary ideas were transmitted to members of Freemasonry lodges throughout France, preparing the way for the revolution to come.

When discontent finally exploded into violence Philippe Égalité was perfectly placed to earn his just reward as the courageous leader of opposition to the King. Why did he, then, to everyone's surprise appear so arrogantly to decline the role of head of the democratic National Convention? Was it out of cowardice, or had he developed a suspicion of democratic bureaucracy? Whatever the reason, his failure to act decisively placed him in increasing danger, for in such volatile times to hesitate was to risk disaster. Realizing that he had made a calamitous mistake in not accepting the challenge offered him, he belatedly attempted to recover his position by throwing in his lot with the Jacobin extremists and their determination to rid France of its monarchy. Yet he need not have voted for the conviction and execution of his cousin and could have abstained as others did.

Inevitably his involvement in the regicide brought him universal execration throughout Europe. That a man, and a French prince at that, could act in this apparently heartless manner towards a member of his own family appeared inexplicable to even the most committed liberals throughout Europe. What is certain, however, is that he voted for the execution of the King from conviction rather than from cowardice. Abandoned by most of his friends and betrayed by his supporters, he became an isolated figure in the political turmoil that followed the fall of the monarchy, as Girondin and Jacobin competed for power. Why, then, did he not escape to America as his family urged him? When his eldest son, the future King Louis Philippe, took his troops and went over to the royalist exiles threatening France his father was doomed. Denounced by Robespierre in the Convention, Philippe Égalité awaited his inevitable conviction and execution with characteristic courage.

Perhaps the greatest enigma of all is why this man brought up as a French prince, with a limited education and with little or no contact with ordinary people, could develop an open mind and, uniquely for his time and background, a social conscience. Yet he clearly appreciated the new ideas of democracy that were spreading throughout France and came to realize the need for a fundamental change that would bring about a more democratic and socially just society. Although he was, in character, withdrawn and aloof, this genuine commitment to principle explains why he attracted the leading liberals of his age. Among them was his mistress, Félicité de Genlis, the greatest female intellectual and educator of her age, and the black composer and swordsman the Chevalier de Saint-Georges, who joined him in founding the first anti-slavery society in France.

Philippe Égalité's undoubted honesty, coupled with his

bold political actions, made him the hero of the people and a ready-made substitute for the despotic Louis XVI. A man of unusual physical bravery, he risked his life in one of the first balloon ascents in history, acting with the same determination with which he challenged the power of the King in the open assembly of the Estates General. This characteristic bold approach to events also led him to embark on one of the most remarkable building projects of the late eighteenth century: the transformation of the gardens of the Palais-Royal into the first modern shopping centre in history.

At a time when England was seen as France's natural enemy, he provoked controversy by championing everything English, from that country's democratic political system to the cut of an English coat or the quality of English racing bloodstock. To Philippe Égalité Britain was the free and peaceful society to which the new France should aspire and for which he would gladly abandon his inherited privileges. This love of England was so profound that he even purchased a house in London and spent as much time as he could in the company of his friend George, Prince of Wales. As he told his last mistress, the Scottish courtesan Grace Dalrymple Elliott, 'I would gladly exchange all that I have for the quiet life of an English country gentleman.' This bold Anglophilia made him increasingly feared and despised by the court at Versailles, annoying Louis XVI and enraging Queen Marie Antoinette, who became his bitterest enemy.

The more one considers his life the more unusual it appears, for no other prince in history embarked on such an odyssey that led from a royal palace to the execution block. No less mystifying was his character, for behind the polished aristocratic disdain that he always displayed was a kind and tolerant person who was able to combine an aristocrat lifestyle with a genuine enthusiasm for radical politics. Never a wholehearted member of the French court, he was equally a stranger to the revolutionary world, where his strange provenance always aroused suspicion. But if a man is to be judged by his actions and not his words, Philippe Égalité passes the test of a true revolutionary with flying colours. Before opposition to despotism became the accepted norm in France he boldly took the lead and in the Estates General as in the later Convention stood up to be counted. That his eldest son Louis Philippe, the best-educated monarch in history, eventually became the first and only democratic King of the French is a tribute to the ideas of freedom that he derived from his father.

In recent years French historians such as Evelyne Lever have begun to reassess Philippe Égalité's importance as well as to consider in more depth the complicated motives that brought about his own self-destruction. It is hoped that this book will introduce British readers to his story, for he remains a unique and fascinating figure in European as well as French history; for, as Thomas Carlyle wrote, 'Probably no mortal ever had such things recorded of him: such facts and also such lies. For he was a Jacobin Prince of the Blood; consider what a combination!'

Contents

Preface 7
List of Illustrations 15
1 Prince of the Blood 19
2 The Libertine 37
3 The Palais-Royal 47
4 Freemasons 57
5 At Sea 67
6 The Developer 79
7 London 89
8 The Intrepid Balloonist 99
9 Leader of the Notables 109
10 Hero of the Hour 119
11 Laclos 127
12 The Estates General 137
13 The Paymaster 147
14 Revolution 155
15 Versailles 163
16 The Diplomat 173
17 Strained Relationships 181
18 Flight to Varenne 191
19 Égalité 201
20 Dilemmas 215
21 The Regicide 225
22 Death and Dishonour 237
Bibliography 249
Index 255

ILLUSTRATIONS BETWEEN
PAGES 144 AND 145

The coat of arms of the Duc d'Orléans
Louis Philippe Joseph, Duc d'Orléans in 1789
Louis Philippe Joseph's cousin, Louis XVI
Louis XVI's wife, Marie Antoinette
Pierre Choderlos de Laclos, political secretary to Louis Philippe
    Joseph and author of *Les Liaisons dangereuses*
The galleries of the Palais-Royal, the Paris seat of the Orléans
    family, *c.* 1785
Historic descent of Louis Philippe Joseph in the Robert brothers'
    balloon, December 1783
Gardens of the Palais-Royal after the great renovation scheme of
    Louis Philippe Joseph and his architect Victor Louis
The courtesan Rosalie Duthé, first of Louis Philippe Joseph's
    many mistresses
Louise Marie Adélaïde de Bourbon, Duchesse de Chartres, Louis
    Philippe Joseph's wife
Louis Philippe Joseph with his children and their governess
    Madame de Genlis, *c.* 1774
Félicité de Genlis, Louis Philippe Joseph's mistress and the
    leading educationist of her age
The little school at Belle Chasse, near Paris, founded by Madame
    de Genlis in 1777 to educate Louis Philippe Joseph's children
    with her own
Harp lesson given by Madame de Genlis to Mademoiselle
    d'Orléans, Louis Philippe Joseph's daughter
Depiction of the Réveillon riots that broke out in Paris in April
    1789, three months before the storming of the Bastille
A contemporary newspaper account of the storming of the Bastille
    that marked the start of the French Revolution on 14 July 1789
'To Versailles!' The women of Paris lead the march to the Palace
    of Versailles to bring the Royal Family back to Paris

French troops uniting with the Paris mob in revolutionary fervour
at the overthrow of the King

Illustrations from a contemporary pack of playing cards, depicting
revolutionary values

Louis Philippe Joseph brandishing the head of Louis XVI on the
steps of the scaffold – a contemporary English print blaming
Philippe Égalité for his part in his cousin's trial and execution

Last known image of Louis Phillipe Joseph in prison

A coin issued to commemorate the execution of Louis Philippe on
6 November 1793

Philippe's son, Louis Philippe, Duc de Chartres and future King
of the French, in officer's uniform, 1792

I

PRINCE OF THE BLOOD

NEVER HAS A man been born into greater splendour and died in more ignominy than Louis Philippe Joseph, fifth Duc d'Orléans, better known to history as Philippe Égalité. So important was his arrival at the Palace of Saint-Cloud near Paris on a spring morning in 1747 that a messenger was immediately sent to inform the King at Versailles a few miles away. For this child, given the courtesy title of Duc de Montpensier, would be fourth in line to the French throne and a Prince of the Blood, a direct descendant in the male line of past Kings of France. He would also be heir to the vast estates of the Orléans dynasty, the equivalent of three modern French *départements*. But as the historian Amédée Britsch has written, 'Philippe would be the fruit of passion rather than of reason.'

Saint-Cloud, presided over by the boy's father, the Duc de Chartres, was then almost as magnificent as the great Palace of Versailles itself, with majestic stone courtyards and a vast marble salon decorated with paintings by Mignard that rivalled the Hall of Mirrors. The wealth that had built Saint-Cloud is almost unimaginable today, for even the greatest of English country houses of the time seemed modest in comparison. Yet this vast palace was but one of a dozen Orléanist mansions scattered throughout the Île-de-France and Picardy. Given by the crown to Monsieur, the dissolute brother of the Sun King, Louis XIV, it had passed to his son Philippe, the second Duc d'Orléans. This brilliant military commander had been Regent of France during the minority of the present king, Louis XV, and in what was to become a family tradition had become notorious as one of the most immoral reprobates of the age. The father of many bastards, he was widely rumoured to have practised black magic and, more dangerously, intrigued with the English enemy. This may well have been true for, unusually for a Frenchman, he openly admired England and all things English, a characteristic that would later be displayed with even greater intensity in his great-grandson, Louis Philippe Joseph.

The Regent's son, the new arrival's grandfather and third Duc d'Orléans, had proved to be the odd man out in this most eccentric of families. Unlike his father and his son, he was a gentle and scholarly soul of such saintly demeanour that he became known as 'Louis the Pious'. Revered by the common people of Paris for his unstinted generosity, particularly in the times of famine that had plagued France for the past century, he had, by the time of his grandson's birth, long retired from the world to lead a life of simple contemplation with the monks at the Abbey of Sainte-Geneviève near Saint-Cloud. Leaving the management of his estates to others, he devoted himself to a rigorous study of natural science and ancient philosophies, in the course of which he mastered the archaic languages of Aramaic, Syriac and Hebrew. Moreover his research into ancient philosophy led him to some very odd beliefs, the most bizarre of which was his certainty that death was merely an illusion and that the dead might return at any moment. This strange delusion even led him to continue to pay a pension to a female retainer long after her death in the conviction that the old lady might reappear at any minute.

More damagingly to his family, he was also convinced that his son, the present Duc de Chartres, was physically incapable of fathering a child. Consequently he regarded the arrival of little Louis Philippe Joseph with the deepest suspicion, his scepticism appearing fully justified when one day, soon after the birth, a peasant woman leapt out of the bushes in the abbey grounds and fell at his feet claiming to be the real mother of the new Orléans heir. Accordingly Louis the Pious refused to send even a congratulatory note to his son at Saint-Cloud, and when complimented on the happy event by the

Queen through her envoy M. de Chalmazel, Louis replied enigmatically, 'Sir, thank Her Majesty for her kind words, whatever the truth of the matter.' When the Queen told her husband of this odd remark she added a mock warning that if His Majesty was ever tempted, like the mad duke, to retreat to the Sainte-Geneviève she would immediately enter the Carmelite order herself!

This strange recluse finally died in 1752, still believing that his grandson was an impostor. Just forty-eight years old, he was already prematurely aged by a life of self-denial. Yielding to his confessor's pleas, he grudgingly agreed to receive his infant grandchildren for a final audience before promptly dying of a heart attack. True to his scientific beliefs and convinced that a man should be useful to others even in death, he left instructions that his mortal remains be passed to the Paris anatomists for dissection. Curiously he did not find this incompatible with his firm conviction that death was transitory and that the deceased would soon reappear in a different guise. His funeral at the Church of Val-de-Grâce complemented the simplicity of his life, as did his many legacies. To the monks of Sainte-Geneviève he left his modest furniture and his much-cherished laboratory equipment; to his doctor he passed a cabinet containing an impressive collection of fossils and botanical specimens. A tormented soul, he had throughout his life displayed the altruism that was the obverse side of the Orléans character. In death he remained revered by the common people of Paris, who flocked to his funeral in a moving tribute to a royal prince who had chosen the life of a simple monk. His bond with the people would have an uncanny resonance thirty years later when his grandson experienced the same popularity, leading him to the very steps of the throne of France.

The new head of the family could not have made a greater contrast with his saintly and eccentric father. Known as 'Philippe the Fat', he represented a return to the Orléans tradition of extravagance and debauchery. Lazy and unprincipled, he was given to a life devoted to hunting by day and gambling and dissipation by night. Then suddenly and unexpectedly he fell in love and abandoned a life of pleasure for one of constancy. The object of this devotion was Louise Henriette de Bourbon Conti, daughter of the formidable and ambitious Princesse de Conti. Educated in an exceptionally strict convent, Louise Henriette had emerged into French society as an attractive young woman. Her fine looks and noble bearing had even attracted the Venetian adventurer Giacomo Casanova when he visited Paris. He described her in his memoirs as the most charming girl he had met in France. The Contis, like their cousins and fellow Princes of the Blood, the Condés, were considered by their contemporaries to be a family with even more questionable morals than the Orléans themselves. More importantly, Louise Henriette's father, the Prince de Conti, was deeply unpopular at court, having led the early opposition to the arbitrary power of Louis XV – a role that Louis Philippe Joseph was later destined to fulfil.

Captivated by Louise Henriette's beauty, 'Philippe the Fat' set his reservations aside and in November 1743 formally asked the King's permission – as required by every Prince of the Blood – to marry her. The King consented, and bride and groom appeared together at Versailles a month later, he dressed in cloth of gold and she in silver brocade. After the ceremony, attended by the entire court, the newlyweds had the honour of being formally escorted to their marriage bed by the King and Queen. The following morning, as was the custom, the court assembled to watch them dress, for little was done in private at Versailles.

Unusually for an age when cynicism and dynastic considerations prevailed over emotion, their union appeared, at first, to be a true love match. The besotted Duc de Chartres confessed to feeling such passion in the presence of his young bride that his entire body felt as if it was on fire. This passion was certainly reciprocated, and the lovers appeared, to the amusement of the courtiers around them, to be physically obsessed with each other to the point of abnormality. So passionate was their behaviour in public that, even in this most sensual of societies, many declared themselves shocked by it. One observer, the Duchesse de Tallard, wryly commented that they were making married love seem positively indecent! A year later this emotion seemed undimmed, for even when they were parted by the Duc's military duties in the War of the Austrian Succession they wrote passionate and erotic love letters to each other every day. Perhaps inspired by his love for Louise Henriette the young Duc performed the part of the warrior prince so valiantly that he was awarded the Order of Saint Louis by the King and promoted to Lieutenant General of the army. When campaigning ended for the winter, as was customary in the warfare of the mid-eighteenth century, the lovers were restored to each other at Saint-Cloud. It proved a productive season, for by the following spring Louise Henriette was six months pregnant. Nevertheless, she still insisted on accompanying her husband when campaigning resumed.

On 13 July 1746 their first child, a daughter, was born, to the ill-concealed disappointment of her father. However, the child soon died and the following year Louise Henriette fell pregnant again, this time with the future Louis Philippe Joseph. When her confinement was safely completed, Louise Henriette again insisted on accompanying her husband on campaign, leaving her baby to be cared for at Saint-Cloud by a retinue that consisted of no fewer than three wet nurses, five nursemaids and two male valets. Chartres, delighted to have produced an heir, continued his military success and was further rewarded with the governorship of the Dauphiné province. When the war finally ended, in October 1748, with the Peace of Aix-la-Chapelle, the young Duc and Duchesse de Chartres, now much in favour at court, returned to Saint-Cloud. Here they began entertaining the French aristocracy in a style said to be worthy of the King's influential mistress, Madame de Pompadour.

As both shared the contemporary aristocratic passion for amateur drama, the little theatre at Saint-Cloud was completely renovated and soon became a great attraction for the court at nearby Versailles. Chartres himself displayed an unsuspected talent for acting, making his début as Rondon in Voltaire's new play, *L'Enfant prodigue*. A few weeks later he repeated his success, this time in the more challenging role of M. de Forlis in de Boissy's *Dehors trompeurs*. On this occasion he had the honour of playing opposite the formidable Madame de Pompadour, no mean actress herself. The Duc de Luynes, a perceptive critic of court theatricals, considered that Chartres gave an exceptionally fine performance for a novice and performed without displaying a trace of nerves.

Offstage he largely ignored his infant son while continuing to pay passionate attention to his attractive young wife. She, however, had begun to follow the advice of her interfering mother, the Princesse de Conti, by attempting to control the extravagance of her feckless husband. A far greater threat to married bliss of the Chartres now arose, for the louche atmosphere at Saint-Cloud, with its constant round of visitors, was beginning to affect Louise Henriette in dangerous ways. Raised almost exclusively in the company of chaste young women, the presence at Saint-Cloud of so many virile and attractive young men began to intrigue and fascinate her. It soon became obvious that her feelings towards her husband had cooled and that they were growing apart. The Marquis d'Argenson, a frequent guest, noted in his diary that 'although they spend the day together the Duc and Duchesse de Chartres now sleep in separate rooms'.

Then, in acknowledgement that all passion for her husband had finally died, Louise Henriette abruptly demanded that he return her love letters. When told by a servant that she had immediately burnt the letters, Chartres was mortified. As bitter confirmation that their passionate relationship was indeed now over he immediately rented a small, charming and discreet villa in the rue Cadet in the smartest area of Paris and invited his friends the Comte d'Estrehan, the Chevalier de Dampierre and several other trusted companions to share it with him. The rue Cadet would be their communal love nest, a venue where they could entertain the attractive and readily available actresses from the Paris theatres. When informed of this arrangement Louise Henriette showed little concern, having recently begun passionate affairs of her own with several young men. Among them was the 26-year-old Comte de Melfort, a man described by the diarist de Cheverney as being as beautiful as a classical statue and as strong as Hercules.

For the next three years the Duc and Duchesse de Chartres went their separate ways, then in late 1749 Louise Henriette discovered that she was again pregnant. When told the embarrassing news her husband insisted that they must be seen together in public again and, above all, that they must spend their nights together in the same bedroom at Saint-Cloud. Perhaps he recalled his wife's indiscreet words when her son's legitimacy was once humorously questioned in her presence: 'When you fall on to a pile of thorns do you know which one has pricked you?' This pretence of renewed conjugality fooled no one, but it did permit a daughter, Louise Bathilde, to be born without the taint of illegitimacy in July the following year.

Predictably the child's arrival did little to mollify the hostility between her parents, and the Duc soon resumed his old promiscuous routine. Each evening he would drive from Saint-Cloud or the Palais-Royal, the Paris mansion of the Orléans family, to the little house in the rue Cadet and spend the night there with one of his mistresses. His favourite was an eighteen-year-old actress known as 'La Chanterie', but she would soon be supplanted by 'La Petite Coupée', a dancer at the Paris Opéra, infamous for her licentious manner.

These comings and goings at the rue Cadet, discreet as they were, did not escape the attention of Louis XV's secret police. A careful record of each girl's movements, including a detailed description of their supposed 'specialities', was kept and regularly reported to the King at Versailles. This practice of using the police to spy on the nobility was unique to France and had begun under Louis XIV, who was prompted by his childhood fear of an untrustworthy aristocracy. This clandestine surveillance would continue until 1789 when the revolution swept it, and the aristocracy it was meant to control, away. Hatred of this constant shadowing by unseen agents was one of the many reasons that would later lead Louis Philippe Joseph to praise the openness and personal freedom of English society. Far better, he believed, to have an uncensored press that openly criticized and mocked both aristocratic and political misdemeanours than to be subject to a network of spies responsible to no one but the King.

In September 1751 the strained relationship between the Duc and Duchesse de Chartres erupted into public scandal. During a royal levee at the Palace of Fontainebleau, Louise Henriette entered the crowded salon alone and approached her lover, the Comte de Melfort. He, in complete violation of established etiquette, remained seated as they engaged in intimate conversation. It was an unwitting but public admission of their intimacy, and all the more shocking for being performed in the presence of the King. When told of her blatant indiscretion, her husband Chartres was furious and as punishment for the humiliation he had suffered wrote formally to his wife informing her that he considered himself no longer responsible for her many debts.

When Louis the Pious died the following year all the dukes moved up a rung, and Louis Philippe Joseph, aged five years and three months, became the new Duc de Chartres. It was time for him to pass from the hands of women into those of men. In a traditional Orléanist ceremony he was led into a salon at Saint-Cloud and in front of an audience of doctors and noblemen was divested of his childish robes. Standing naked yet unembarrassed, he submitted to a close inspection of his body by the physicians before being declared, as required, undoubtedly male and perfectly healthy. At a command from his father, servants then entered carrying a diminutive set of richly embroidered male courtier robes and carefully dressed the child. A prince in miniature, he stood patiently while his ringlets were drawn back into a man's queue and his hair anointed with white powder. The child had become a man. That evening he returned, not to the nursery at Saint-Cloud and the familiar female faces that he had known since birth, but to new apartments in the Palais-Royal and unfamiliar companions, now exclusively male.

His appointed guardian was to be the Comte de Pons Saint-Maurice, First Gentleman of the Palais-Royal. The King, who had as a courtesy been consulted on the proposed appointment, declared that he thought the urbane Pons an excellent choice. Whatever his suspected intellectual inadequacies, Pons was certainly a man of supreme style and fashion and obsessed by the meticulous etiquette that was so important in France at the time. Admired for his exquisite manners, Pons was a skilful player in the comedy of manners that characterized the French court under Louis XV. Unusually for a man of the world, he was said to have remained celibate until the age of forty-two, when he suddenly fell in love with and quickly married the rich widow of the Parisian banker Mazade. It appeared to be an idyllic and practical union as his wife's fortune enabled Pons to refuse graciously any remuneration for his new responsibilities as governor of the young Duc de Chartres. Nor did he consider his educational duties onerous enough for him to relinquish his other positions in the Orléans household, including that of Colonel of the Regiment of Dragoons. Yet for all his urbanity Pons was later to be castigated by his successor, Madame de Genlis, for having selfishly neglected the intellectual development of the young duke. Many, including the Prince de Montbarrey, the Minister of War, shared her opinion. He later wrote that Pons 'had been too concerned with his own affairs and had left too much of his young charge's education in the hands of underlings'. This charge of intellectual neglect seems odd seeing that Pons chose as his principal assistant Étienne Laureault de Foncemagne, a most eminent member of the Académie Française and an expert on monarchy in general and Salic law in particular. So formidable was Foncemagne's reputation as a scholar that Louis XV had even considered him a worthy tutor for his own son, the Dauphin, not least because Foncemagne had written a powerful defence of the divine right of kings – a subject close to the heart of any Bourbon king. But Foncemagne had modestly declined that honour while securing for himself the more lucrative and far less arduous position of Keeper of Antiquities at the Louvre. When approached by Pons, who was convinced that this famous scholar would more than compensate for his own intellectual inadequacies, Foncemagne accepted the post with alacrity, suggesting as his own assistant and principal instructor to the young duke the formidable educationalist, the Abbé Allaire.

Pons appeared happy enough to leave the mundane business of pure education to his well-qualified assistants while reserving for himself the sole responsibility for inculcating taste and good manners in his young charge. These were important concerns in mid-eighteenth century France, for as George Sand later wrote of the age: 'There was an accepted way of walking, of sitting down, of saluting, of picking up a glove, of holding a fork . . . in short a complete mimicry that children had to be taught at an early age so that it became second nature.'

In general Pons followed the same policies that had been adopted twenty years earlier in the education of Louis Philippe Joseph's father and were contained in the most famous educational tract of the time, the anonymous *Reflections on the Education of a Prince*. Vice and sensuality were to be discouraged by promoting a rigid self-control in the child. All intercourse between the pupil and his instructors must be conducted in an atmosphere of unbending formality. Any expression of emotion, either approval or disapproval, must be discouraged in his presence. Above all, the little duke must never be exposed to anything base or vile such as dogs or the familiarity of common servants. Nor must he be touched, caressed or even physically comforted in any way, even if he fell and injured himself. It was an emotional regime that made the cold ambience of an English public school a century later appear warm and friendly. Predictably it would produce an undemonstrative man devoid of the normal expressions of emotion; a passionless being who was never once seen either to cry or even laugh openly. 'The young Duc', wrote Guignol a decade later, 'was more like a wooden puppet than a real man composed of flesh and blood.'

Above all, his instructors and servants were informed by Pons that Louis Philippe Joseph must never be left alone to daydream, as idle thoughts were known to sow the seeds of future vice. So in a form of gentle yet exquisite cruelty he was, from the age of five, never once allowed one minute of simple privacy. In rare moments of play time, at the table, in his bed-room – even in the lavatory – no fewer than three instructors or servants had always to be present. Furthermore, every-thing that he said or did at any moment of the day or night was to be reported back to either Pons or Foncemagne. Nor as he wandered the corridors of the Palais-Royal, an attendant never far behind, was the child to be allowed the least contact with or even sight of the ordinary people who thronged the streets outside. It was a deprivation that would later lead to his lifelong fascination with the lives of the poor and their strange and, to him, exotic poverty.

With his young mind carefully controlled and regulated, it was now the turn of his body, and consideration was given to the terrible scourge of smallpox. Threat of this contagion was never far from the minds of even the greatest princes in the eighteenth century. In 1715 it had killed three succes-sive dauphins. The only one who appeared to have escaped became Louis XV, but he was eventually fated to succumb to the infection, dying in 1774 after weeks of the most appalling suffering. Naturally the Duc d'Orléans was anxious lest his own young son and heir should contact the disease particularly when, in the autumn of 1752, the child suddenly went down with a high fever and what appeared to be the ominous red blotches of incipient smallpox. Luckily it proved a false alarm and the boy recovered, but his father took it as a warning from God and began to consider the controversial new practice of inoculation that was becoming increasingly popular across the Channel.

The English adventurer Lady Mary Wortley Montagu had witnessed the procedure when travelling in Turkey in 1721 and had insisted that her own two infant sons be inoculated by the Turks. When her written account of this revolutionary practice reached London some of the more radical doctors of the day began experimenting with it. Such was their success that by 1750 it had become so popular with the British nobility that even the Princess of Wales had been success-fully inoculated. In France, however, medical opinion remained more sceptical and more concerned with the small number of fatalities that the procedure had produced. The Duc d'Orléans, who had himself survived smallpox in his youth, soon found that no Parisian doctor was prepared to risk his reputation or income by experimenting with inocula-tion. In desperation he wrote to a London doctor, Kerpatry, for advice but receiving no reply he then contacted Théodore Tronchin of Geneva, the leading Continental practitioner of vaccination. Tronchin, who had successfully demonstrated the procedure on a child at the inaugural meeting of the French Academy of Science earlier that year, agreed at once to return to Paris. Yet before risking such a controversial pro-cedure on a child so close to the succession of the French throne, the Duc d'Orléans thought it prudent to seek per-mission from the King himself. He was told to proceed as he thought fit.

After carefully examining the young Louis Philippe Joseph and stretching him painfully from a doorframe to investigate a suspected inherited tendency to spinal curvature, Tronchin agreed to proceed. The entire Orléans household, together with invited guests, gathered to witness the inoculation of the young duke and his sister on 24 March 1754. Predictably the audience found itself divided into pro- and anti-inoculation camps. One brave courtier boldly thrust a pamphlet entitled *The Case Against Inoculation* into the Duc's hand as he arrived. He brushed it impatiently aside, but turning suddenly to his estranged Duchesse seated beside him asked her permission, as the children's mother, for Tronchin to continue. Louise Henriette, although from her tearful demeanour clearly fearing the worst, told him to proceed but to leave her in peace to weep as a mother. So at nine o'clock Tronchin started to inoculate little Louis Philippe Joseph and his sister, regaling the assembled company throughout with a dramatic commentary on what he was doing. Ten minutes later he declared the process complete and the inoculation of the two children a total success. As he bowed to the audience they applauded him with wild enthusiasm. A few days later his optimism appeared justified since the children were obviously still in perfect health.

Tronchin's bravura display at the Palais-Royal provoked such interest in Paris that when the Orléans family attended the opera a few days later the entire audience rose to its feet and applauded them far more enthusiastically than they did that evening's performance. Even that old cynic, Voltaire, was impressed by this miracle of modern medicine and declared his great satisfaction that the Orléans children were now safe from the shadow cast on his generation by the dreaded smallpox. As a token of his relief and gratitude, the Duc d'Orléans presented Tronchin with a reward of 24,000 livres together with two small diamond-studded caskets, one bearing the portrait of the children, the other that of the Duchess. These were indeed generous gifts but paled in comparison with the millions of livres that Tronchin would now earn as his fame spread throughout French society. Within a week he was invited to Versailles, where the Queen implored him to examine the royal children.

With his son's health assured, at least from the dreaded smallpox, the Duc d'Orléans decided that it was time for the boy to begin to play his part in public life. So, accompanied by the ever-watchful Comte de Pons, the young Louis Philippe Joseph, who had just completed an intensive course in equitation at the riding school at Saint-Cloud, made his first public appearance that June to lay a foundation stone for a new portico at the Cathedral of Saint-Eustache in Paris. He performed this duty with aplomb, displaying such impressive grace and bearing that the Comte de Pons was convinced that the young prince would soon be mature enough to make his public début at Versailles. Meanwhile his father, to the disgust of the royal family, appeared to have resumed his old life of dissipation, spending his days hunting and drinking and his evenings gambling and whoring. Ominously, the King also noted that whenever Orléans did deign to appear at Versailles he was now surrounded by the growing band of nobles opposed to the increased power of the monarchy.

The hostility between Versailles and the Palais-Royal that was to have such tragic consequences was further exacerbated when, at the outbreak of the Seven Years' War in 1756, Louis XV summarily dismissed the Duc d'Orléans' formal request to be given command of the army and compounded the insult by appointing his own son, the Dauphin, instead. The disgruntled Orléans had to content himself with a lesser command but led his troops so valiantly at the Battle of Hastenbeck against combined British and Hanoverian forces that, to the King's consternation, he was immediately acclaimed a national hero. When news of his success reached Paris the Duchesse, putting aside her personal hostility, appeared on the balcony of the Palais-Royal and announced her husband's victory to the cheering crowds. Returning from the battlefield, his laurels still green, the Duc, true to character, celebrated his triumphs with a new round of unsuitable affairs with young girls from the opera. One of them, a beautiful young Italian singer called Marquise, even managed to persuade him to set her up in a sumptuous apartment near the Palais-Royal and then wasted little time in getting herself pregnant. When news of the imminent and embarrassing confinement reached the palace, Louise Henriette, who had always managed to ignore her husband's previous indiscreet behaviour, was mortified. This proved to be literally so, for in January 1759, aged just thirty-two, she fell so ill with consumption that it was decided she be given the last rites. As always with the House of

Orléans, this could not be an appropriately quiet and intimate occasion but was an elaborate ceremony established by custom and involving a long and exhausting ritual. Every Prince of the Blood was summoned and Louis Philippe Joseph's sister, the little Louise Bathilde, brought from the Madeleine Traisnel Convent to see her mother for the last time. Flanked by his children and escorted by a column of Swiss guards carrying flaming torches, the Duc led the procession into the great salon where his wife lay on a dais surrounded by her ladies in front of the entire Orléans household. Having received the sacrament the Duchess blessed her children and was carried back to her chamber, where she died peacefully on 9 February.

Since she was considered by many of her contemporaries to have been just as licentious as her husband, Louise Henriette's obituaries were certainly contentious. The poet Charles Collé described her as a black-hearted and debauched witch and was particularly scathing of her attempts at writing verse. Others who knew her more intimately, such as Baron Grimm, a German witness of French society at the time, were more generous, praising her as a true heroine for all that she had endured. As befitted her rank, the French court went into a solemn six-day mourning for Madame Orléans, during which period she was finally interred in the grounds of yet another family palace, Val-de-Grâce.

Young Louis Philippe Joseph appeared to share his father's unexpected grief, falling into such a depression that the Comte de Pons decided to try and restore the boy's spirits by engaging for him a younger and more approachable teacher. This time Pons chose not an academic but Louis de Carmontelle, the son of a humble shoemaker who had risen in the army to become a most capable artillery officer and who had served with distinction in the recent Westphalian campaign. As a man of the world Carmontelle brought a new dimension of practical experience to the closed world of the young prince. His legacy was to kindle in him a lifelong interest in mathematics and all things military. Under

Carmontelle's urbane influence Louis Philippe Joseph began to show a greater degree of self-confidence, so that by the end of the summer of 1759, when he was twelve years old, his father agreed with Pons that the boy was mature enough to be presented to the King at Versailles.

Since the building of the great palace a century earlier the majority of French nobles had obeyed the King's wish and gathered at Versailles. Successive Ducs d'Orléans, however, had chosen to assert their independence and to remain in Paris and keep their own court at the Palais-Royal. This constant presence in the capital had enabled the family to retain the goodwill of the ordinary citizens, and their popularity had been further augmented, since the days of the Regency, by the custom of giving generous relief to the poor. Although famine had disappeared from England by the late seventeenth century, it lingered on in France for a further hundred years, bringing death and disease throughout the country. Nor was it confined to the countryside, for Paris too suffered from its deprivations and crowds of beggars would often gather at the doors of the Palais-Royal waiting for bread to be distributed by the Duc's servants. The goodwill and respect that these charitable actions generated were unique to the House of Orléans, and two decades later would ensure that the Palais-Royal became the most important power base in the social upheaval that was to come.

Yet Versailles in 1759 remained a place of peace and prosperity under the powerful cultural influence of the King's mistress, Madame de Pompadour. Her innate good taste, combined with the astute financial management of the King's First Minister, the Duc de Choiseul, had regained for Versailles much of the splendour that it had enjoyed under the Sun King a century earlier. Now a constant round of balls and masques, operas and dramas provided diversion for the nobility. To the young Louis Philippe Joseph, who made his formal appearance there that June, it would have seemed a pleasure palace after the sombre atmosphere of the Palais-Royal. As befitted a Prince of the Blood, an apartment was always kept ready for the Duc d'Orléans, and two days after their arrival father and son, accompanied by the Comte de Pons, set off to the Hall of Mirrors where Louis XV and the entire royal family waited to receive them. As well as the Dauphin and Dauphine there stood their four sons, the Duc de Bourgogne, the Duc de Berry, the Comte de Provence and the Comte d'Artois, all ranged in order of succession to the throne. Thoroughly briefed on the required etiquette, the young Duc de Chartres bowed solemnly to each of his cousins in turn, addressing them as 'Monsieur'. He was then conducted to a separate salon to meet their sisters, the royal princesses, an experience he later confessed to have found far more relaxing and enjoyable. To his father's obvious satisfaction Louis Philippe Joseph conducted himself impeccably that day without making a single *faux pas* and was rewarded by being given the singular honour of handing the Queen her napkin at dinner and the King his nightshirt at bedtime.

According to custom, Princes of the Blood were officially baptized and given their final Christian name only when they were considered to have attained the age of reason. By his impeccable behaviour at Versailles, the young Duc de Chartres had clearly demonstrated that he had attained this state. When approached by the Duc d'Orléans for his permission, the King not only gave it gladly but announced that he and the Queen would be delighted to act as godparents at the ceremony. So on a dark November evening, dressed in a robe of silver silk embroidered with diamonds and with a matching tricorne hat, his hair tied back with a white ribbon, the young Duc de Chartres presented himself again before the King. In solemn procession the entire royal family, accompanied by the Princes of the Blood and other nobles, paraded through the vast palace of Versailles to the royal chapel, lit for the occasion by a thousand candles. The mass completed, the King and Queen rose from their seats and led the young Duc de Chartres to the altar where, after handing his hat and sword to the Comte de Pons, he knelt before them to receive the name 'Joseph' to add to that of Louis Philippe. As they all returned to the royal apartments, the Duc d'Orléans was seen to be almost beside himself with delight and gratitude to the King and insisted on personally distributing the traditional small gifts of sugared sweets to all those who had been present. The baptism of Louis Philippe Joseph had shown that the House of Orléans, in spite of past differences, now enjoyed both the confidence and the affection of the King. The following spring, as the young Duc de Chartres went to make his first communion at the Church of Saint-Eustache in Paris, the cheering crowds lining the streets confirmed that the family was as popular in the capital as ever.

2

THE LIBERTINE

AT THE AGE of fifteen Louis Philippe Joseph differed little from other young princes of the age. In appearance he was tall and slim, with a predictably aristocratic bearing and an open if expressionless face. Always impeccably dressed, he invariably wore across his chest the blue ribbon of the Saint-Esprit and on his coat the black collar of the Order of Saint-Michel. A fine horseman, since the age of fourteen he had hunted regularly with Louis XV and attended the endless levees and receptions that filled the day at Versailles. His conduct and manners at these important social events continued to be faultless. But one aspect of his character began increasingly to worry his father. Although he had evidently reached puberty the young Duc de Chartres appeared to have a strange and inexplicable indifference to the presence of women. Had he inherited the homosexuality that had made his ancestor Monsieur, the brother of Louis XIV, so reviled? Rather than risk a repeat of that near catastrophe, the Duc d'Orléans decided in March 1766 to deal with the matter personally and to engage the services of a young lady well known to him.

Rosalie Duthé, a blonde and attractive fifteen-year-old, was nominally a dancer at the Paris Opéra, but she was better known as one of the most alluring young courtesans in Paris and had been painted nude by Fragonard, Vestier and Le Beau. Honoured to be chosen for this essential work, Rosalie soon became a regular visitor at the Palais-Royal. So expertly did she perform her task that within a month she had taught Louis Philippe Joseph all he would ever need to know about the art of making love. Indeed, so accomplished was she that her visits to the Palais-Royal were soon eagerly awaited by her young pupil, who would watch for her from his window. Predictably these assignations were closely observed by the same secret police that were already keeping watch on the young Duc's father. Daily records, now in the Bibliothèque Nationale in Paris, were regularly presented to Louis XV who followed them with great relish and no little amusement. Marais, the officer responsible, confirmed in his reports that 'the young lady has been so successful that the Duc de Chartres has been carried round to her house at full speed in a sedan chair every morning last week'. News of Rosalie Duthé's success certainly boosted her already formidable reputation with the French aristocracy, and it was reported that even such distinguished English visitors as Lord Egremont now beat a path to her door. Her status among her fellow courtesans too was so enhanced that she was now compared to the most famous of them all, La Brissaude.

Graduating with honour from Rosalie's embraces, Louis Philippe Joseph progressed through many more courtesans over the following months, each short-lived affair being meticulously documented in Officer Marais' reports. Like some eastern potentate he experimented with group sex, spending the night at the Palais-Royal with three dancers, La Guérin, Emilie and Zelmire, who left at five in the morning each clutching six gold louis. The young libertine was clearly making up for lost time. Once launched, his career of debauchery, in an age when boredom was the most dreaded misfortune and amusement the main objective, continued apace. It was not long before he was being compared with such established roués as the Comte de la Tour du Pin, the Vicomte de Rochechouart, the Duc de Fronsart and the acknowledged leader of them all, Maréchal Richelieu.

His preferred companions in these amatory revels were his closest and most trusted friends, the Chevalier de Durfort, fourteen years his senior, and the Duc de Lauzun; both would remain loyal to him for the rest his life. Born on the same day as Louis Philippe Joseph, Lauzun would later be described by Madame de Genlis as his only true friend and one who stood by him throughout all the intrigues and catastrophes that were to follow. Like his father, Louis Philippe Joseph had also now acquired a love nest that he shared with his friends. When not entertaining dancers and actresses here at 10 rue Saint-Lazare, they could be found at the infamous establishment of Monsieur Brissault, a glorified brothel in the centre of Paris. Here aristocratic clients when taking a rest from the constant lovemaking that took place in the surrounding boudoirs could dine with their women on oysters and champagne. Nicknamed 'The President', Brissault would often join in the bacchanalia himself. None of his clients was aware that he was in reality a police spy supplying the most compromising details of their activities to the authorities.

On one occasion the ubiquitous Officer Marais took it upon himself to question closely some of the young ladies, among them a Mademoiselle Durancy, about the Duc de Chartres' sexual behaviour. He discovered, to his surprise, that in spite of his impeccable social manners Louis Philippe Joseph's sexual conduct appeared to be astonishingly coarse. This opinion was confirmed by another courtesan, who told Marais that she thought the Duc's behaviour in bed more appropriate to a common coachman than a Prince of the Blood. Marais, who seems to have taken a particular interest these matters, noted in his report that, in his opinion, what the young gentleman needed was a relationship with an 'honest' woman – a rare commodity at the time, for as an English visitor, Lord Chesterfield, wrote to his son, 'such a creature does not exist in Paris'.

However, another of Louis Philippe Joseph's profligate friends, the Duc de Fitzjames, a member of the exiled Stuart dynasty, claimed to have found such a one. One evening he announced his discovery to his friends and told an astonished Duc de Chartres: 'Monseigneur, I now wish to marry and live like an honest man with my wife. So I am giving up these nocturnal activities and will not be coming here any more.' Chartres' response was to invite him a few days later to a valedictory dinner at the rue Saint-Lazare. When Fitzjames arrived he found the house draped throughout in mourning black and dimly illuminated with flaming torches. Naked girls lay on silken couches pretending to weep so convincingly for their lost patron that Fitzjames immediately succumbed and spent a last, enjoyable night in passionate debauchery. But there were many rich aristocratic young men only too willing to take Fitzjames's place and Louis Philippe Joseph's carousel of pleasure continued unabated, seemingly driven by an unswerving adherence to the Comte de Voyer's cynical precept that 'all true feelings are ridiculous and all moral scruples merely a distraction. We act solely from self-interest and the quest for pleasure alone should dictate our actions.' Or, as his disciple would later write of himself, 'The pursuit of pleasure was my sole motivation at that time.'

In 1758 the Duc d'Orléans decided to leave Paris and retire to another family mansion, Bagnolet, ten miles to the east of Paris. There he was joined by his own mistress – yet another actress, Étiennette Perrine, known as Marquise, and their three illegitimate children. His departure left Louis Philippe Joseph as sole master of the Palais-Royal and for the first time in his life he could exercise domestic control rather than be its recipient, which he did with a remarkable degree of tolerance, his only recorded transgression being a tendency to tease and embarrass the respectable ladies of the household with the sexual innuendo of his conversation. Yet in spite of his own lax morals he became increasingly annoyed by his father's close relationship with Marquise. The problem for Chartres was that his father was not just having an affair with a mere actress but that he was giving her the status of a wife. Relations between father and son rapidly deteriorated and were further exacerbated when Chartres discovered that Marquise had violated decorum by appearing in the hunting field dressed in a man's breeches and smoking a cigar. To her contemporaries this was a far more heinous offence than mere adultery. Father and son ceased to be on speaking terms.

In the summer of 1766 a new and attractive figure appeared

in the Orléans household. This was Madame de Montesson, a real marquise and a gifted amateur actress who specialized in comedy. A wealthy widow, she had been married to a banker fifty years her senior. Attractive and witty, she soon caught the Duc d'Orléans' eye and posed an obvious threat to the incumbent Marquise. When told of his father's keen interest in this eligible newcomer, the Duc de Chartres went immediately to Villers-Cotterêts, another of the Orléans palaces where his father was staying, and proposed a *rapprochement* between them. His sole condition was that his father should renounce Marquise and replace her with the more socially acceptable Madame de Montesson. Orléans, who had clearly been debating the matter himself, readily agreed and by the autumn a real marquise had replaced the comic one and the Duc d'Orléans and his son were again on the best of terms.

A year earlier, in December 1765, the Dauphin, heir to the French throne, had suddenly died, the latest royal victim of smallpox. Now all that stood between the House of Orléans and the throne itself were the late Dauphin's three infant sons. Yet even their survival was uncertain given the risk from the childhood diseases that ravaged the most cosseted members of the royal family. If the Bourbon dynasty was to survive it was imperative that the Orléans play a more prominent and visible role in the affairs of state. Consequently at the funeral services for the Duke of Parma, King Stanislaus of Poland and Elizabeth Farnese, Queen of Spain, the following year it was the young Duc de Chartres who officially represented Louis XV. Later when King Christian VII of Denmark visited France it was the turn of the father, and the Duc d'Orléans presided over the state banquet given in the visitor's honour at the Palais-Royal. Almost 700 guests sat down to dinner and King Louis, relieved for the day of his official duties, clearly enjoyed himself by dancing with his host's daughter, Louise Bathilde d'Orléans. Nor was the evening's pleasure spoilt when their grossly fat host went sprawling on the floor, badly rupturing an Achilles tendon, and had to retire leaving his son to take his place. Having demonstrated that they were prepared to play their part in the many tedious ceremonies that were required of the monarchy, the Orléans had consolidated their position close to the throne. It was now imperative that the heir to the dynasty, the young Duc de Chartres, should make a good and suitable marriage.

The ideal bride would be a princess of royal blood and a Catholic and, given the balance of power in contemporary European politics and the need to strengthen the Continental alliance, a German. The obvious choice was Marie-Josephe de Saxe, who met all these qualifications admirably, but when approached her elderly father proved reluctant to contemplate uniting his illustrious family with the mere cadet branch of the Bourbons. The responsibility for finding a bride was then passed to the Abbé de Breteuil, Chancellor of the Orléans household. Ignoring the dozens of European princesses available, he suggested, to the Duc d'Orléans' initial surprise, a candidate far closer to home. This was Louise Marie Adélaïde de Bourbon, daughter of the immensely wealthy Duc de Penthièvre, Grand Admiral of France and bastard son of Louis XIV and Madame de Montespan.

As Penthièvre's only surviving child, Marie Adélaïde was by far the richest heiress in France and consequently in the world at that time. Just sixteen years old, she was tall and slim with unusually pale, almost translucent skin, blue eyes and golden hair. Educated by the nuns of the Montmartre convent, she had been raised in an atmosphere of the strictest moral rectitude. This was in complete contrast to her notoriously degenerate brother, the Prince de Lamballe, a young man of almost Gothic debauchery who had married the shy and virtuous Marie-Thérèse de Savoie-Carignan, the future confidante of Queen Marie Antoinette. Fortunately for his young wife, he had died of syphilis a short time after their marriage. Embarrassingly the blame for his early death had been attributed to Louis Philippe Joseph, who was said to have encouraged Lamballe to take up with a courtesan whom he knew had the disease. This accusation is contradicted by one of Officer Marais' reports in which he clearly states that it was not the Duc de Chartres who introduced Lamballe to the courtesan but a well-known Parisian procuress. True or not, this slur on Louis Philippe Joseph's character appeared not to have reached the ears of the Duc de Penthièvre, who willingly gave his assent to the match.

Unpredictable as ever, the Duc d'Orléans at first opposed the Abbé de Breteuil's suggestion, telling him that he would have much preferred a royal bride for his son. His formal excuse was that he was reluctant to bring the descendant of a royal bastard into the family as it could be seen to compromise his own family's status as legitimate Princes of the Blood. But his opposition was short-lived, for he and Penthièvre were old friends, having served together in the army. Moreover the prospect of an introduction of vast wealth, including some of the finest châteaux of the Loire, into the family coffers soon prevailed. After more half-hearted prevarication by the Duc, the advice of the Abbé de Breteuil finally prevailed and the Duc de Choiseul was appointed to conduct the marriage agreement between the two families. When during the course of these negotiations the full extent of the Penthièvre dowry was revealed, the Duc d'Orléans quietly abandoned any lingering reservations. But when the King discovered the truth he was furious at the prospect of the largest private fortune in France passing to the rival, cadet branch of the Bourbons. Yet, unable to find a valid reason to withhold his permission for the union, he finally and reluctantly gave it.

As befitted an alliance between one of the noblest and one of the wealthiest families in the land, the wedding took place in the Chapel Royal at Versailles in the presence of the King and Queen. Early on the morning of 5 April 1769 Louis Philippe Joseph took to his bride an offering of orange flowers that she would later wear in her hair. Then, formally dressed in his wedding finery, he presented himself to his father for inspection. The Duc was delighted and pronounced his son as looking, in his cerise and cloth of gold robes, more like a character from a romantic legend than a living prince. Later, when standing at the altar beside his bride, dressed in pale silver, his natural height made Louis Philippe Joseph appear to tower over her diminutive figure. No expense had been spared on the ceremony, a papal blessing had been obtained from Rome and the archaic office of Master of Ceremonies revived for the occasion. Decorum and observation of rank were punctiliously observed throughout the ceremony although it was sourly noted that the bride's mother, the Duchesse de Penthièvre, apparently already considered herself above her true station since she was wearing a type of long prayer shawl traditionally reserved for members of the royal family. In total contrast to his wife's supposed arrogance, the Duc de Penthièvre appeared humbled by his daughter's elevation to the rank of Princess of the Blood. After the signing of the marriage documents the King presented the couple with a wedding gift of 150,000 livres for the groom and 100,000 for the bride. Orléans' personal dowry was more ambiguous, a promise of all the residences and servants they would require, under-written by a recompense of 400,000 livres if he failed to comply. But both gifts were dwarfed by Penthièvre's contribution, for he settled on the young couple an immediate 6 million livres in cash and another 4 million's worth of lands, châteaux and rents. A further 2 million would accrue to the new Duchesse de Chartres on his death. It was to be the most fabulous dowry in French history. That evening, when the Comte de Pons, on behalf of the Orléans household, presented the new bride with many of the family jewels, including diamond necklaces, pearls and other items decorated with precious stones of great value, they seemed almost trivial in comparison.

The ceremony completed and a sumptuous banquet served, the wedding party progressed to the gold and white Salle de Guerre, where, beneath a huge bass relief of Louis XIV crushing his enemies, the King sat at a card table with the new bridegroom to play his favourite card game, lansquenet. At a separate table his sons, the Dauphin and the Comte de Provence, entertained the new bride with a game of cavagnole, the most popular pastime at the court of Versailles. Then, at a sign from the King, the newlyweds rose and were accompanied to their bedroom by the members of the royal family. As the new Duchesse de Chartres disrobed in her dressing room, her husband became obsessed by a point of subtle yet important etiquette. Should he remain in his day clothes, out of respect for the King, or change into night attire for the ceremony of blessing the marital bed? After much whispered debate, the Grand Almoner of France ruled that removing his coat would be sufficient for the occasion. To add to his bewilderment the King then told the confused Chartres when he reappeared to put it back on again. Such details of sartorial procedure required a great deal of consideration at Versailles. The blessing completed, the Duc d'Orléans handed the King a nightshirt, which he, in turn, graciously presented to the bridegroom. Finally the bridegroom reappeared in full night attire, his hair tied back with a ribbon beneath a large, white nightcap. The bed curtains were then ceremoniously drawn and the party began to retire discreetly from the bedroom, only for the King to order the drapes to be pulled momentarily apart again in a humorous attempt to embarrass the young couple.

The next morning the entire court was already aware that the marriage had been successfully consummated, for life at Versailles, even for Princes of the Blood, could never be lived in privacy. That afternoon, escorted by servants dressed in the Orléans livery of red and blue, the newlyweds made the short carriage drive to Paris. At her new home, the Palais-Royal, Marie Adélaïde was formally introduced to the members and staff of this formidable household. Everyone was impressed by her open character and noble bearing, not least Dr Tronchin, now resident surgeon in the household. He wrote admiringly of her, 'I find Madame Chartres a most honest, sensible and modest person. She has won all hearts at the Palais-Royal and will make a most charming princess.' When the young Duc and Duchesse later drove out informally together for the first time, Parisians, who had never once seen their own king take the trouble to visit them in such a manner, applauded them enthusiastically. Their popularity was further confirmed that evening when they went together to the Comédie Française to see Sedaine's new drama *The Deserter*. As they entered their box cries of 'Long live the royal family' rang throughout the theatre. A few days later the Duc de Penthièvre gave a splendid dinner for his daughter at his Paris house, the Hôtel de Toulouse. As she entered the dining room, Louise Marie Adélaïde, as she had always done, went to kneel and kiss her father's hand. Penthièvre gently refused this gesture of filial obeisance, lifting her to her feet and telling her that now she had become a Princess of the Blood he must, if anything, kiss hers.

For the next month the wedding celebrations continued as the newlyweds progressed to each of their châteaux in turn. At Saint-Cloud they watched the King review a large detachment of his troops before proceeding on to Marly, a palace that had obviously decayed since its great days under Louis XIV. Dismayed at the visible deterioration and walls that dripped with moisture, ruining the glorious colours of its frescos, they soon made their escape to L'Isle Adam, the home of the Prince de Conti. Here all the Princes of the Blood awaited them for yet another grand reception in their honour. On 26 May the Duc de Chartres and his new wife finally reached the Palace of Villers-Cotterêts. Marie Adélaïde was led to a rustic bower, where she received each of the household servants and retainers in turn. The following morning, in an idyllic scene that resembled a painting by Watteau, twenty-four local maidens dressed in pink and white gowns and carrying shepherdesses' crooks appeared in the garden and greeted her with verses composed in her honour by the poet Collé and set to music by the composer Monsigny. Never before had the French court witnessed such a sumptuous wedding or enjoyed such protracted celebrations. They were to be last of their kind, for the French aristocracy was soon to be swept aside by the first great social upheaval of modern times.

3

THE PALAIS-ROYAL

THE GREAT PALACE of the Palais-Royal, to which the newly-weds returned in October 1769, was to be a rival to the Louvre both politically and architecturally in the coming decades. It had originally been designed by the architect Jacques Lemercier as a theatre for Cardinal Richelieu and was the first in France to have movable scenery wings and a proscenium arch. Following Richelieu's death the Palais Cardinal, as it was then known, became a royal property before passing to the Orléans family. Still a theatre, it was used for courtly entertainment and became the home of Molière's drama company until his death in 1673. The greatest dramatist of the age was then followed by the most celebrated composer, Jean-Baptiste Lully, who moved his Academy of Music there.

In 1763 the theatre was destroyed in a disastrous fire and it was decided to rebuild it as part of the Parisian seat of the House of Orléans. At the time this was seen as a mildly provocative gesture, given its close proximity to the Louvre. A new and imposing portico of Tuscan columns beneath a bas-relief in stone of the family coat-of-arms now embellished the façade. Unusually for a royal mansion the architect Pierre Constant d'Ivry had designed gates with open ironwork tracery that allowed the passing citizens to gaze into the front courtyard. This visual accessibility together with the custom of allowing the public to walk in the gardens of the Palais-Royal was unique in contemporary France and in complete contrast to the elaborate security measures that prevailed at Versailles. The message was clear and unambiguous – the House of Orléans recognizes and identifies with the ordinary people of Paris. The garden in particular had drawn people to the Palais, resembling as they did a more informal and less dangerous version of the Vauxhall Gardens in London. As the light faded each day it became a place of assignation and a Mecca for whores and their clients. Louis Philippe Joseph's own mother had been accosted there one afternoon by a drunken Dutchman who assumed that she was a prostitute arriving early for work. Her cries brought the palace guard who dragged the confused visitor away. There were less controversial attractions too, such as pavement cafés, including the famous Café Foy, and a small lake and gravel walks with seats placed at regular intervals for pedestrians to rest. Even the philosopher Denis Diderot, taking time off from the composition of *L'Encyclopédie*, was drawn there most evenings for the five o'clock promenade when he would stroll with his friend the Marquis d'Argenson discussing politics and philosophy as they passed throngs of pretty girls and their beaux.

Visitors could also watch the arrival of aristocratic guests at the Palais who attended the levees and receptions that took place most evenings, together with audiences assembling for performances at the new opera salon that had been constructed. A year later the last of the renovations were completed with the opening of a vast oval salon able to accommodate over 2,500 people, an event that was celebrated with a lavish production of Rameau's opera *Zoroastra*. Those entering the house could enjoy a superb collection of paintings second only in importance to that of the King at Versailles. Most of the great French, Italian and Flemish masters of the previous two centuries were represented, including masterpieces by Raphael, Titian, Rembrandt, Veronese and Rubens. These were complemented by a fabulous collection of over 800 miniatures and medallions, some of which had been commissioned by Louis the Pious when a near recluse at the Abbey of Sainte-Geneviève. Finally there was a splendid collection of gold and silver cups, precious stones and vast Brussels and Gobelin tapestries, one series from the drawing of Le Brun, presented to the Regent Orléans by his brother Louis XIV, depicting *The Triumphs of Alexander the Great*.

Three large apartments had been reserved for the exclusive use of the Duc de Chartres and his new wife. These were reached by a new and elaborate oval-shaped stairway designed by the most celebrated interior designer of the age, Pierre Constant d'Ivry, and featuring palm trees and putti made of wrought iron and bronze. To the right at the top of the stairs lay the apartment reserved for the Duc d'Orléans, to the left that of the Duc de Chartres. This led, in turn, to the rococo rooms created for the Duchesse d'Orléans but never occupied by her. These had caused such a stir in Paris that no less than eight pages of illustrations in Diderot's *Encyclopédie* had been devoted to them. Each room had its own character, many featuring elaborate bas-reliefs and *trompe-l'œil* paintings, all with the theme of the triumph of womanhood. Their new occupant, Marie Adélaïde, would live there in far greater splendour than the new Dauphine, Marie Antoinette, would enjoy at Versailles when she arrived there the following May.

Now that the Duc d'Orléans had retired with his mistress, Madame de Montesson, to the more modest comfort of his mansion at Barège, Louis Philippe Joseph was sole master of the Palais-Royal and its entire complement of servants, stewards, retainers and ladies-in-waiting. Not that his new duties precluded a return to his old amorous ways and regular visits to the love nest at 10 rue Saint-Lazare that had been maintained in his absence by the Duc de Fitzjames. A regular stream of pretty actresses and dancers continued to be supplied for the establishment by the well-known procuresses, Madame Brissault and Madame Gourdan. Fitzjames, his promise to marry and settle down with his wife long forgotten, remained master of the revels and determined to be the first to sample the charms of each new *ingénue*. One such newcomer was the voluptuous Le Cocq, who declared a particular interest in the Duc de Chartres. To oblige his old friend and to test the prowess of this bold young woman, Fitzjames took her for what he described as 'a two-furlong canter'. Much impressed, he rewarded her with the appropriately princely sum of 100 louis before passing her on to his dissolute companion.

Meanwhile Marie Adélaïde, barely seventeen years old and serious and virtuous by nature, was settling into life at the Palais-Royal and enjoying the attention paid to her by the largest household in Paris. This was a novel if challenging experience for a young woman who a year earlier had been a shy and innocent schoolgirl locked away in a convent. Yet she now assumed her new role with an ease and elegance that won the hearts of her more worldly and sophisticated companions such as the elderly Comtesse de Rochambeau and the Marquise de Polignac. In contrast with the constrained and formal atmosphere of the royal court at Versailles, the Palais-Royal was a haven of free speech and relaxed manners. Both the young Duc de Chartres and his Duchesse encouraged an ease among their friends and retainers that soon began to attract the more enlightened members of Parisian society as well as retaining such long-established companions as the Comte de Schomberg, the Chevalier de Durfort and the Vicomte de la Tour du Pin. Yet some of the oldest courtiers, remembering the glories of Louis XIV, lamented the passing of the more formal manners that then prevailed. 'Such men', wrote Madame de Genlis, 'were but the debris from that golden age.' Yet de Genlis, who would soon play a catalytic if divisive role in the lives of the Duc de Chartres and his wife, considered the present ambience at the Palais-Royal far more conducive to a civilized life as new ideas could be openly discussed without provoking acrimony, nor was there undue deference to social rank.

Each day the Chartres held court at the Palais-Royal, and in the evenings everyone still present, whether formally invited or not, would be expected to join them for dinner. After the meal they would often retire with their friends to the opera salon. Occasionally they would leave the palace and visit a public theatre or opera house, although Marie Adélaïde's first visit to one on 9 April 1769 had been somewhat spoilt by the crowd of young courtesans who insisted on waving to her husband from the stalls. The evening was redeemed, however, when an actor, having spoken the line 'Long live the

King', turned towards her box, bowed and shouted impromptu, 'and long live the royal family'. Marie Adélaïde is reported to have burst into tears, an emotional affectation said to be highly popular at the time. Some days, known as 'little days', guests at the Palais-Royal would number no more than a modest fifty or so and the company would spend the evening in one of the lesser salons with Marie Adélaïde and her ladies seated at one end quietly embroidering samplers while the men strolled about the room exchanging gossip. It was the bourgeois lifestyle on a grand scale.

Frequently the Chartres were summoned to Versailles where the ageing Louis XV kept a keen eye on the progress of their marriage. While observing due respect and politeness for his cousins, the remote and withdrawn Dauphin, soon to marry the Archduchess Marie Antoinette of Austria, and his more amiable brother, the already portly Comte de Provence, Louis Philippe Joseph maintained a wary reserve. Nor was the King pleased to be informed by Louis Philippe Joseph of the proposed marriage of his sister Louise Bathilde to the Duc de Bourbon, son of the Prince de Condé. This alliance would unite the two cadet branches of the Bourbon royal family, putting further pressure to breed on the mainstream branch. Yet the marriage began in near scandal as the Duc de Bourbon, driven as he claimed by passion, arrived at the convent where his fiancée was staying the night, put a ladder against the wall, climbed up and carried her off. Instead of the condemnation that he expected, Bourbon was fêted for his deed and the playwright Laujon wrote a charming little comedy in his honour entitled *The Fifteen-Year-Old Sweet-heart*. Sadly, within a year of their marriage the uncontrolled passion of the Duc de Bourbon swept him 'like a fire in a haystack' from the arms of Louise Bathilde into the embrace of dozens of other women. Meanwhile the more dynastically important marriage of the Dauphin had taken place on 16 May 1770 at Versailles, the Duchesse de Chartres being given by the King the particular honour of handing the nightdress to Marie Antoinette as the newlyweds retired to bed.

A year later another event that would affect the destiny of France occurred when Marie Adélaïde found herself pregnant. Typically her husband celebrated the good news by holding a lavish supper party for his friends and girlfriends at their new love nest in the rue Saint-Lazare. It seemed to Chartres the ideal occasion to introduce two pretty newcomers to the house, Guimard and Aby. The event was again closely observed by the lugubrious Inspector Marais and carefully documented in his report to Versailles. At first the pregnancy progressed uneventfully. The Comte de Pons presented the prospective mother with a magnificent layette and the Archbishop of Paris gave permission for the new arrival to be baptized privately by the Chartres' personal chaplain. Then on 10 October Marie Adélaïde went suddenly into labour and gave premature birth to a stillborn daughter. Desolate at the loss, the Duc de Chartres implored those around him to keep the sad secret, and the baby was quietly buried in a part of the Saint-Eustache cemetery reserved for such little tragedies. Marie Adélaïde was told that the baby had been taken to Saint-Cloud for health reasons, but three months later the truth could no longer be kept from her. This sad event even moved the court at Versailles to tears and Marie Antoinette wrote sorrowfully about it to her mother in Vienna.

However, sympathy for the House of Orléans was now in short supply at Versailles as political events and the increasing dissent between the two branches of the Bourbon dynasty began to threaten the very survival of the monarchy. For as senior Prince of the Blood and notwithstanding his obligations to the King, the Duc d'Orléans was also President of both the Council of Princes and the Parlement of Paris. Traditionally these assemblies, which administered the law throughout France, were quietly opposed to the power of the King and watchful of any attempt to emasculate their influence in the country. The trouble had begun in January 1769 when the President of the Cour des Aides, Chrétien Malesherbes, presented the Duc de Chartres with an alarming report on the new taxation demanded by the King to finance the crippling debts incurred by France in the Seven Years War. Both Chartres and Malesherbes agreed that such proposals were inequitable, but more importantly they violated the tradition that taxes should not be levied without the consent of the people assembled in the Estates General. Their protests were abruptly dismissed by the King, and in March 1769 he summoned Malesherbes to Versailles and much to the amusement of the foppish courtiers present informed him that both the Cour des Aides and the Parlement were suspended. This event had a profound effect on Louis Philippe Joseph, kindling his political awakening and inspiring his subsequent opposition to arbitrary royal government and his involvement with the radical opposition. Equally inspirational were the words of his uncle, the Prince de Conti, addressed to Chartres and his fellow Princes of the Blood:

> Forward, gentlemen, no equivocation; if we falter we shall be treated like valets, as already we are only too much. We must make the court realize that we are Princes and peers of the kingdom and that, as such, it is up to us to set an example of resistance to arbitrary authority and to prevent the court from invading our privileges and those of the nation

In 1771 the mutual resentment came to a head when Chancellor Maupeou persuaded Louis XV to abolish the existing courts altogether and replace them with appointed bodies that would do the King's bidding without dissent. The Parlements responded by refusing to confirm the new system, describing it derogatively as the 'Parlement of Maupeou'. When their letters of protest began to flood into Versailles, each had been countersigned by the Duc de Chartres. This was not the behaviour expected of a Prince of the Blood, and the King reacted with fury. When news of this resistance led by the House of Orléans and their kinsmen the Condés and the Contis became public knowledge, the Paris crowds were jubilant. Already seeking the popularity that would be his making and eventually his downfall, Louis Philippe Joseph went out of the Palais-Royal and strolled around for an hour accepting the plaudits of the people. At that moment a myth was born: the belief that the Palais-Royal was the centre of resistance to despotic royal power and its inhabitants the aristocratic champions of a new and more enlightened democracy. The King's response to the opposition was swift and decisive. Firstly he wrote to the Duc d'Orléans reproaching him more in sorrow than in anger, then he issued in January 1771 a *lettre de cachet*, the personal edict of the sovereign, banishing the Duc and his son to internal exile at their estate of Villers-Cotterêts. On the night they left Paris a placard appeared on the wall of the Palais-Royal. It bore these prophetic words: 'Rise up, great Prince, and place the Crown on your head.'

Having decided to act against his recalcitrant kinsmen the King had no alternative but to continue his attempt to still the opposition. Two months later he signed the edict abolishing the traditional privileges of the Parlements and it passed into law. His action confirmed to the country his determination to assert the absolute power of the Crown at all cost over any elected court or assembly. In a document drafted for him by one of his counsellors, Gilbert de Voisins, Louis stated his own position unambiguously:

> In my person alone rests the sovereign power and it is from me alone that the Parlements hold their existence and their authority. That authority can only be exercised in my name and can never be turned against me. For it is exclusively to me that the legislative power belongs without any qualification or partition. The whole public order emanates from me since I am supreme guardian. My people and my person are one and the same and the rights and interests of the nation that some presume to make a body separate from the monarchy are necessarily united with my own and can only rest in my hands.

Alone among the Princes of the Blood, the Comte de la Marche openly supported the King by attending the emasculated Parlement while his colleagues sent a letter of protest and stayed away. Louis is reported to have read it swiftly, then thrown it on the fire. On 13 April the Princes appeared together again in Paris, but without the exiled Duc de Chartres, and were acclaimed as the leaders of the gathering revolt against despotism. Politics in France, as the Austrian ambassador Mercy d'Argentau reported to Vienna, had suddenly come alive. The rebellious princes, led by the House of Orléans, had shown the way to the rest of society in defending their ancient freedoms. 'They have opened the eyes of the entire nation,' wrote the lawyer Guy Target before launching himself into a series of pamphlets attacking Maupeou and what he stood for in the most vitriolic terms.

To his surprise, the Duc d'Orléans found himself the nominal head of this opposition and drawn into a quarrel not of his making. His son, however, had begun to relish the contest and to enjoy the plaudits of the crowd when he reappeared from his temporary exile at Villers-Cotterêts. When he deliberately cut the Comte de la Marche at an assembly the news spread throughout Paris and was taken as a harbinger of future acts of rebellion against Versailles.

That same year an event occurred that would offer Louis Philippe Joseph a new and unexpected power base through which he could expand and communicate his fast-developing ideas on constitutional reform. On 16 June the Comte de Clermont had died, leaving the Grand Mastery of French Freemasonry vacant and the opportunity for the young Duc de Chartres to extend his influence and gain new adherents to his developing opposition to absolutist monarchy.

4

FREEMASONS

FREEMASONRY HAD BECOME all the rage in France after having been introduced into the country in the first decade of the eighteenth century by English Masons, some of whom were Jacobite officers exiled at the Stuart court at St-Germain-en-Laye near Paris. The atmosphere of secrecy and intrigue that permeated Freemasonry had an immediate appeal to a society in which open political and philosophical discussion were discouraged. The more adventurous of the bourgeois came to see their lodge meetings as the ideal forum for discussing the radical ideas of Voltaire and Rousseau and as the only place in France where they could mix socially with those members of the nobility who were equally enthused by the new learning of the Enlightenment. A network of lodges was soon established under the aegis of the inappropriately named English Grand Lodge of France with, bizarrely, the English political adventurer the Duke of Wharton as its Grand Master. This curious structure was soon reformed and the lodges became entirely French; they excluded Jews, actors, workers and servants but encouraged membership by the nobility and, in spite of papal condemnation, the clergy. Who, after all, would not want to join an organization that counted some of the great minds of the age – Montesquieu, Condorcet, Helvétius, d'Alembert – among its numbers? One Parisian lodge, the Nine Sisters, even claimed both Voltaire and Benjamin Franklin as members. Such was the appeal of Freemasonry that by the time of de Clermont's death in 1771 even the King and his two sons were said to have been secretly initiated and there were over 40,000 Masons in France distributed among more than 1,000 lodges.

The Comte de Clermont, Louis de Bourbon-Condé, was another Prince of the Blood with a grudge against Louis XV, believing himself to have been treated churlishly by the King and ill rewarded for his many successes on the battlefield. For the last twenty years of his life he had conducted a clandestine but vitriolic campaign to blacken the monarch's name in a series of unsigned pamphlets defending the rights of the Parlements and attacking the growing despotism of Versailles. Impressed by the Orléans' unequivocal opposition to Maupeou and his royal master at Versailles, de Clermont made it clear that he saw the young Duc de Chartres as his logical successor. The great majority of rank-and-file Masons agreed, for not only was Chartres a Prince of the Blood and close to the succession but he had also shown an interest in and commitment to the ideas of the Enlightenment that now enthused Freemasonry. Still only twenty-four years old, he was clearly the 'coming man' in France and as such the ideal figurehead for a progressive and ambitious organization committed to liberal but non-violent reform.

Thus it was not surprising that barely a week after de Clermont's funeral, on 24 June 1771, Louis Philippe Joseph, Duc de Chartres, was unanimously elected Grand Master of all the regular lodges of France. His initiation ceremony, as related by the contemporary historian Christophe Montjoie, was macabre in the extreme. Chartres was brought into a darkened room, at the back of which was a dimly lit grotto where bones were displayed and a mannequin dressed up in the accoutrements of royalty was standing. The five brothers present then ordered Chartres to lie on the ground, as if he were dead. In that position he was told to recite all of the Masonry grades that he had received, and to repeat all of the oaths that he had made. He was then given a detailed description of the grade he was about to receive, and told to swear never to reveal anything of this to any Knight of Malta, the Catholic order that opposed Freemasonry. After this, Montjoie continues, the Duc was told to get up and to climb to the top step of a ladder that was placed against the wall and then to let himself fall off. Immediately after his fall he was given a dagger and ordered to strike at the crowned mannequin. As he did so a liquid, the colour of blood, squirted out on to him and dripped on to the floor. He was then told to cut the head off the figure and to hold it up in his right hand, with the dagger dripping blood in his left. It was then revealed to him that the bones in the grotto were those of Jacques de Molai, Grand Master of the Templar Order, and that the man whose blood he had spilled, and whose head he was holding in his right hand, was that of Philippe le Bel, King of France. Then he was shown the secret hand-shake of the Kadosch Knight, which was done in a stabbing gesture. Montjoie insists that this was the Duc de Chartres' initiation to cruelty, and that his slaying of the mannequin meant the assassination of Louis XVI. Perhaps this story was no more than an invention, an early example of the demo-nization of his character that would later be used to blacken Louis Philippe Joseph's name.

There was one final hurdle to surmount before Louis Philippe Joseph could take up the position of Grand Master. As with every major decision taken by a Prince of the Blood, even to visit a neighbouring country, the King's permission must first be obtained before the new Grand Master could take up his appointment. As both Orléans were still excluded from Versailles and nominally confined to their estate at Villers-Cotterêts, the Duc d'Orléans plucked up courage and wrote directly to the now ailing Louis XV.

Sire. I ask you to reconsider the severe restrictions placed on my son and myself. For two years we have remained in dis-grace and deprived of both your majesty's company and good opinion . . . I assure you, Sire, of our total loyalty to you and to the throne. Nor have we any wish to see your role or authority diminished in any way . . . Look into your heart and you will find assurance that the ancient bonds of loyalty that bind us together are undiminished and allow us to present to you in person the token of our love and loyalty.

The letter had the desired effect, for the *lettre de cachet* was quietly withdrawn and both members of the House of Orléans were once more welcomed to Versailles. Royal approval was also given for the Duc de Chartres' new appointment as Grand Master of the Grand Orient of France, and he immediately took up his duties. Those of his friends who were not already Masons also joined, including his old friend the Duc de Lauzun and his future secretary Pierre Choderlos de Laclos, who would soon use the network of lodges throughout France to promote the radical ideas emanating from the Palais-Royal. That same year much of intelligent French society appeared intent on becoming Masons. The eager newcomers included lawyers, journalists, industrialists, artists, philosophers, men as varied in their interests as the ballooning pioneers the Montgolfier brothers and the penniless future revolutionary Camille Desmoulins. It has been claimed that the lodges of the 1770s were the precursors of the Jacobin Clubs twenty year later. Certainly the apparently spontaneous spread of the revolution throughout France that followed the fall of the Bastille can be attributed to the highly efficient communications network provided by the Masonic lodges. So thorough was the Duc de Chartres' own commitment to the cause of Freemasonry that within the year he had persuaded his own Duchesse to join the female lodge of Folie-Titon in Paris. This was a rare public appearance for the reserved Marie Adélaïde but she was now emboldened by the presence of a new and highly influential lady-in-waiting at the Palais-Royal, Félicité Ducrest de Saint-Albin, better known as Madame de Genlis.

Twenty-six years old, pretty, cultured and above all determined, Félicité de Genlis was the niece of Madame de Montesson, the Duc d'Orléans' mistress. It was claimed that her aunt had engineered her entry into the Palais-Royal in order to bring about a reconciliation between Louis Philippe Joseph and his father, still estranged over the issue of Orléans' choice of mistress. Within a few months Félicité had become the inseparable companion of Marie Adélaïde and, without her knowledge, the lover of her husband. In an age when ladies of society led a repressed life dominated by gossip and trivia, Félicité was a true intellectual but able to conduct herself so diplomatically that her learning never appeared boorish or pedantic. A polymath, she was accomplished at everything from discussing philosophy with Diderot, Talleyrand or Voltaire at the salon she attracted to the Palais-Royal to acting brilliantly in the many plays and comedies devised by her aunt and playing the harp with professional skill. These qualities, combined with an innate knowledge of the techniques of seduction, made her a formidable operator in French society.

Even as a child she had displayed an unusual precocity, once insisting on wearing for several months the stage costume of Love that she found in a hamper at the family home in Burgundy. Although her family were in straitened circumstances, Félicité was given an excellent education and by the time she was sixteen had acquired many of the skills that were to make her famous. When her father, César Ducrest, was captured by the enemy fleet at Santo Domingo he was taken as a prisoner of war to England. Here he showed a fellow naval officer, the young Charles Alexis Brûlart, Comte de Genlis, a miniature portrait of his attractive daughter playing the harp. This, together with the letters from Félicité that her father allowed him to see, persuaded Genlis that he was already in love with her. On his release and return to France Genlis found the reality as desirable as the image and showed his honourable intentions by paying for her father to be released from the debtors' prison into which he had been thrown on his arrival back on French soil. Broken by the experience, Ducrest soon died, leaving his wife and daughter in near penury until Félicité's marriage to the Comte de Genlis in October 1763. Tellingly the marriage contract involved a settlement of 1,200 livres a year on the bride's mother too. Very much the poor relations of the Genlis family, the new bride and groom were nevertheless presented at court before Charles Alexis resumed his military service, this time with the army.

By now her aunt, Madame de Montesson, had introduced Félicité to the circle of the Duc d'Orléans, who suggested to his son that this gifted young woman would make an ideal companion and lady of honour for his wife. After much discussion it was agreed Félicité would join the household at a salary of 4,000 livres a year and that her husband would leave the army and take up an appointment as Captain of the Guard at the Palais-Royal for 5,000 livres. Her appointment was an immediate success for she was very different in character from the other ladies at the Palais-Royal. Within a few weeks she had already enthused Marie Adélaïde with her knowledge of English and Italian and her deep interest in all the arts and sciences. 'She attached herself to me,' she wrote in her *Memoirs*, 'with a kind of passion that lasted in full force for more than fifteen years.' To the young Duchesse, brought up in the stultified world of the high aristocracy, Félicité's company brought mental liberation and admission to a world of ideas that she had previously thought the exclusive province of men. Using her unrivalled charm and social skills Félicité managed to captivate her mistress without provoking the dangerous jealousy of the older and more socially elevated ladies of the household such as the Marquise de Polignac. Soon she was drafting letters for the Duchesse and dealing with her correspondence, for the lady-in-waiting had become both tutor and friend.

Louis Philippe Joseph was equally captivated by this vivacious newcomer, who was clearly far better read than himself; he confessed at this time to having read no more than six books in his entire life. It was a new experience for him to be able to abandon mere pleasantries with a woman and to discuss the ideas of Rousseau and Voltaire with her while still feeling a physical attraction. Tall, vigorous and alert, he had already shown a sartorial predilection for all things English, insisting that his coats and hats be made in the English style and affecting an interest in fast carriages and horse-racing. Predictably he fell completely in love with Félicité de Genlis, although he realized that this could be no passing affair and that he must retain her friendship at all cost, for the Palais-Royal could not afford to lose the talents of such a remarkable woman. Madame de Genlis had already become a prize asset of the Palais-Royal, her presence encouraging some of the liveliest minds in France to gather there. Twice a week she held a reception that attracted such politicians as Jean-Sylvain Bailly and Marie-Jean Hérault de Séchelles, men who would play an important role in the coming revolution, as well as artists and the composers Gluck and Monsigny. Not even Versailles had been able to attract such distinguished visitors, as Félicité soon realized when Marie Antoinette invited her to play the harp at Versailles in person – an invitation that was politely declined.

An opportunity for intimacy between Louis Philippe Joseph and Félicité first arose that July when the Duchesse, always in poor health, decided to travel to the spa at Forges and take the waters there in the hope of becoming pregnant again. It was his intention, Louis Philippe Joseph revealed in a letter discovered almost 200 years later, 'to live in closer relations there with Madame de Genlis'. Scarcely had the intimacy commenced when the Duc was summoned back to Paris where his sister was about to give birth. Frustrated by this unexpected separation, he wrote a series of passionate letters to Félicité addressing her as 'my child'. Her replies are equally passionate. 'Yes, my dear friend, I have given myself to you, abandoned myself to you in a transport of delight. Never was a friend or child so loved as you.' Yet in spite of these endearments most letters from the high-minded Félicité contained passages of moral rectitude exhorting Louis Philippe Joseph not to neglect his young wife and praising her for her purity, honesty and sensibility. All of this compromising correspondence was naturally intercepted by Louis XV's secret police, who passed on copies that were carefully locked away in the King's infamous *cabinet noir*. Yet within a year the romance had cooled and such terms of endearment as 'mon cher' and 'mon enfant' had been replaced in their letters by the more formal and conventional

'Monseigneur' and 'Madame'. Yet mutual respect and admiration remained as strong as ever, for they both realized that they had found a common cause. Using the Palais-Royal as their power base, they would promote the House of Orléans to real political power in France, perhaps even to the throne itself, while at the same time Félicité would discover the real and more important vocation of her life.

The waters of Forges were efficacious, for early the following year Marie Adélaïde was pregnant again. On 6 October 1773 she gave birth to a son in the presence of her husband, her father, the Prince de Condé, the Duc and Duchesse de Bourbon and almost the entire household of the Palais-Royal. Within an hour the news had spread through the streets of Paris and a cheering crowd assembled while the church of Saint-Eustache nearby echoed to the sound of a congratulatory *Te Deum*. The continuance of the Orléans dynasty was thus assured. The following year a second son would be born, followed by twin daughters in 1777 and a third son in 1779.

Meanwhile Madame de Genlis' celebrity continued as the *beau monde* of Paris flocked to her receptions and theatrical evenings at the Palais-Royal, where even a salon that seated 500 people now proved insufficient to accommodate them all. Her morally improving dramas, specially written for these occasions, were performed by her own daughters, Pulchérie and Caroline. It seemed that nothing Madame de Genlis did could fail, and when she wrote a book based on the fate of four Bordeaux gentlemen thrown into prison for life on a trumped-up charge of debt it became an overnight success, selling at a premium price to the Queen, the royal princesses, the Empress of Russia and the Electress of Saxony, among others. These unexpected triumphs encouraged her growing belief that she was destined to share her knowledge and tastes with a wider audience and to bring the new learning to the wealthy but generally poorly educated aristocracy of France. If this audience responded to the arts, would it not, in the true Enlightenment manner, also be intrigued by the fascination of science? To this end she commissioned a series of talks by the most eminent scientists of the day at the house of M. Sigault de la Fond and chemistry classes given by the royal apothecary, M. Mittouart. These activities confirmed to her that her true destiny was that of an unusually gifted educator able to enthuse an audience without pedantry.

Long before the birth of her daughters, the Duchesse de Chartres had promised Félicité, presumably with the Duc's approval, that she would entrust her with their education. This would have been a controversial decision, for traditionally women had never been involved in the education of the aristocracy in France. Now the time had come to implement it, and with typical boldness Félicité decided to set up a small school in Bellechasse convent near by where she would personally teach the Orléans girls together with her own daughters. At the Duc's expense a small building was erected in the grounds of the convent, every detail being designed by Madame de Genlis herself, including her own room with a glass door through which she could watch the children at work. On the classroom walls were hung pictures of the Roman Emperors, the Kings of France and great heroes from the past. The stairway was devoted to geography and hung with maps showing all the countries of the world. Foreign maids were hired to encourage a multilingual atmosphere that involved the children in speaking Italian at breakfast and English at dinner. Each Saturday a reception was held at which the pupils could mix with the celebrated visitors, some of the finest minds in France, who in turn were enthralled to visit such a progressive institution that embodied the very spirit of the Enlightenment. Still only thirty-one years old, Félicité de Genlis had found her true vocation as the most gifted and influential educationalist of her time.

5

AT SEA

NOW THAT HE had a son and heir, the Duc de Chartres was determined to find a more serious role for himself that would be appropriate to his place in French society yet remain non-political and uncontentious. A military career beckoned, but unlike his fellow European princes he decided to ignore the army and opt for the less fashionable navy. The reason for this unusual choice was that his father-in-law, the Duc de Penthièvre, was Grand Admiral of France, a highly prestigious and surprisingly lucrative office. Furthermore Penthièvre was nearing retirement and it seemed logical to Louis Philippe Joseph that he should be the natural inheritor of the post.

The first step would be to persuade Penthièvre to agree, but when the subject was broached the Duc insisted that he had given Chartres enough already in the form of his daughter and that he wanted to remain as Grand Admiral. Louis Philippe Joseph was furious at this supposed intransigence for it was well known that Penthièvre had never once put to sea and that his naval experience had been confined to mock manoeuvres with toy boats on his lake at Rambouillet. His refusal made Chartres even more convinced that his destiny lay at sea and that he had a natural, if yet unrevealed, talent for naval warfare. There was also the matter of the salary, for the office of Grand Admiral was worth 400,000 livres a year as well as the lucrative prize money and ransoms for prisoners-of-war taken at sea. Even with his own prodigious wealth Chartres was finding the cost of maintaining his huge establishment increasingly difficult to meet, and with the King's three sons ahead of him in the queue for royal preferment he could expect little from Versailles. When, in 1771, he had requested the vacant, and lucrative, Colonelcy of the Swiss and Grisons Regiment it had immediately been given to the Comte d'Artois.

Despite Penthièvre's rebuff Chartres remained persistent and again wrote and asked him to cede the office, claiming that if naval service was denied him he would be condemned to perpetual idleness and that all future army commands would automatically go to one of the King's three sons anyway. His only hope, he claimed, was the navy where he could make a reputation for himself and justify all expectations. Although this letter appeared sincere and thoroughly convincing, Penthièvre again refused, claiming that circumstances did not permit him to satisfy Chartres' request.

Denied the highest post in the navy, Louis Philippe Joseph then swallowed his pride and settled for one of the lowest by enlisting as a simple *garde de la marine* for the summer naval manoeuvres at Brest under the command of Admiral d'Orvilliers. His claim to talent as a naval officer must have been justified, for by the end of his second cruise he was pro-moted to the rank of full captain and the King wrote thanking him for popularizing the navy as a fashionable career for young aristocrats.

This marked the beginning of a period of improved rela-tions with the court. Louis Philippe Joseph not only became a frequent guest at Versailles but also acted as master of the revels to the Dauphin and his new bride. On each visit he would flirt with Marie Antoinette and her companion, the Princesse de Lamballe, paying them the most outrageous compliments. The Dauphin's younger brother, the seventeen-year-old Comte d'Artois, was equally delighted for his cousin to be back in favour and to be taken off for nights of debauchery by Chartres and his fellow reprobate, the Duc de Lauzun.

Then in May 1774 Louis XV displayed the first signs of the smallpox that he had so far managed to elude. His express wish, as his illness progressed, was for the Duc de Chartres to remain at Versailles and to continue the evening games of billiards and piquet that he had come to enjoy. This Louis Philippe Joseph, fully protected by childhood inoculation from the disease, willingly did, even accompanying the King to what would prove to be a last supper with his mistress, Madame du Barry. After a long agony Louis XV finally died on 10 May.

Before departing for Paris later that same day the Duc de Chartres requested an audience at which he pledged his loyalty to the new King. The Duc d'Orléans too was quick to assure Louis XVI of his fidelity, putting his 'long experience of public affairs and unrivalled knowledge of human nature' at the monarch's disposal. However, the new King, insecure and inexperienced but wary of any offers emanating from the Palais-Royal, chose instead to call upon the services of the Comte de Maurepas, one of his father's ex-ministers who had been dismissed in 1740 for daring to mock Madame de Pompadour. A traditionalist with little interest in reform, Maurepas pledged his personal loyalty to Louis, assuring him that he would listen to no one but himself. But the House of Orléans was reluctant to let the chance of influencing the new monarch pass uncontested, and father and son both wrote letters to the King urging him to at least examine the possibility of restoring the independence of the Parlements. Louis was unimpressed but diplomatically avoided a blank refusal, insisting that his cousins continue their regular visits to court. A warm friendship appeared to have developed between the new Queen and the Duchesse de Chartres, the latter entertaining Marie Antoinette with the latest gossip from Paris and advising her on the right dressmakers to choose.

The mutual suspicion between the two branches of the Bourbon dynasty now reasserted itself when Chancellor Maupeou, still in office, persuaded the King that Maurepas was secretly in collusion with the Orléans. Nor had the deliberate absence of the Duc d'Orléans and his son from the late King's funeral at Saint-Denis, a protest against the new Maupeou-inspired Parlement, helped matters. Maurepas suggested to the King, in order to take suspicion away from himself, that both Orléans be exiled. Rather than take this drastic measure, Louis made it clear that they were both in disgrace and ordered father and son immediately to leave Marly where the court was in session. On their first evening back in Paris the Duc and Duchesse de Chartres attended the opera, where they were loudly cheered by the audience for what was seen as another stand on principle against Versailles. A few days later the new King and his consort visited Paris and were greeted with silence.

Louis must have had doubts about Maupeou's policies, for by the autumn he had taken the advice of his more moderate advisers Miromesnil, Turgot and Malesherbes and capitulated to the opposition by restoring the power of the old Parlements. The Duc d'Orléans was exultant at his triumph. 'I am drunk with joy,' he wrote to his Chancellor, Lemoyne Bellisle. Whatever the political disagreements, the personal relationship between the Chartres and the new royal family appeared to have remained intact, at least until the following year when Marie Antoinette's younger brother Maximilien visited the French court. Delighted and perhaps distracted to see her brother again after many years, the Queen eagerly introduced the young man to the court and the King's ministers but unwisely failed to do the same to the Princes of the Blood. The Duc d'Orléans was outraged, seeing this as a personal insult delivered to the Bourbons by the Habsburgs, and ordered his kinsmen not to attend court; thereby transforming a purely domestic spat into what could have been an international issue. For the first time since she had arrived in France Marie Antoinette was incensed by the behaviour of both the Orléans. The Comte de la Marck later insisted that this seemingly petty incident marked the start of the bitter war between Marie Antoinette and Louis Philippe Joseph that would help to bring about both their deaths.

Once more out of favour at Versailles, the Duc de Chartres thought it opportune to resume his naval career by signing on for nine months' service, joining the fleet on 1 May 1775.

However, the Duc de Chartres was no ordinary officer, and the fleet was unable to sail until he had attended the coronation of the new King in Paris. Finally on 3 July he arrived at Rochefort and received all the honours due to his rank before inspecting the port and its garrison. Two days later he received the good news from Paris that Marie Adélaïde had given birth to their second son. The customary celebrations completed, the Duc set sail on board the *Tourterelle*, a twenty-six-gun frigate, before transferring to the flagship *Terpsichore* when the fleet reached La Rochelle. Untroubled by seasickness, the Duc found life on board most agreeable as the fleet cruised slowly along the coast of France and northern Spain. In fact it seems to have been little more than a pleasure cruise, the Duc going ashore to spend a leisurely day touring the Îsle de Ré and later visiting the cathedral at Compostella for the Festival of St James. As he informed the King by letter, naval life seemed to be very agreeable. Louis replied by congratulating him and without the least irony added, 'There can be no more promising start to his naval career than not to suffer from seasickness.'

Chartres returned to Paris on 12 September, only to be disappointed to find that he had again been passed over for two lucrative royal appointments, the Governorship of Languedoc and the Priory of the Order of Malta. Disgruntled and bored by his own inactivity, he consoled himself by commissioning the eminent architect Piètre to build him an observatory at the Palais-Royal but still spent most of his day idling or gambling at faro and dice. Yet he remained a dedicated admirer of all things English and the lifestyle of George, Prince of Wales, in particular. Having caught the latter's enthusiasm for fast carriages he now equipped himself with a smart new carriage and four and challenged his friends Lauzun and Fitzjames to race against him from Paris to Versailles. All three set off from the Palais-Royal at breakneck speed, Lauzun coming to grief at the halfway stage and Chartres soon after, leaving Fitzjames as the winner. On another occasion he raced the Comte de Genlis to

Fontainebleau for a substantial wager. Professing to be bored by everything around him, he even made one of the most futile bets in history by challenging Genlis to prick 500,000 holes in a piece of cardboard in under an hour. Yet his most consistent passion throughout this period of inaction was horse-racing, a sport that had been introduced from England in the reign of Louis XIV by his ancestor the Regent. A primitive course had been established at Longchamps decades earlier and it had become the custom for French enthusiasts to travel over to Newmarket each summer to watch the more professional racing there. Now in March 1775 Chartres persuaded the Comte d'Artois, his apprentice roué, to join him in establishing the first authentic English-style racetrack in France at Plaine des Sablons. Complete with English jockeys it was such a sensation that the Queen and her ladies came along and applauded Lauzun, who rode the first winner of the day.

The following year the prospect of war with England returned when France gave its support to rebellious British colonies in America. On 1 April Louis Philippe Joseph was promoted admiral and ordered to sail on board the *Solitaire* to Cape St Vincent where his ship would join the Toulon fleet. Second in command was a Comte de Bougainville, who was destined to become one of France's most famous explorers. Off Lagos the fleet began its manoeuvres under the direction of the Duc de Chartres, who had spent the past weeks improving his seamanship. His performance was generally much praised, being marred only by a minor collision between the *Solitaire* and the *Terpsichore* that Chartres readily admitted was his own fault. Nevertheless both ships needed to put into Cadiz for repairs. Louis Philippe Joseph, ever restless, went ashore and stayed with the French consul, who took him to his first bullfight. He was much heartened when a letter arrived from Sartine, the navy minister, saying, 'Only great men have the courage to own up to their mistakes. Take this slight mishap as a lesson for the future, Monseigneur, and be assured that His Majesty has the greatest confidence in you.' The King's faith in his kinsman's abilities as a naval commander must have been sincere, for on 4 January the following year the Duc de Chartres was promoted to the important post of Lieutenant General of the Navies of France. Perhaps the inevitable war with England over the American colonies would allow him the chance of military glory that he longed for.

However, when by August the French and British fleets were still at peace, Louis Philippe Joseph, bored with being at sea, left his ship and returned to Paris where his wife had just given birth to twin daughters, Mademoiselle d'Orléans and Mademoiselle de Chartres. Although both children were in good health their father came close to death himself, for having drunk a large glass of iced redcurrant juice he appeared poisoned and was seized by a violent fever and appalling stomach cramps. At four in the morning Tronchin, the resident physician at the Palais-Royal, had to be summoned, and he prescribed a hot bath and four sessions of bleeding. Marie Adélaïde was warned of the seriousness of her husband's condition, and for several hours he lingered near death until the fever suddenly lifted. When news of his recovery was released, the whole of Paris seemed to celebrate. *Te Deums* were sung, and the Freemasons ordered masses said by every lodge throughout France.

On 6 February 1778 France recognized the rebellious American colonies, bringing war with Britain even closer. Given the nature of the conflict on two continents sea power would play an important role in the hostilities. When Louis Philippe Joseph left suddenly to join the fleet at Brest, Marie Adélaïde deputized for him at a lavish ball to inaugurate a new salon at the Palais-Royal again designed by Piètre. Within a week he was back to lobby Minister Sartine for overall command of the fleet. Sartine advised patience. There were domestic problems to be dealt with too, for his sister, the Duchesse de Bourbon, had dismissed one of her ladies, Madame de Canillac, as her husband had become infatuated with her. Yet the Duchesse herself, in the sexual musical chairs of the time, had recently become the mistress of the King's brother the Comte d'Artois. Furious at her treatment, Madame de Canillac had taken revenge at a masked ball by openly flirting with the Comte d'Artois. This had in turn enraged the Duchesse de Bourbon, who strode up to her lover and ripped the mask from his face, an unforgivable breach of etiquette at a masked ball. As the scandal escalated the Duc de Bourbon sought to defend his wife's honour by challenging the Comte d'Artois to a duel in the Bois de Boulogne. At the last moment the combatants fell into each other's arms before a shot was fired and honour appeared satisfied. But the incident did little for the deteriorating relationship between the two branches of the ruling dynasty and even less for the respect in which the aristocracy was held. Marie Antoinette in particular was angered by this wild behaviour, having attempted to bring about a discreet reconciliation between the parties on behalf of the King. Although he was clearly not the main protagonist, she suspected that the Duc de Chartres was behind the scandal, motivated by his hatred of the royal family.

The Duc, who considered himself innocent of all blame, was delighted two months later to meet Voltaire for the first time. The great man was in Paris for the opening of his new play, *Irène*, and had asked to meet the man who had so valiantly led the nobles' opposition to Maupeou's reforms. His visit to the Palais-Royal was a great success, Voltaire spending hours deep in conversation with Louis Philippe Joseph, admiring the good looks of his children and praising the vision and fortitude of the House of Orléans. In contrast Louis XVI had refused Voltaire's request to visit him at Versailles, considering the eminent philosopher to be one of the most odious and dangerous men in his kingdom.

Scarcely had Voltaire departed than Chartres was ordered to return to Brest where on 13 May he boarded the *Saint Esprit* as Inspector General of the Fleet with responsibility for ensuring that each vessel was properly armed and provisioned for battle. He was also given naval command of the third or blue squadron but not, to his chagrin, responsibility for the whole fleet. He had again been passed over, this time in favour of the more experienced Comte d'Orvillier. As a sop to his pride Sartine had diplomatically asked Chartres to keep an eye on operations on behalf of the King and himself and to deal with a delicate problem of protocol that was causing concern at the Ministry. The regular officers, all of them with aristocratic connections, resented having to serve alongside mere merchant navy commoners drafted in to supplement the numbers. This petty dispute could well have compromised the performance of the fleet in battle. Louis Philippe Joseph proved unusually adept at dealing with the problem, inviting officers from both sections to his table and encouraging a relaxed and friendly atmosphere that soon resolved the problem.

Finally the long-awaited hostilities began on 17 June when the French frigate *La Belle Poule* encountered the more heavily armed *Arethusa* just off the French coast. After an engagement lasting several hours, *La Belle Poule* limped into Brest with forty dead on board. Until this encounter there had been no official declaration of war between the two nations but this inevitably followed and on 30 June the French fleet consisting of thirty-two ships left Brest in search of the enemy. As the forty-five-gun *Saint Esprit* was about to sail Chartres sent a last letter to his wife in Paris reassuring her of his safety, and even Marie Antoinette was moved to call incognito on Madame de Chartres that evening. For the next few weeks the two fleets manoeuvred without making contact until on 23 July the English Admiral Keppel discovered the French sailing to windward and set off in pursuit. A strong gale was blowing, making battle impossible until the 27th when the wind dropped and the French fleet divided into three sections off Ushant, with the Duc de Chartres commanding the vanguard. At a critical point in the battle Admiral d'Orvilliers ordered Chartres to bring his ships about and to attack the English rearguard, but Chartres appears to have made his move too late and the English were able to evade contact. The rest of the battle proved inconclusive, with both sides claiming victory. Keppel's version appeared in the London *Morning Post* a few days later:

> The gale abating, the enemy steered a leeward course and drew into line of battle. Immediately on perceiving this Mr Keppel gave the signal for running to windward and came to a general action . . . The French soon crowded all their sails and *gallantly* ran into Brest harbour, but not till they were pretty severely handled . . . His Royal Highness, the Duc de Chartres, had a grapple with the *Victory* but thought proper to retire on receiving her fourth broadside, with the rest of her squadron, leaving once more the British flag to ride in triumph over Brest.

Beyond dispute was the fact that the French had lost over 160 dead and over 500 wounded by the time they regained Brest. Unwisely Louis Philippe Joseph decided to personally carry the news of the 'victory' to Paris and then on to Versailles. He arrived there at two in the morning on Sunday 2 August and insisted that the King be woken and told the good news. Then it was back in triumph to the Palais-Royal to appear on the balcony with his wife and to accept the acclamation of a huge crowd. Later that day the mob celebrated Monseigneur's great victory by burning an effigy of Admiral Keppel in the gardens of the Palais-Royal. That evening the Duc and Duchesse de Chartres were given a twenty-minute standing ovation when they arrived at the opera. Celebrations continued the next day with a hastily arranged concert that included the recitation of a heroic poem in his honour while the inhabitants of streets surrounding the Palais-Royal decorated their windows with burning candles. The risk of hubris was imminent. Galloping back to Brest he rejoined his ship, and the fleet immediately put to sea. When he returned to Brest just over a month later there would be a far different welcome awaiting him.

In his absence the true nature of the battle was revealed in both London and Paris. The King and his ministers were informed that, far from being the hero of the hour, the Duc de Chartres had either misunderstood or had deliberately ignored d'Orvilliers' order to engage the enemy. Ominously the King wrote at letter of commiseration to d'Orvilliers. At the instigation of Maurepas, ballads mocking the Duc de Chartres began to appear on the streets of Paris and he was told that the Princesse de Lamballe and the Duchesse de Polignac were secretly laughing behind his back. Wounded by such ridicule, Louis Philippe Joseph informed Sartine that he intended to resign from the navy, but before this could be formalized news arrived that an inquiry held on board ship had already found that confusion rather than dereliction of duty was the reason why the French fleet had failed to defeat the English. Whatever Chartres' failings, lack of courage was not among them, and after landing at Brest on 18 September he went immediately to face the King and Queen at Choisy, where they were staying. As he entered not a single courtier applauded, and at the opera that evening only a polite welcome, appropriate to a Prince of the Blood, greeted his arrival. Even then a voice from the stalls shouted, 'Gentlemen, you are applauding an actor, not a Prince!' For the King and his ministers the Ushant Affair was just revenge on Chartres for all the trouble he had caused them with his vigorous opposition to Maupeou's reforms.

Profoundly wounded by the derision, Louis Philippe Joseph appealed to his friends to defend him, particularly the Comte de Genlis who had been on board the *Saint Esprit*. This de Genlis willingly did, urging the second in command, de la Motte Picquet, to give his account of events. Picquet confirmed Chartres' version, completely exonerating him and describing the Duc as an example to everyone on board, 'a man who had foregone his rank, his comforts and had even risked his health to set a good example to everyone on board and who remained cool and confident even in the heat of battle'. Furthermore the officer dismissed the question of the missed signals as pure invention by the newspapers. However, the Admiral begged to differ. 'I have reason to believe', d'Orvilliers wrote, 'that if the commander of the blue squadron had obeyed my signal then our day's work would have been crowned with glory.' Other officers clearly shared d'Orvilliers' opinion but hesitated to openly challenge a Prince of the Blood.

Whatever the truth of the matter, Louis Philippe Joseph had seen enough of the sea. In a letter full of passion and indignation he wrote to the King protesting his innocence and rebutting the slur on his name, his family and his honour and asking to be released from his naval command. As a face-saving gesture and in recognition of his service to the country he suggested that Louis appoint him to the vacant post of Colonel General of Hussars and Light Troops. When the Prince de Montbarrey, Minister for War, was told of this he objected strongly, pointing out to the King that other Princes of the Blood had accepted less exalted appointments and that they would certainly protest at this gratuitous and inappropriate appointment of a man who was still the centre of controversy. Montbarrey was also shocked to discover, as he told the King, that the Duc de Chartres had even attempted to bribe one of his War Ministry commissioners, offering the man 3,000 louis if he could get the Colonel Generalship approved in less than eight days. Louis wrote angrily to the Duc d'Orléans telling him that his son was forbidden to come to court for a month. This attempt at bribery appeared to infuriate the King far more than Louis Philippe Joseph's controversial behaviour at sea. As a result he endorsed Maurepas' advice that never again should a Prince of the Blood be given a military command merely because of rank; in future talent and experience would be the main criteria.

6

THE DEVELOPER

T HE CONTROVERSY OVER Louis Philippe Joseph's performance as a naval officer had come at a time when the
King was worried and distracted by his wife's imminent
confinement. This was resolved on 18 December 1778 when
Marie Antoinette gave birth to a son. That night Versailles
was illuminated with thousands of celebratory lights, while
the Palais-Royal, it was noticed, displayed only the meanest of
illuminations. The Ushant controversy marked a watershed in
the relationship between Versailles and the Palais-Royal, and
the historic rivalry between the two branches of the Bourbon
dynasty now degenerated into a mutual hostility that would
eventually become open hatred.

For Louis Philippe Joseph, his treatment at the hands of
the King and Queen was a bitterly wounding and humiliating
experience that he could neither forgive nor forget. Smarting
from the derision heaped on him, he attempted to save what
little was left of his military reputation by announcing that he
would rejoin the fleet at Saint-Malo where it was preparing to
support the army in a proposed invasion of England. But a
message from Versailles, written by Marie Antoinette at the
King's instructions – another petty and unnecessary insult –
ordered him to remain in Paris. 'So I am condemned to a life
of perpetual idleness,' he wrote to a friend. He now saw the
Queen as his greatest enemy at court, a realization made all
the more painful because of the efforts he had made to welcome
and entertain her when she had first arrived from Vienna. But
there had been a subtle change at Versailles that may have
contributed to the Queen's increasing hostility. Her closest
companion, the Princesse de Lamballe, one of Louis Philippe
Joseph's ex-lovers, had recently, as the result of a scandal, been

temporarily dismissed from the Queen's presence. Her place
had been taken by Yolande, Duchesse de Polignac, a woman
with a proven dislike of the Duc de Chartres and a deep contempt for the very name of Orléans. With his naval career in
ruins the Duc de Chartres attempted in the summer of 1780 to
escape abroad and distract himself by travelling in Turkey and
Egypt. But Princes of the Blood still required the sovereign's
permission to leave the country, and this was refused.
Grudgingly Louis did allow his cousin to visit Rome that
autumn as compensation.

On his return, Louis Philippe Joseph was faced with a
financial crisis that had developed over the past decade. His
household chancellor, Seguin, informed him that although
Marie Adélaïde had brought a generous wedding dowry with
her and the annual revenues from his vast estates exceeded
800,000 livres these were heavily mortgaged and insufficient to
maintain the upkeep of the Palais-Royal and his other houses,
let alone support his heavy gambling and extravagant lifestyle.
With a retinue of over 1,000 officials and servants to support,
the House of Orléans was in serious financial trouble. An
appeal to the generosity of their respective parents, the Duc de
Penthièvre and the Duc d'Orléans, produced a stop-gap contribution of 60,000 livres, a useful sum but insufficient to
prevent eventual financial disaster. A more radical solution was
urgently needed to avoid an embarrassing and humiliating
bankruptcy.

The solution came unexpectedly from Madame de Genlis'
brother, the Marquis Ducrest, who made the novel suggestion that the Palais-Royal be developed to take advantage of
the current building boom that had seen the rapid expansion
of Paris over the past few years. There was now a scarcity of
shops, cafés and commercial premises in the city centre, and
Ducrest believed that the extensive gardens of the Palais-
Royal would make an ideal venue for such businesses. Chartres
immediately agreed, but as his father remained the legal owner
his permission must also be obtained. Cleverly Ducrest
recruited his aunt, Madame de Montesson, to persuade the

Duc to cooperate and to see it as an opportunity to please his son and improve the fractious relationship between them. Orléans grudgingly agreed on condition that he retained ownership of all the furniture and paintings in the house and that certain rooms be retained for his exclusive use. So on 30 December 1780 Louis Philippe Joseph became the legal owner of the Palais-Royal and prepared to embark on one of the most comprehensive urban developments that Paris had ever seen. That same day he summoned the architect Piètre to discuss plans and prepare drawings with the help of Victor Louis, a young architect whom the Duc had met in Bordeaux. Three different schemes were produced, only the last receiving the Duc's approval on 12 June 1781. It comprised a regular colonnade on three sides of the gardens decorated by a façade of Corinthian columns. All opened on to a covered promenade lit by 188 street lamps suspended above the centre of the walkway – a successful design that remains unaltered to this day.

When news of this radical development was revealed, many of the local householders in the surrounding rues Montpensier, Beaujolais and Valois were horrified at the prospect of the demolition that would take place. Furthermore the gardens of the Palais-Royal had become a civic institution, a place of calm and shade in the hot Parisian summers. Free access to the gardens, originally a privilege, was now taken as a right, and when the Duc entered the gardens with his architects to survey them he was surrounded and abused by an angry crowd. Nevertheless he approached the project boldly and in a thoroughly modern way, putting all the plans on display and publishing a booklet explaining and defending the development. But the public remained hostile and he awoke one morning to see that the name of a nearby street had been painted over with 'Rue Ushant' and 'Rue Saint-Esprit', an unpleasant reminder of his recent troubles.

Over seventy surrounding properties would be affected by the development, and their legal status and that of the

Palais-Royal was unclear. Most of the owners were aristocrats, lawyers or financiers, and with the Marquis de Voyer at their head they knew how to defend their rights. At an audience granted by the Duc and Duchesse de Chartres they put their case forcefully, but their host replied that he needed the money and that was that. When they threatened to continue their resistance, pointing out that they had two million livres at their disposal, the Duc scornfully replied, 'Yes, but I have four.' To support their case the protestors researched old documents relating to Marshal Richelieu, who had left the Palais-Royal to Louis XIII and to Louis XIV who had then passed it on to his Orléans brother, Monsieur. Eventually the dispute arrived at Versailles and the royal council decided that Louis XIV's gift to his brother had legal validity and that work on the gardens could proceed. The disgruntled neighbours continued to protest, but the people of Paris were mollified by an assurance from Louis Philippe Joseph that the public would continue to have unhindered use of the gardens. Predictably the court at Versailles sneered openly at the project, predicting that he would never find the money and, even if he did, then the Duc de Chartres would soon tire of his pet scheme. But all were reduced to silence when on 8 August it was announced that he had raised one million livres from a firm of Genoese bankers and work could begin. On 9 November the builder, Berthault, was commissioned to begin the development, which must be completed by 1 April 1784. The first step was to remove all the iron gates and railings from the gardens, and these were sold for an immediate and very useful sum.

With this important enterprise under way Louis Philippe Joseph turned to the problem of the education of his children. Now the father of three sons and two daughters, he was concerned that they were growing up as playthings of their nurses, spoilt and indulged and without a proper intellectual education. Their present governor, the Chevalier de Bonnard, was a worthy ex-artillery officer who was responsible for the daily supervision of the children, who were now between four months and five years old. Bonnard had himself become worried by the little princes' pale complexions and asked the household physician, Tronchin, to suggest a regime that would improve their health. Tronchin recommended that the children's diet be strictly controlled, that they be kept in an unusually cool temperature and be washed only in cold water. But it was Bonnard's educational curriculum that really gave cause for concern, for it deliberately ignored the ideas of Plato, Locke and Rousseau and concentrated instead on his own idiosyncratic opinions of what was good and moral. Yet he was a kind and generous man and the children looked on him with real affection as he taught them a variety of subjects including history, geography and the rudiments of mathematics. The boys proved so adept at reading and writing that their father began to doubt if their letters to him were really their own work. Their mother loved them dearly, showering them with kisses whenever they met, and each summer they were taken to Saint-Cloud to play with their grandfather 'Papa Orléans', who was equally affectionate towards them. But Madame de Genlis had begun to question the wisdom of leaving such important children in the sole care of Bonnard, for their precocious behaviour, and that of the Duc de Valois in particular, was beginning to cause alarm. In January 1781 she took it upon herself to summon Bonnard and tell him of her concerns.

Matters came to a head the following year when Valois' behaviour – refusing to mount a horse with his father, running away in fear of dogs and generally being unruly – began to concern his father too. At a meeting to discuss the problem Félicité proposed that the elderly Comte de Schomberg, the Chevalier Durfort or the Comte de Thiard should replace Bonnard as governor. When the Duc had abruptly rejected all three candidates Félicité said suddenly, 'Then why not I?' The Duc, showing no surprise, replied, 'And why not?' Encouraged by Louis Philippe Joseph's positive response she immediately accepted the offer, later writing in her journal:

The manner and tone of the Duc de Chartres made a very strong impression on me. I saw the possibility of something quite out of the common, something famous, and I hoped that it might be possible for it to be realized. I told him quite frankly my thoughts. The Duc seemed charmed and said to me, 'Well, it's done. You shall be their governor.'

The next morning he summoned Bonnard and his deputy, the Abbé Guyot, and told them of his intention to appoint Madame de Genlis. Both men were speechless with amazement but could do little but accept their dismissal. Two days later he took his children to Bellechasse and presented them to Madame de Genlis, saying, 'My children, here is your new governor. Embrace her and love her well.' News of this radical appointment created a sensation in French society, reinforcing the growing belief that the Duc de Chartres was a master of the unexpected. It is hard today to realize what a radical appointment this was, for in the late eighteenth century women, particularly in France, were involved only in the education of small children. The idea of putting a woman in charge, not just of aristocrats but of important Princes and Princesses of the Blood, was revolutionary. When the proposal was put to the King for his approval he replied dismissively, 'Happily I have the Dauphin. The Comtesse d'Artois has her children. You have the right to do as you please with yours.' Nor was the excitement confined to France. A German visitor wrote back to a friend, exclaiming, 'What new theory of education has led this father to entrust his sons to the hands of a woman so long after the time when all princes take theirs away from them?' Versailles used its familiar weapon of ridicule to mock the Duc de Chartres, suggesting that the Duc de Luynes, the stupidest man at court, had asked the King if he might take over the governorship of the little Dauphin. There were doubts too whether Madame de Genlis' disingenuous account of her spontaneous appointment was really true, for the son of the Chevalier de Bonnard later claimed that papers in his possession proved that Madame de Genlis' appointment had been planned for months ahead.

The controversy must soon have become public knowledge, for as Louis Philippe Joseph arrived at the theatre with Madame de Genlis one evening in April to watch a performance of the new play, appropriately entitled *The Knowing Woman*, their entry was greeted by an odd mixture of cheers and catcalls lasting ten minutes. Chartres and his party treated their hostile reception with disdain, ignoring the cacophony as they smilingly took their seats.

Madame de Genlis was now the most controversial woman in France. The once penniless harpist had achieved her social and intellectual apotheosis and was now spoken of as an equal to the two great female intellectuals of the period, Madame de Sévigné and Madame de Staël. None of this furore appeared to affect the new governor, who the next day went about the business of introducing her new pupils into the little school at the Bellechasse convent with cool determination. She had refused the Duc's offer of 20,000 livres a year for her troubles, saying that her only reward would be his continuing friendship. She did, however, demand complete authority and control over the children, beginning with the immediate resignation of the Chevalier de Bonnard. To coincide with her new appointment Félicité now published three volumes of a tract on education that she had been preparing, *Adèle and Théodore. Letters on the Education of Princes and Young Persons*. The supposed pretentiousness of this best-selling work annoyed some at court who saw themselves satirized in the work. Madame d'Oberkirch, for example, wrote that 'Madame de Genlis is a vain woman who has exchanged her gown for the plain spun skirt of a pedagogue.' But Félicité was determined to apply the principles outlined in her book to the practical education of her pupils, and her success in doing so would make them the best-educated royal children in history.

Her curriculum was based on the ideas concerning education that Rousseau had described in *Émile* and included instruction in both practical and academic skills, so the children were taught carpentry, gardening, architecture and book binding as well as gymnastics, moral science, botany and six modern European languages as well as Latin and Greek. This was a revolutionary concept in education for until then no other school in the whole of Europe had thought to combine learning and practicality in such a manner. Madame de Genlis' radical system was to have a political significance that may not have been apparent at the time. Her star pupil, the future King Louis Philippe, would later write, 'Madame de Genlis turned us into honourable and virtuous republicans but in her vanity she wanted us to continue to be Princes of the Blood. There was much here that could not be reconciled.'

Having encroached into one area of the male domain with the governorship of the Orléans children, Madame de Genlis now proposed to invade another by publishing a book that attacked the *encyclopédistes* and their philosophy. So important had she become in the intellectual life of the time that one of their number, Dalembert, the Secretary, was dispatched to Bellechasse to offer her an unprecedented reward, full membership of the French Academy, if she promised to withdraw her book. This was indeed an offer of immortality, for she would be the first woman to be among the exalted ranks of 'The Forty'. To her credit Félicité refused the offer, saying that she was not prepared to compromise her freedom of thought and expression for such a reward.

Much of her time was now spent teaching the children at Bellechasse, who included the two elder sons of the Duc de Chartres and their sister, her own daughter Pulchérie de Genlis, her nephew and niece, César Ducrest and Henriette de Sercey, and two other little girls, Victorine de Chastenay and Josephine Louise de Montaut-Vavailles. On the walls and stairway of the school hung pictures depicting scenes from ancient and religious history commissioned from the painter Myris, for Félicité was convinced of the importance of images in the learning process. The children slept on simple plank beds with hard mattresses and were encouraged to work in the open air at the nearby farm of Saint-Leu that the Duc de Chartres had purchased at Félicité's request. Here they looked after animals, made cheese and baked bread while dressed in simple smocks made of a coarse cotton. Servants were kept to a minimum and the children served themselves at meals. All this was highly shocking to members of the court, who considered that the children of the highest family in the land were being brought up as mere peasants.

7

LONDON

I N 1777 THE Duc de Chartres had met, appropriately at the
Barbeau racecourse, a fellow owner, the Irish-born financial
entrepreneur and spy Nathaniel Parker Forth. Forth flitted
between England and France and had acquired a reputation
as an excellent judge of bloodstock, in which capacity he had
acquired the most successful racehorse of the time, Comus,
for the Comte d'Artois. Chartres was intrigued by Forth and
introduced him into his circle of friends who were eager to
buy promising English bloodstock in order to participate in
the new French craze for racing. Forth appeared to know
where anything could be found or done in England, from
discovering the right staghounds for the Chartres estate to
knowing the correct procedure for entering a horse for a
Selling Plate at Doncaster. So indispensable did Forth
become that the Duc paid him the singular compliment of
calling at his house in Paris rather than summoning him to
the Palais-Royal. Their friendship was enhanced by their
common interest in Freemasonry and by the fact that both
were out of favour at Versailles, Forth having been barred
for bringing his mistress into the royal presence and
attempting to pass her off as his wife. Such *faux pas* were
taken very seriously at Versailles.

Two years later, when the war over the American colonies
had ended, Forth, who was then in London, received at the
instigation of Madame de Genlis a strange request from
the Duc de Chartres to find him a little English girl from a
foundlings hospital. She must be:

> Pretty, with dark hair, not more than six years old: she must
> absolutely have a long nose, and she must not know one

word of French . . . My plan is that she will be brought up with my three-year-old daughters who will learn English by playing with the child . . . I should like the child to arrive this winter.

This was no easy task for such a busy man, so Forth recruited the help of a local clergyman who eventually found a likely prospect living in Christchurch in Hampshire. Her name was Nancy Syms and she was the illegitimate daughter of Mary Syms, a local woman who had recently married a ship's captain. As her daughter was now an embarrassment, she was prepared to part with her in return for the modest sum of twenty-four guineas. The deal was done and on 12 February 1780 Forth informed Louis Philippe Joseph that he was sending the little girl over to France with his next consignment of bloodstock. Chartres had his doubts about the arrangement, fearing that the child's family might some day want her back. 'I should have preferred a child who was completely alone in the world,' he told Forth, but the latter remained confident of his choice, saying, 'I am sending you the finest mare and the prettiest little girl in England.' On her arrival at the Palais-Royal Chartres took the child's hand and led her into Madame de Genlis' presence with the words, 'Here is our little treasure.' Both agreed that she was delightful, and Forth received a letter thanking him for his trouble and praising his excellent discrimination:

> I don't know whether you are a god or a devil, but one or the other you assuredly must be to have found the little angel you have sent us . . . I hope very much that you may wish for something from this country; I assure you that nothing could give me greater pleasure than the chance to prove to you the extent of my obligation.

Félicité de Genlis was so smitten by the girl that she immediately decided to adopt her and persuaded the Archbishop of Paris to rechristen her in the Catholic faith as Anne

Caroline Stéphanie de Genlis. One of the English books that Félicité was reading at the time was Samuel Richardson's *Pamela*, and it was by that nickname that Anne Caroline was to be known for the rest of her life. But the child's new guardian remained obsessed by the fear that her natural mother would one day return to reclaim her and it was not until Forth had persuaded the mother to swear an affidavit in front of no less a person than the Earl of Mansfield, Lord Chief Justice of England, that her fears were allayed.

Pamela, who was to become one of the great beauties of the age and the wife of the United Irishmen's leader and hero, Lord Edward Fitzgerald, had such an attractive personality that Félicité decided to repeat the experiment, and Forth was instructed to find another little English girl who would be brought up by her fifteen-year-old daughter Pulchérie. So in the spring of 1785 a second little English child, Hermine, arrived in France to join Pamela. Naturally French society chose to believe that the two girls were the natural offspring of the Duc de Chartres and Madame de Genlis and that the little school at Bellechasse had been established specifically to allow them to appear openly. Their birth dates seemed to correspond suspiciously with the visit to Forges and two mysterious trips to Spa that Chartres had undertaken when Madame de Genlis was known to have been there. In spite of repeated denials from the Palais-Royal the gossip persisted and was given more credence when it was revealed that one of Madame de Genlis' own novels, *Les Mères rivales*, unfortunately told the story of a mother who adopts her own illegitimate daughter. The truth of the matter will never be known but it seems more likely that the two little girls were not the natural children of Louis Philippe Joseph and Félicité de Genlis but were seen by them as the symbolic representation of their once passionate affair.

The success of his mission to procure the little girls had made Nathaniel Parker Forth indispensable to the Duc de Chartres. Acting as his English agent Forth continued to provide him with the latest hats, gloves and saddlery as well as supplying him with London gossip and news from the English racetracks. But the main business was buying and transporting racehorses for the Orléans' stable. One consignment alone comprised forty horses and required three ships to carry them over to Calais. Even when France and Britain went to war the correspondence continued with Forth who, on a secret mission to ascertain the French conditions for an armistice, was confident enough of their friendship to ask the Duc if he might stay at one of his houses in Paris. Respect for Forth's business acumen had grown into a genuine friendship between the two men and when Forth declined to take his profit from one transaction Louis Philippe Joseph wrote reproachfully to him: 'You have always endeavoured to do what would please me; I always have been and always shall be grateful. I have never seen any sign that you were looking after your own interests . . . For that reason I am distressed that you won't profit from one of my business undertakings.' Such honesty must have been a rare commodity in Paris at the time and only increased the regard that Chartres had already for this forthright and plain-dealing man and the English society he represented.

Such feelings of respect for England were in complete contrast to those held by Louis XVI, who remained an unabashed Anglophobe, despising a nation that had violated the Divine Right of Kings by decapitating its sovereign a century earlier and continued to exclude Catholics from most public offices. His wife shared his distrust of the English, believing that there 'peace and natural honesty were threatened by the spirit of unbridled liberty'. Louis also knew that many of the pamphlets attacking him and the Queen with scurrilous libels, such as *The Pleasures of Antoinette*, a scandal sheet depicting the Queen as a rampant lesbian, were being published in London. It was costing Versailles thousands of livres each month to buy them up when they arrived on the streets of Paris. In contrast Louis Philippe Joseph had for decades longed to visit the country he most admired; but he needed the permission of the sovereign, a restriction introduced by Louis XIV for all Princes of the Blood, not only to travel abroad but also to visit any part of France other than his own estates.

The war with Britain over the American colonies had made such a request pointless, but in July 1782, with peace imminent, Chartres wrote to Forth informing him of his intention to visit London in the near future and asking the agent to find him a suitable house to rent. The property should be in a pleasant part of the city but need not be large, although it must have stabling for at least twelve horses. In appearance it must be elegant but not too grand, a residence where he could live as a visiting French gentleman under the incognito of the Comte de Joinville. A month later Forth had found the ideal property, 35 Portland Place, at a rent of 350 guineas a year. When Chartres asked him to find a reliable concierge, Forth suggested that he live there and perform the role himself, even offering to pay a third of the rent. The Duc was delighted with the offer but declined to accept any rent. Both Madame de Genlis and the Marquis Ducrest, Chartres' financial adviser, were to use the house whenever they were in London. Félicité was, if anything, an even greater Anglophile than Chartres, adoring the great works of English literature and claiming to know much of Milton's *Paradise Lost* by heart. She wholeheartedly encouraged his desire to visit the land of Shakespeare and had written to the eminent historian Edward Gibbon in October 1779 telling him how much the Duc de Chartres admired his country and assuring him that if Chartres was not already French 'he would assuredly be English'.

In May 1783, three months after hostilities between Britain and France had ended, the King gave grudging permission for the Duc de Chartres to visit England and he set off accompanied by the Marquis de Conflans and the Duc de Fitzjames. Characteristically he used the prospect of the journey to bet a friend that he could travel from Paris to London in less than thirty hours. They arrived in England on a gloriously sunny day in May at the start of the flat-racing season, a coincidence that led the then French ambassador in London, the Comte de Moustier, to suggest sarcastically that this was the only reason he had bothered to come at all.

London had been rebuilt after the Great Fire of 1666 and now possessed broad avenues, fine houses and paved streets that contrasted dramatically with those of Paris. Not until the late nineteenth century would the redevelopment planned and executed by Baron Haussmann transform Paris into the most elegant capital in Europe. The house in Portland Place, part of a fashionable new development, delighted Chartres and proved the perfect base from which to explore the city he had longed to see for decades. Within a few days he had immersed himself in the London social scene and was seen everywhere. One of his first visits was to realize a long-held ambition and attend a debate in Parliament where he witnessed the British democracy at work. The club-like atmosphere in the House of Lords was, he thought, more appropriate to an agreeable coffee house: 'The members come in their greatcoats and boots and spurs. It is not uncommon to see a member lying stretched out on one of the benches while others are speaking. Some crack nuts; others eat oranges or whatever else is in season.' As befitted his rank he was invited to dine with George III, whose lifestyle at Windsor he found so much simpler and more contented than that of Louis XVI at Versailles. Unfortunately the King and Queen, although polite, were cautious of their foreign guest and wary of his dissolute reputation, fearing he would be a bad influence on their already wayward son George, Prince of Wales. The first meeting of the two princes, so similar in character, was not auspicious, George telling his brother Frederick, Duke of York, that the Duc de Chartres 'was rather clever but a great beast'.

London itself was a revelation to Louis Philippe Joseph. Everything seemed positive, buzzing with commerce and open to new ideas in a manner that would have been impossible in France. There seemed to be a friendly mixing between the classes, and he noted that, unlike the French nobility, the British aristocracy was not averse to investing in trade and manufacture. He made a resolve to explore the possibilities of himself becoming involved in such activities when he returned to France. A Prince of the Blood involved in trade was a strange prospect, but such a happening would be another opportunity to shock society and annoy the King. Nor did he neglect the pleasures that London offered, and he was soon attending Brooks's Club and travelling to New-market with some of its members, where his distinctive racing colours of pink and black were becoming recognized. On 12 May the *Morning Herald* noted caustically that the Duc de Chartres had the previous day watched the running of the Claret Stakes, and his face, rather than reflecting his lily ancestry, was suffused with a rosy glow, a reference to the vast amounts of claret drunk to celebrate the race. But his obvious eccentricity and the haughty manner of the grand seigneur startled some members of society, among them Lady Bessborough, who was shocked to see that the buttons on his elegant coat depicted stallions mounting mares and dogs copulating with bitches. She thought these accessories in poor taste for a member of the French royal family, unaware of his compulsion to outrage convention and assert his own individuality.

When he returned to England the following year Chartres found that his relationship with the Prince of Wales was much improved and verging on a warm friendship. Now they began going about together, visiting the races and theatres in the company of the prettiest actresses. Invited to join George in July at his pleasure dome, the Brighton Pavilion, Louis Philippe Joseph stayed on until late August. Later he wrote to his host: 'Nothing has given me greater pleasure than your assurances of friendship. Please count me as one of your closest and most devoted admirers.' Returning to London, he insisted on attending another parliamentary debate, this time at the House of Commons, a democratic institution that did not exist in France. By chance the debate included a powerful speech by Pitt the Younger attacking the power of the crown and blaming it for the growing corruption and infringement of civil liberties that were against the interests of the British people. Chartres was ecstatic at the conclusion, telling several MPs as he left that he had just witnessed the workings of a true democracy. His words were overheard and reported back to Versailles, for throughout his stay in London French agents closely observed his movements and eavesdropped on his conversations.

His visit that year coincided with a general election, and Chartres was able to observe at first hand the rumbustuous campaigning carried out by the Whigs and Tories. To his astonishment the candidates openly abused each other, provoking rioting and mayhem and generally behaving in a manner that would have been impossible in France. What was particularly surprising was the involvement of the British aristocracy on the political hustings. The sight of the attractive Duchess of Devonshire riding in an open carriage with the commoner Charles James Fox, openly campaigning for him and even offering kisses for votes, delighted Louis Philippe Joseph's sense of the absurd and the theatrical. A society that could conduct its serious political business so openly and so amusingly was for him something to aspire to. Although the new French ambassador, the Comte d'Adhémar, wrote approvingly of Chartres' behaviour in London, the King considered his flirtation with the English Whigs shocking and near traitorous. Even the English realized that their visitor's new political friendship was causing problems at home. The *Morning Herald* was uncannily accurate in a report that stated: 'The court of Versailles, it is said, are really afraid that the Gallic Prince should imbibe certain Whig principles during the present political struggle in England which may not be easily shaken off.'

That Chartres should be drawn to the Whigs was understandable, given that the Prince of Wales consorted openly with their leader Fox and spoke approvingly of them to his French guest. George and Louis Philippe Joseph had by now discovered that they had much in common, for both were in conflict with the ruling monarchs of their respective countries and both were seen to support the political opposition. They also shared a controversial lifestyle characterized by sexual scandal and heavy drinking. The *Morning Herald* reported seeing them both walking arm in arm in Hyde Park: 'The Prince appearing rather *pale* and the *Mons le Duc* very *rubrified*, it was observed that the Heir of Great Britain had taken up with the *lilies of France* and resigned the *rose of England* to the Prince of Bourbon.' Fifteen years the senior, Chartres soon assumed the role of elder brother to George, offering him advice and support in the numerous scrapes and embarrassments that plagued him. As a token of their new-found friendship they agreed that summer to exchange portraits. Forth was instructed by Louis Philippe Joseph to commission the greatest English portraitist of the day, Sir Joshua Reynolds, to paint a full-length portrait of him as Colonel General of Hussars. Reynolds's bill was 250 guineas, a large sum but Chartres promptly settled it before taking the painting to Carlton House and presenting it to the Prince.

During his London sojourn Louis Philippe Joseph did not neglect his reputation as one of France's greatest libertines, seeking out notorious places of debauchery and attending such scandalous entertainments as *The Calendar of a Man of Pleasure* and *Nocturnal Revels.* Behaving like an early sexual tourist he also sampled, with the help of Charles James Fox, the ladies of easy virtue who frequented the numerous taverns in the Strand, and as testimony to his growing taste for democracy he did not avoid encounters with even the cheapest whores. Ironically Chartres' first mistress, the lovely Rosalie Duthé, was now living in London, married to a rich merchant, but he thought it diplomatic not to contact her.

He did take the opportunity, however, to try and raise more capital for the Palais-Royal development that was fast draining his limited reserves. One scheme suggested by Ducrest was to set up a life insurance company in London as well as investing in the London stock market. This may well have been the reason that Chartres was rumoured to be depositing large sums of money, believed to total over twelve million livres, in English banks. The suspicion at Versailles was that this money would be used to foment future unrest in France. His most implacable critic, the historian Christophe Montjoie, had no doubt of this and caused further alarm at Versailles by claiming that Chartres had made several mysterious loans to Lord Stanhope and Dr Price, both members of the Revolution Society.

In spite of the escalating cost the Palais-Royal project was nearing completion and promising to be a great success. What was left of the gardens was being replanted with trees that restored the venue to its former glory. Now all he needed was the permission of the King before the shops and premises could be let to their new tenants. All Paris had watched the work with interest, and with completion imminent Chartres' success as an urban developer was assured. Soon it would inspire imitators, for both the King's brothers, the Comte de Provence and the Comte d'Artois, were planning to develop the gardens of the Luxembourg Place and the Roule area of the Faubourg Saint-Honoré, respectively.

8

THE INTREPID BALLOONIST

THROUGHOUT HIS LIFE Louis Philippe Joseph appeared to be seeking new experiences that tested both his courage and his nerve. Once he had descended into the depths of a lead mine for no other purpose than to test his nerve and to see how men could work in such an environment. Having been down he now, back from England, decided to go up and to experience the new passion for ballooning that captured the public imagination in the 1780s. It had begun with the Montgolfier brothers' pioneering flight on 19 September 1783 from the courtyard outside the Palace of Versailles when their balloon took off in the presence of the King and the entire royal household. The passengers on this historic flight were a sheep, a cock and a duck. After a flight of eight minutes the balloon, kept aloft by hot air from a burning brazier, landed safely in a nearby wood at Vaucresson, the only casualty being the cock who suffered a broken leg from a kick by the sheep. Two months later Pilâtre de Rozier and the Marquis d'Arlandes became the first human beings to take to the air when their balloon stayed aloft for half an hour and travelled seven kilometres across country. Yet the danger of these early aerial expeditions was soon revealed, for the following year de Rozier and his friend Pierre Romain were killed near Boulogne while attempting to cross the English Channel. Their balloon, kept aloft by a dangerous mixture of hydrogen and hot air, exploded at a height of almost 3,000 feet.

Louis Philippe Joseph was fascinated by these adventures and had witnessed the first de Rozier flight, following the balloon on horseback, and was there to greet them when they landed. Six days later, accompanied by the Duke of Cumberland, who had accepted an invitation to stay at the Palais-Royal, and his friend the Duc de Fitzjames he arrived at the Tuileries on a bitterly cold morning to watch de Rozier's rivals, the Robert brothers, take flight. As Chartres and his guests held the guy ropes his sister, the Duchesse de Bourbon, cut the last retaining line and the bright blue canopy soared into the air. On this occasion the flight lasted over two hours, Chartres leading an accompanying posse that followed it on horseback until it landed in open country, twenty-seven miles from Paris. The triumphant aviators were then rushed back to Paris by Chartres to accept the acclamation of a huge crowd before being fêted at the Palais-Royal by the new royal patron of ballooning. That same day Chartres commissioned a new and even more revolutionary balloon from the Roberts that would be the largest canopy yet built, cylindrical in shape and thirty feet in diameter. It would also be constructed from a radical new material, rubberized taffeta produced by the Réveillon factory in Paris. At either end would be two large cylinders acting as aerial rudders to steer the contraption. When built it was an amazing sight, a vast flying boat in which the Duc de Chartres intended to attempt the near impossible and make the first aerial crossing of the English Channel.

By early July 1784 the balloon was ready for take-off; all that was needed now was good weather. It was decided that an ascent be made from the park at Saint-Cloud, but technical problems delayed the flight until the 15th when conditions were perfect, and in front of a huge and excited crowd the Duc de Chartres climbed into the basket with the two Robert brothers. As the crowd pressed forward the wives of the Roberts released the ropes holding the gondola and the great canopy began slowly to rise. However, when level with the tops of the surrounding trees the balloon came to a halt and seemed unable to ascend further until several bags of ballast were thrown overboard, allowing it to continue its stately ascent. As the historian Montjoie wrote:

> Within three minutes the spectators lost sight of it. It rose to such a height that the voyagers not only lost sight of the earth

but felt themselves borne into a region very different from what they had left. Suddenly, although the weather was calm they were enveloped in a thick vapour, an impetuous wind turned the balloon around three times and the travellers abandoned all hope of being able to steer their ship.

So unexpectedly violent was the wind that the aviators feared it would rupture the canopy as the balloon started to rotate dangerously. Desperate to control the revolving balloon, they decided to discard the two taffeta-covered steering rudders at either end of the gondola. This had little effect and the balloon continued to spin out of control. 'Monseigneur,' cried one of the brothers, 'we are lost.' But Louis Philippe Joseph remained remarkably cool and phlegmatic. 'Is there nothing we can do?' he asked. 'Our only chance is to pierce the canopy,' replied one of the Roberts. Without another word Chartres prised off one of the ornamental wooden spears that decorated the gondola and drove it into the rubberized fabric, tearing a seven-foot-long hole in the canopy. At once the balloon began to descend rapidly while the desperate crew jettisoned the last remaining bags of sand ballast over the side. Below them they saw the surface of Lake Garenne fast approaching. Knowing that the chances of the gondola staying afloat were slim even if it survived the impact, they prepared themselves for the worst. Yet by some miracle the gondola struck the water at an angle and skimmed lightly across the surface, coming to rest near the shore. With great presence of mind Louis Philippe Joseph grabbed a dangling rope and threw it to a small boy, one of many spectators, who secured it to a tree. The other spectators were a herd of curious cows that had gathered to watch the spectacle. Forty minutes later the intrepid aviators were back in the park at Meudon, bruised but victorious after having set a new height record of almost 5,000 feet. The Duc de Chartres was again the hero of the hour, having had the courage to make the flight and then arguably saving the lives of himself and his companions by his prompt action. Surely the mockery that he had endured since the Battle of Ushant would now be dispelled.

This was not to be, for it was immediately suggested at Versailles, without justification, that the Duc de Chartres had been terrified throughout the flight and had pleaded with the Robert brothers to make a rapid return to the ground. Satirical verses and pamphlets appeared, mocking the brave aviator. One, a work of black propaganda, was entitled *The Private Life or an Apologia for the Serene Prince, Monseigneur the Duc de Chartres.* Much of the later vilification of Louis Philippe Joseph emanates from this highly damaging book as it purports to be a real autobiography, apologizing for Chartres' panic in the balloon and for his lying and degenerate behaviour in general. Written in the most cloying and expiatory language, it appears to blame his many failures on the moral degeneracy of his parents and repeats the old calumny that he had brought about the death of the Prince de Lamballe by deliberately introducing him to diseased prostitutes in order to marry his sister and gain the entire Penthièvre inheritance. All of his other supposed vices are mentioned in great detail: his subservience to the Freemasons, his greed, his licentiousness, his obsession with horse-racing, and above all his lickspittle Anglomania. Even his choice of a woman as governor for his children and the renovations at the Palais-Royal appear as mock apologies. The author of this piece reveals his true sympathies and his closeness to the court at Versailles when he goes on to praise the reigning monarch as 'that most just and righteous of kings'. As a riposte to the numerous tracts emanating from London, supposedly financed by Chartres, attacking Louis XVI and Marie Antoinette the *Apologia* was a very convincing and highly successful work of black propaganda. The King's brother, the Comte d'Artois, was so impressed with it that he personally placed a copy in the royal library.

Marie Adélaïde was both wounded and infuriated by the *Apologia*, personally offering a reward of 2,000 livres to whoever would reveal the identity of the author. Chartres, however, treated the libel with his customary disdain, saying that to him public opinion was not worth a single écu. It was a brave statement at a time when lack of money was again troubling him, for in spite of the success of the Palais-Royal development, revenues from the Orléans estates were still insufficient to meet the formidable overheads. New sources of income must be found or, as his new treasurer the Abbé Baudeau warned him, the House of Orléans would soon be bankrupt. The problem was that before any action could be taken to develop the Orléans' estates the permission of the King must be obtained. In the meantime Chartres attempted to introduce some economies into his lavish lifestyle. He began by selling his hunting dogs and their accoutrements to the Queen and the Comte d'Artois and dismissing about a hundred servants and retainers. On 13 August 1784 the King finally signed the letters patent that allowed him to sell the leases on the Palais-Royal development at a very reasonable rent. At the suggestion of the Abbé Baudeau he ordered more premises to be constructed on the fourth side of the garden. These would be of wood decorated with *trompe-l'œil* designs and significantly cheaper to rent than the more substantial stone buildings in the arcades. Soon the new buildings, grandly named 'The Tartars Camp', were being mocked by his enemies, who dubbed them 'The Pinewood Palaces' instead. The German diplomatic Baron Grimm, however, found the development 'the prettiest little marketplace I have ever seen'.

Once more Parisians were able to enter the gardens of the Palais-Royal, finding to their delight that rather than being defaced by commercial development they were enhanced. The first establishment to open was Dubuisson's Cellar Café at numbers 89–92 in the main arcade. No porters were allowed in the arcades, and rents must be paid six months in advance. Soon the 145 new boutiques, cafés, bookshops, hairdressers and chemists were attracting a huge and admiring crowd. The style and presentation of the develop-ment immediately won over the remaining detractors as the gardens became the new and most fashionable shopping centre in all Paris. The obvious success of the venture soon attracted speculators, and early in 1787 a company offered the Duc twelve million livres for the right to future rents. Encouraged by the rewards that his investment promised, Chartres now invited Nathaniel Parker Forth to come to Paris and help investigate the possibilities of building a cotton-spinning factory, a bleach manufacturing works and a network of canals across the whole of northern France.

One of the best locations in the arcade had been specially reserved for Jousserand, the proprietor of the famous Café Foy, a Parisian institution for the past fifty years. Jousserand was also allowed the unique distinction of being able to put a small pavilion on the lawns of the garden itself in summer. His rival Dubuisson replied with a large and elegant under-ground gallery, the Café du Caveau, which drew both political agitators and men of letters. Throughout the gardens there were also small kiosks selling refreshments where visitors could rest as they toured on foot or in their carriages. In every direction there were attractive vistas that caught the rising and setting sun at every season. The courtesans had also returned, the lights and bustle of the arcades making it far easier for them to ply their trade in safety. Baron Grimm thought the whole scene resembled some open-air ball. Indeed in June 1784 Louis Philippe Joseph had suggested the gardens should be the venue for just such a ball to celebrate the visit of the King of Sweden. As the King was travelling incognito a masked ball, in the Venetian manner, would be most appropriate. But Louis XVI vetoed the idea on moral grounds, anxious lest the masks encourage immoral and diplomatically embarrassing behaviour. Yet in spite of the bustle, the gardens of the Palais-Royal had retained their reputation as a meeting place for men and women interested in the arts, politics and philosophy where friends could sip a coffee or eat an ice in summer while engaging in lively conversation. There were literary salons too, and museums such as that of the balloonist Pilâtre de Rozier devoted to the new science of aeronautics. In October of that first year a puppet theatre opened that set the pattern for other theatrical and musical companies to perform and entertain there.

In contrast to the atrophied and stuffy atmosphere of the court at Versailles, the Palais-Royal and its gardens were a place of vivacity and innovation with the Duc de Chartres as its patron and figurehead. This naturally aroused the jealousy of the King and Queen, who saw the development as a deliberate attempt to gain popularity with the people at the expense of Versailles. Perhaps as a riposte, Marie Antoinette suddenly demanded that the Duc d'Orléans sell the royal family the great Château of Saint-Cloud with its magnificent gardens which was symbolically closer to Paris and its people than Versailles. Orléans was in a quandary, not wanting to sell but fearful of offending the King and above all the Queen if he did not. After long and tortuous negotiations, the financial controller, Calonne, managed to extract the vast sum of six million livres from the royal family and Saint-Cloud passed into the hands of Louis XVI and Marie Antoinette. Louis Philippe Joseph was predictably furious at losing Saint-Cloud, knowing that it was passing to his great enemy at court. To placate him his father agreed to pass over four million livres of rents that allowed Chartres to discharge some of his most urgent debts.

Now without Saint-Cloud, the elderly Duc d'Orléans continued living quietly and happily with Madame de Montesson, dividing his time between his remaining houses at Sainte-Assise, Raincy and the Hôtel de la Chaussée d'Antin in Paris. He adhered strictly to the condition imposed by the King, in return for permission to marry the Marquise, that she should not assume the title of Duchesse and that she must never be presented at court. Yet she accompanied her husband to public functions and was treated elsewhere as the Duchesse in all but name. In 1783 they together attended a ceremony at the military academy at Brienne where the fourteen-year-old winner of the prize for mathematics caught Madame de Montesson's attention by addressing her as flatteringly as

'Your Highness'; his name was Napoleon Bonaparte. But Orléans had the further distress of knowing that his son and daughter were scarcely less hostile towards their stepmother than the King himself. An air of rigid formality was maintained between them, somewhat alleviated by Madame de Montesson's tact and understanding in what was a very difficult situation. Even the Duc's kinsman, the Prince de Condé, refused to accept Madame de Montesson, and Orléans became used to wounding slights such as that from the Comte du Nord, who having accepted his invitation to dinner then refused after being told that he would have to meet Madame de Montesson.

In October 1785 the lady herself discovered that the Queen would be passing their house at Sainte-Assise as she travelled by boat along the river Seine en route for Paris. It seemed an ideal opportunity for Madame de Montesson to present herself on the river bank as Marie Antoinette passed, but a few days before the event she received an anonymous package containing a voluminous silk ribbon of gold and silver that was to be erected on the river bank to act as a symbolic barrier between herself and the passing Queen. Possibly as a result of this last wounding insult, the old Duc fell suddenly ill with what his doctor described as a 'fluxion of the chest'. Although he was himself suffering from an attack of jaundice, the Duc de Chartres hurried to his father's bedside. The whole family assembled, and even the King, who had retained an affection for Orléans in spite of his son's behaviour, ordered that he be kept informed of the old man's condition every quarter of an hour. On 17 November the *curé* of Saint-Eustache arrived to hear the old man's confession and give him the last rites before he died at dawn the following day.

As was his duty, the Duc de Chartres rode immediately to Versailles to inform the King of his father's death. The King replied in accordance with custom, 'Monsieur the Duc d'Orléans, I am truly vexed by the death of the Prince your father.' Madame de Montesson was then accompanied by the Duchesse de Castres and the Duchesse de Bourbon to

Paris, where at the King's orders she entered a convent, having been told that she must not decorate the doors of her carriage with the Orléans arms. After twelve days of official mourning the old Duc's heart and entrails were buried at the church of Saint-Port and his body interred at Val-de-Grâce. Louis Philippe Joseph was now sole master of the Orléans dynasty and about to embark on the most dramatic and controversial period of his life.

9

LEADER OF THE NOTABLES

NOW APPROACHING THE age of forty, Louis Philippe Joseph had changed little in character in the past twenty years in spite of his increasing involvement in politics. He was still more concerned with enjoyment than responsibility, and the passage of the years had begun to leave their mark on his physical appearance. His nose now had a slightly bulbous aspect and his face had become permanently flushed from overindulgence in strong wine. His best feature, his piercing blue eyes, remained impressive, but his receding hairline was evidence of the passing years. Nor was it a comfort that many young aristocrats, in emulation of this master of style and libertinage, had also shaved the front of their own heads in tribute. The characteristic faint yet sardonic smile remained constantly on his lips, reflecting the assumed lassitude and ennui that he had made his own. Still bored by the inaction imposed by his position as the senior Prince of the Blood, he soon lost interest in ballooning and returned to hunting and fencing, in which he was known to be proficient. He also maintained his remarkable sexual vitality, exploring sensuality in all its forms as his huge cache of pornography, discovered at the Palais-Royal after his death, revealed.

The mistresses still came and went with regularity. Over the years there was Mademoiselle de Cambis, soon followed by the Princesse de Lamballe, who was in turn supplanted by Madame de Genlis. Then shortly after the death of his father he met the woman who would remain his principal mistress until his death. Françoise-Marguerite Bouvier de Cépoy was the daughter of Georges-Louis Leclerk, Comte de Buffon, an author who had published the first authoritative encyclopedia on natural science. Better known as Agnès, Madame de Buffon was twenty years old in 1785 and a ravishing beauty. Before her early marriage to the Comte de Buffon she had been the mistress of the Comte de Genlis, the husband of Madame de Genlis. Félicité had persuaded the new Duc d'Orléans that the pretty Agnès would make him a highly desirable young mistress. This was a clever move on her part, for at a stroke she had prised Agnès away from her husband and handed her to her ex-lover as a controllable and unthreatening replacement for herself. Orléans was completely smitten by her, telling his friend the Duc de Lauzun that she was a little animal in bed and possessed of a wonderful body. Within a week Agnès was established in a splendid little bourgeois house on the rue Bleue and ready to receive her new lover.

However, fidelity to one woman was an impossibility for Louis Philippe Joseph, and the following year he added a second mistress to his entourage. This was another twenty-year-old who had recently arrived from England and would later give him much-needed comfort and support. Grace Dalrymple Elliott was the daughter of a Scottish gentleman whose family had fallen on hard times. At the age of fifteen she was persuaded to marry Sir John Elliott, a man even older than her father. The marriage proved a disaster, the dissimilarities in age and taste making life a misery for the lively and exceptionally beautiful young girl. Bored and discontented, she soon took a lover, but unlike his contemporary, Sir William Hamilton, who tolerated Emma's passionate affair with Lord Nelson, Elliott was not prepared to condone his wife's relationship with a younger man and, unusually for the time, sued for divorce. His young wife was disgraced and fled to France where she was discovered by Lord Cholmondeley, who brought her back to England where she soon became mistress to George, Prince of Wales, by whom she secretly gave birth to a daughter, suggestively named Georgiana Augusta Frederica Seymour. Grace's portrait, painted in 1778 by Thomas Gainsborough, is emblematic of the age, showing her slim figure in a golden gown, her powdered hair piled high on her head, a single black velvet band around her neck. She was now one of the leading courtesans in the land and was naturally introduced to the Duc de Chartres when he came to stay at Brighton. Mutual admiration of each other's tastes led to the Duc de Chartres becoming fascinated by his friend's beautiful mistress, and to his host's chagrin he invited Grace to visit him in Paris. A passionate affair followed, but within a year the relationship had cooled, as so often in Louis Philippe Joseph's life, into a friendship that would last for the next seven years.

Agnès de Buffon, however, remained the fixed point in his emotional life, a position she ensured by providing a unique combination of domestic comfort and erotic stimulation. She proved to be so charming that she even won over Marie Adélaïde, who grudgingly accepted her presence in her husband's life as long as she was not accorded the rights of second wife and her husband's respect and affection for herself as his wife was maintained. For the virtuous Marie Adélaïde the louche atmosphere of the Palais-Royal must have been hard to stomach, for both Félicité's husband, the new Marquis de Sillery, and her brother, the Marquis Ducrest, were infamous libertines who were constantly to be seen 'glass in hand chatting to a pretty girl on one of the dozens of sofas that lined the corridors of the Palais-Royal'. There were others, too, officials in the Orléans household who would play an important role in the coming revolution, among them Jacques-Pierre Brissot, the future leader of the Girondins, Camille Desmoulins, Jérôme Pétion, Mayor of Paris at the time of the Terror, and Bertrand Barère, one of the most extreme of the Jacobins. All enjoyed the patronage of the Duc d'Orléans and shared his hatred of the Queen.

Constantly abused and libelled by Versailles, Louis Philippe Joseph had his chance of revenge when an embarrassing scandal involving Marie Antoinette was revealed. It began in 1784 when the Parisian jeweller Bohmer offered the Queen a large and vulgar diamond necklace consisting of 647 brilliants for just over one and a half million livres. This was the equivalent cost of two fully fitted-out warships, making it impossible for her to accept, but an enterprising minor retainer at Versailles, Jeanne de la Motte, saw an opportunity to benefit from the situation. She persuaded Louis, Cardinal de Rohan, then in disgrace for having behaved badly when on a diplomatic mission to Vienna, that the Queen would be delighted if he used his vast wealth to purchase the necklace for her. To convince the hesitant de Rohan, de la Motte, in a charade similar to the tricking of Malvolio in *Twelfth Night*, persuaded a local prostitute to pose as the Queen and meet de Rohan at night in the gardens of Versailles and express her longing for the necklace. De Rohan was duped and agreed to buy it as a gift for the Queen, who in gratitude would then make sure that he was restored to favour at court. De la Motte collected it on the Cardinal's behalf, but instead of handing it to the Queen she had it broken up and sold the diamonds in small lots. With the money she bought herself a substantial estate at Bar-sur-l'Aube. When asked to pay by the jeweller, de Rohan was mystified, having failed to see the Queen appear with her new necklace. His notes to the Queen enquiring about it produced first bafflement, then anger. When the King was told of the débâcle, he had de Rohan and de la Motte arrested and thrown into the Bastille. The subsequent inquiry revealed de Rohan as a fool and de la Motte as a thief. She was flogged and branded with the letter 'V' for *voleuse*, but de la Motte became a popular hero with the crowd for she had exposed the greed and extravagance of the Queen. Marie Antoinette's embarrassment was a godsend to her enemies at the Palais-Royal and provided an unexpected opportunity to heap further calumny on her, portraying the unfortunate woman as a depraved and vindictive slut. A flood of scurrilous pamphlets now appeared on the streets of Paris proclaiming her depravity. One of the more extreme claimed that the Queen and Jeanne de la Motte were lesbians and that Jeanne's rejection of her erstwhile lover had provoked Marie Antoinette into fabricating the episode of the necklace in order to take revenge on the poor and vulnerable woman.

This wave of anti-Versailles propaganda emanating from the Palais-Royal was certainly funded out of the vast inheritance that Louis Philippe Joseph had gained with the death of his father. It was an astonishing legacy. With the Duchies of Orléans, Valois, Chartres, d'Étampes and de la Ferté-Alais came the great houses of the Palais-Royal, the Hôtel du Plessis-Châtillon in Paris and the Hôtel de Grande Ferrare at Fontainebleau. Moreover there were the domains of Domfront, Carentan, Saint-Lô, Coutances, Valognes, d'Auge, de Mortain and the huge forest of Bondy too. The legacy comprised in all an astonishing one twentieth of the whole of France – approximately two and a half million hectares – and included some of the most fertile land in the kingdom as well as dozens of canals and forests. Although some of it was encumbered by historic debt and burdened by the maladministration of thousands of inefficient officials and tax collectors, only the King himself enjoyed a greater income.

With these funds the new Duc d'Orléans could now afford to back the political activities of those who, like himself, were determined to curb the power of the French monarchy and introduce democratic reform. Over the past year Félicité de Genlis had been assiduously courting the liberal intelligentsia, the artists, writers, philosophers and politicians opposed to 'the despotism', and encouraging them to look on the Palais-Royal as the most important salon of free speech in Paris. Her brother, the Marquis Ducrest, having demonstrated his administrative talents in overseeing the commercial development of the Palais-Royal gardens, was now the official chancellor of the Orléans household with an impressive salary of 100,000 livres a year. Although described by Talleyrand as 'a mere charlatan', Ducrest played a powerful role with his sister in the emergence of an efficient and politically significant regime at the Palais-Royal. One consequence of Ducrest's arrival was Louis Philippe Joseph's new interest in the workings of his vast estates and of the commercial activities at the Palais-Royal, where work on a new theatre, today the home of the Comédie Française, began in August 1786. The gardens were further embellished with the addition of a central circus comprising classical columns and fountains that created a cooling oasis for hot summer days. It was here that Louis Philippe Joseph received the ambassadors of Prince Tipoo Sahib, the bane of English rule in India.

A sound judge of character, Ducrest recruited much new talent to assist him at the Palais-Royal. Jérôme Geoffroi de Limon became financial controller and Henri Shée, an Irish officer in the service of France, personal secretary to the Duc, while another Irishman, Henri Clarke, took charge of the military personnel. But his most significant appointment was that of Jacques-Pierre Brissot, already a renowned and subversive journalist under surveillance by both the police and the Ministry of Foreign Affairs. Brissot, the son of a cook, was a firebrand who had championed the cause of the American colonists and opposed absolutism in France, but unlike his patron the Duc d'Orléans he was no admirer of the British and their constitution, having spent some time in London as a journalist. There he had attempted to set up an academy for the benefit of European liberals in exile involving such leading intellectuals as Jeremy Bentham. Returning to France, Brissot decided to counter police harassment by seeking the protection of a powerful public figure. He therefore approached Louis Philippe Joseph who, after consulting Ducrest, suggested that he join the household of the Palais-Royal as a teacher working under the direction of Madame de Genlis. This had been a wise move by Brissot, for he was soon suspected by Versailles of being the author of yet another pamphlet attacking the Queen and was arrested in September 1784 and thrown into the Bastille. His new patron, however, came immediately to his rescue and Brissot was soon released, becoming an invaluable publicist for the ideas of Mirabeau, Talleyrand, Barthès and other liberals associated with the Palais-Royal.

He was also instrumental in interesting his patron in the cause of black emancipation by introducing him to the great swordsman and composer the Chevalier de Saint-Georges, the 'Black Mozart'. Saint-Georges had been born in Guadeloupe, the son of a French aristocrat and a black slave mother. Brought to France to be educated, the boy showed a remarkable talent for music, eventually joining the theatrical company that Madame de Montesson had established at Raincy. Here he was introduced to Louis Philippe Joseph, who found him stimulating company and offered him a post at the Palais-Royal. On two of his visits to England Chartres had taken Saint-Georges with him and they had met Thomas Clarkson and other members of the Society for the Abolition of the Slave Trade. The anti-slavery issue appealed to Louis Philippe Joseph's liberal instincts, and on his return to Paris he determined with Brissot to help establish a French society that would work to eradicate slavery from the French colonies. This became a reality in 1788 when Brissot founded the Société des Amis des Noirs, which brought to France the growing abolitionist movement that had swept Europe.

However, Brissot's most valuable contribution was to change the public image of the Duc d'Orléans and to present him to the public, already intrigued by his eccentricity and impressed by his courage in opposing Versailles, as the ideal candidate for the post of liberal monarch if the current sovereign could be overthrown. It would be one of the first public relations exercises in modern history, transforming the image of a supposedly arrogant, cynical and distant prince into a man of the people dedicated to pulling down an overweening monarchy and improving the lot of the ordinary citizen.

Brissot began using his unique talent for communications to issue statements in the Duc's name that attacked the power of the King and praised the efforts of true democrats to bring about a fundamental change in French society. Cleverly he also encouraged the Duc to associate more with the leading philosophers, scientists and political thinkers of the day, often providing them with sinecures in the vast administrative apparatus of the Orléans estates throughout France. This patronage not only provided these intellectuals with a valuable income but also gave them the political protection of one of the most powerful men in the land. The Duc d'Orléans played his part by allowing Brissot considerable power to make appointments himself, such as appointing Jérôme Pétion, later republican Mayor of Paris, to the Orléans office at Chartres, and two other future Convention members, Chasset and Blot, to positions at Villefranche-en-Beaujolais and Lyon respectively. Men of lesser education who were enthused with liberal ideas and a commitment to bringing about a reform of French society were also recruited to the Orléans patrimony by Brissot and the Marquis Ducrest. Dozens of appointments were made without Louis Philippe Joseph even being involved, his lieutenants not caring to bother him with such trivia.

Gradually the Palais-Royal was becoming the base for real political resistance to the power of Versailles, and the Duc d'Orléans was increasingly seen as the democratic king in waiting. For his part Louis Philippe Joseph showed little concern for the august future that his acolytes had ordained for him, maintaining his self-indulgent lifestyle and content to leave the manipulation of his pubic image to others. Only his hatred of Marie Antoinette could provoke a strong reaction, as when she strongly objected to the proposed marriage of his little daughter to the twelve-year-old son of the Comte d'Artois. As a response he refused to accompany his eldest son, now Duc de Chartres, when he was formally presented to Louis XVI on 26 December 1786, persuading his father-in-law, the Duc de Penthièvre, to go in his place. The young man was received coldly at Versailles, neither the King nor the Queen deigning to take his proffered hand and his cousins refusing to embrace him. The mutual embarrassment was only relieved when the amiable Comte d'Artois stepped forward and offered him a chair to sit on.

This event led to a further deterioration of the relationship between Versailles and the Palais-Royal, for it came a few days before the country was plunged into a dramatic financial crisis by the revelation of an enormous debt of over

100 million livres. The new Controller-General, Charles Calonne, a man with a reputation for *laissez-faire* economics, decided that strong measures were now unavoidable. A harsher tax regime to raise new revenue was urgently needed, and another confrontation with the Parlements became unavoidable. The first step was to convene the Assembly of Notables, which had not met since 1626. Ominously for Calonne it decided to elect the new Duc d'Orléans as its president. But when the members assembled at Versailles on 22 February 1787 their new president was found to be missing; he had with his habitual insouciance gone hunting instead, only arriving at Versailles in the late afternoon. In the following days Calonne warned the 144 delegates that the nobility must expect to bear the brunt of the new taxation in the form of a tax on landed property and another on contracts and patents. Most importantly, a single customs tax would end for ever the peculation and smuggling that was bleeding the state of revenue. As expected, his proposals were greeted with such outrage that Louis Philippe Joseph immediately bet the Duc de Lauzun fifty louis that they would never be accepted. That their new president was taking the mounting crisis less seriously than the occasion warranted was confirmed a few days later when he failed again to appear at the Assembly. His excuse was that he had been delayed hunting and by chasing a stag into the heart of Paris along the Faubourg Montmartre and the Faubourg Saint-Honoré and dispatching it before an excited crowd in the Place Louis XV.

Calonne's proposals had united the nobility and the clergy, who for the first time were also now expected to pay taxes. With the sole exception of the Comte d'Artois, the Assembly of Notables rejected the reforms. They had taken particular offence that Calonne, a known spendthrift and dandy who had insisted that the seats in his coach be lined with fur in winter, should have the effrontery to be so harsh with others. For the first time Calonne and the King faced a near-united Assembly, politically aware and determined to frustrate their proposed reforms. Their case was not helped by the discovery that Calonne was involved in some murky financial transactions himself, including speculation over royal land, the Company of the Indies and even the supply of water to Paris. He responded by appealing to the people over the heads of the Notables and denouncing them as rich egotists concerned only with preserving their own privileges at the expense of the common good. Having alienated the nobles, the clergy and most importantly Marie Antoinette by not promoting her favourites, Calonne had little support left and was abruptly dismissed by the King. As his effigy was burnt on the Pont Neuf he was stripped of his honours and forced to surrender his country estate before being allowed to go into exile.

His successor, Loménie de Brienne, a member of the Assembly of Notables who had previously opposed the reforms, soon recognized that there was little alternative but to persist with them. He did, however, offer to trade their imposition for a promise by the King to restore the older and more comprehensive representative body, the Estates General. This was seen as a victory for the Assembly of Notables and for their president, the Duc d'Orléans. Although he had more to lose financially from the reforms than any of the others he was consoled by the prospect of the King losing even more. Above all, there was a new political climate in France, a feeling that royal power was no longer inviolate and that the same probing and questioning that had led to the downfall of Calonne would prevail with his successors. As Talleyrand wrote: 'Everyone now realized that by criticism and opposition to the dictates of ministers real change could be brought about.' People now began to speak openly of liberty and equality and to even contemplate a reformed monarchy similar to Britain's.

10

HERO OF THE HOUR

A LTHOUGH HE HAD played little part in the deliberations of the Assembly of Notables, the Duc d'Orléans continued to be seen as the leader of the opposition. As a figurehead his credentials were impeccable for not only was he the senior Prince of the Blood but he had also openly challenged the arbitrary power of Versailles. Many, not just his supporters at the Palais-Royal, saw him as a king in waiting, dispassionate, open minded and prepared to embrace reform. Jacques Brissot, who had, albeit temporarily, abandoned his republican beliefs, even described his patron enthusiastically as 'the one man who is capable of reuniting France'. Both Brissot and Ducrest were now convinced that they must work tirelessly to bring the Duc d'Orléans to the throne and that he should rule under a democratic constitution based on the British model. Their problem, as ever, was to stir their patron from his habitual apathy and to persuade him to share their enthusiasm for the task.

The Orléans threat had certainly been recognized at Versailles, and the King's advisers attempted to counter it by devising a strategy that would remove the troublesome Duc d'Orléans from the country altogether. Their plan was to persuade the people of Brabant, in near revolt against their Dutch masters, to accept him as the first ruler of a new and independent Belgium in return for French support to allow them to break away from Holland. When the idea was put to him, Louis Philippe Joseph showed little enthusiasm for the role or for being domiciled in the provincial city of Brussels. Yet he was not averse to inspecting his proposed domain and set off with a large entourage including his family and Madame de Genlis to take the waters at the town of Spa. As they passed through eastern France cheering crowds brandishing red, white and blue cockades, the Orléans colours, greeted their carriages. The journey also provided a good opportunity to introduce his thirteen-year-old son and heir, the new Duc de Chartres, to his future responsibilities. At Lille Chartres was received with full military honours by the Prince de Robecq before travelling on to Spa with the Marquis Ducrest. Using the pretext of his role of governor to the young prince Ducrest was able to continue secret negotiations with local politicians about the future of the Brabant throne. Independence for Belgium would require a change of regime in Holland, which in turn would require French military intervention, but Louis XVI, under the advice of Loménie de Brienne, eventually announced that it would not be forthcoming, which allowed the King of Prussia to send troops in support of the ruling Stadholder, the Prince of Orange.

On 17 June 1787 the historic first meeting of the new Estates General took place at Versailles, the opening sessions passing without controversy as the delegates adopted measures that reformed the provincial administration, encouraged free trade and modernized the collection of customs revenues. Every speaker was careful not to mention the critical issue of taxation. To avoid an immediate confrontation, Louis XVI had decided that he would not call a traditional *lit de justice*, a form of privy council that could endorse but not discuss the dictates of the crown, but would rely instead on the open sessions of the Estates General instead. However, as soon as the reform of stamp duty was mentioned Le Coigneux de Belabre leapt to his feet and to great acclaim vehemently opposed it, demanding that the King reveal to the Estates the full details of all tax receipts before any reform was debated. He was then seconded by Emmanuel Fréteau and the Abbé Sabathier. Faced with such an obvious and determined revolt the King reluctantly withdrew the motion. At stake for the crown was an urgently needed loan of 400 million livres. When the Estates refused to debate it for a second time a royal minister, the Marquis de Lamoignon, lost his temper and harangued the delegates, accusing them of the grossest disloyalty and pointing out that the King had already set a good example by making draconian economies in his own household expenditure. In reality he had merely disbanded a couple of packs of hunting dogs and pensioned off a few retainers.

Matters came to a head on 19 November when the King, closely guarded by troops, arrived to confront the Estates in person. Silence fell as he entered the hall and began addressing the delegates in his high-pitched, snuffling voice. He did not prevaricate but told them firmly that he expected their cooperation in approving these urgently needed reforms. The debate then commenced, each speaker determined to show that he was not cowed by the presence of the King. To a man they criticized the conduct of the royal ministers and refused outright to endorse the motion. After a seven-hour debate and just as the vote was about to be taken the King suddenly intervened. Rising to his feet he said in a calm voice, 'After having listened to your advice I find that I have no alternative but to insist on the motion being passed at my express command. I ordain therefore that the edict be entered into the register of my Parliament and it is to be executed according to its form and tenor.' There was complete silence throughout the hall, for these were the words customarily used by the King in a *lit de justice*. The Duc d'Orléans then rose slowly to his feet and in a voice shaking with emotion astonished the entire assembly by uttering the following words: 'If the King holds a royal session of Parliament the votes should be collected and counted . . . but if this is a *lit de justice* he imposes silence on us all.' The King, attempting to control his anger, replied that it was indeed a royal session. 'In which case, sir,' Orléans said quietly, 'allow me to lay at your feet the illegality of your order.'

This was an astonishing event; a Prince of the Blood was in open Parliament challenging the rights of a French king. There was no precedent for this. Angry but determined,

Louis continued. 'But it is legal because I wish it,' he asserted, and then, face scarlet with anger, he strode from the hall. As pandemonium broke out the King's ministers attempted to close the proceedings but the excited members refused to let this happen until the minutes of this historic session had been recorded for posterity as follows:

> The Parliament, considering the illegality of what has just passed at the royal session in which the votes were not counted in the manner prescribed and the debate not completed, declares that it has not taken part in the due process regarding the loans, gradual and successive, for the years 1788 to 1792 and postpones its decision until the next meeting of the Estates General.

As Louis Philippe Joseph left the hall he was swept up by the crowd and carried in triumph to his coach before returning to great acclamation at the Palais-Royal. His had been a unique intervention, for in the past French princes had often taken up arms against their sovereign but none had ever opposed him in an open, democratic forum. Characteristically he later told Brissot that he had not made his stand against the King to please his friends or to side with the Parliament but merely because the King had 'treated me with so much insolence'.

Although the King would have preferred to take no action against the malcontents, rightly suspecting that strong measures would only make them even greater heroes, Marie Antoinette insisted that he do so. Determined that Orléans should pay for his insolence, she persuaded her husband to issue *lettres de cachet* against Fréteau, Sabathier and the Duc d'Orléans. The following day at six in the evening Baron de Breteuil, Minister of the Royal Household, handed the Duc d'Orléans a *lettre de cachet* ordering him to leave Paris and to confine himself to his estate at Villers-Cotterêts. As expected, Louis Philippe Joseph treated the punishment with amused contempt, setting off from the Palais-Royal at eleven that evening to cheers and cries of 'Long live the Duc d'Orléans!' from the huge crowd gathered outside. As he mounted his carriage he turned to the Baron de Breteuil, who had been sent to enforce the royal dictate, and snapped contemptuously to him, as if to a lackey, 'And you, get up behind.'

The following day Fréteau and the Abbé Sabathier were arrested and confined in the citadel of Doullens and Mont St Michel respectively. The King was also prepared to punish every other member of the Estates who had encouraged the Duc d'Orléans to make his insolent challenge, but the Estates presented a determined face, sending a delegation to Versailles a week later to defend their actions and protest at the exiling of the Duc and his supporters. 'If they are guilty then we all are,' their petition asserted. At Villers-Cotterêts the Duc fretted 'like a child deprived of his toys' and mourned the absence of Madame de Buffon, although he did manage a weekly tryst with her in a pavilion at Bourg de Nanteuil near by. Every day he was urged by Brissot to become more active in the mounting political opposition to Versailles and to play up his role as martyr for democracy and justice, but he remained more concerned with alleviating the terms of his exile and persuading the few friends he retained at court, such as the Princesse de Lamballe, to plead his cause. To all entreaties Louis XVI patiently and persistently replied, 'Remember I am only treating him as a responsible father would.' Loath to appeal directly to the King himself, Louis Philippe Joseph persuaded Madame de Montesson, a close friend of Loménie de Brienne, to ask the minister to intervene on his behalf. Again the request was politely refused. Finally he wrote directly to the King himself, pleading that he must return to Paris as his financial controller, the Marquis de Limon, was desperately ill and the weather at Villers-Cotterêts at this time of year was particularly unpleasant. As a sop to the King a rather implausible stratagem was agreed with the Marquis Ducrest by which the latter would resign his post at the Palais-Royal and take the blame for organizing anti-royalist activity there. That done, Ducrest would prudently leave

Paris and spend the next few months in England. Yet neither the letter nor Ducrest's 'confession' carried any weight with the King, who merely advised his cousin, through Montmorin, the Minister for Foreign Affairs, to remain patiently at Villers-Cotterêts.

Meanwhile in Paris the Duc d'Orléans was even more of a popular hero, being portrayed in dozens of pamphlets as the innocent victim of royal despotism who had nobly rejected the offer of his own liberty until his comrades, Fréteau and Sabathier, had received theirs. One anonymous writer added to his reputation as a man of singular courage by claiming that he had once seen the Duc jump into the river Aisne to rescue a jockey from drowning. It was an event to set alongside his established reputation as one of France's most intrepid balloonists. At last, on 20 December, his father-in-law the Duc de Penthièvre managed to persuade the King to allow him to move to Raincy, a short distance from Paris, but the change of venue served only to make Louis Philippe Joseph even more discontented as he realized that he much preferred the grandeur of Villers-Cotterêts.

The continuing impasse between Versailles and the Estates General had produced a crisis in the administration of France that made the transaction of normal, legal business virtually impossible. Unrest had, ominously, begun to spread to the streets of Paris too. There was even the first mention of civil war and talk of a march on Versailles to force the King to observe the wishes of Parliament. One morning the words 'Palace for Sale, Ministers for Execution, and Crown on Offer!' were found scrawled on the walls of Versailles. For their part the King's ministers, Loménie de Brienne and Chrétien Lamoignon, began making secret provision for a royal coup d'état that would see France controlled by the army, Parliament abolished and the King ruling alone. First they must attempt to bring the figurehead of opposition, the Duc d'Orléans, back into the fold. Meanwhile the Duc had been informed by letter that if he was prepared to renounce both politics and his opposition to the King his exile would be rescinded. Wisely he ignored the approach, but his continued exile had become such an embarrassment to Versailles that in the following spring, on 16 April 1788, he received a letter that all but conceded victory:

> My cousin. I wish to have the support of all the Princes of the Blood when next I attend Parliament. It is with pleasure therefore that I revoke the order that confines you to Raincy. I am told that you will no longer oppose me and I welcome you back with the warmest affection.

The very next day Orléans was back at Versailles ready to ceremonially assist the King from his bed and to endure a fifteen-minute lecture on the perfidy of those presumptuous lawyers who, thinking themselves the new aristocracy, were seeking to usurp the timeless bond that existed between the sovereign and his people. Yet the King appeared so friendly that Louis Philippe Joseph seized the opportunity of asking him, together with the Queen, to stand as godparent at the forthcoming baptism of his two infant sons, the Ducs de Montpensier and Beaujolais. Quick to capitalize on this thaw in relations between Versailles and the Palais-Royal, he then overplayed his hand by proposing that his daughter, Mademoiselle Orléans, become engaged to the Comte d'Artois' son, thereby further uniting the two branches of the Bourbon dynasty. When told of this suggestion Marie Antoinette raised her arms in horror and the project was immediately abandoned.

True to his word, Orléans kept apart from the political controversy that continued to escalate in the face of the King's continuing threat to suspend the Estates General. Although Orléans was free, Fréteau and the Abbé Sabatier remained in prison, the latter at the curious fortress of Mont St Michel. This prison was in reality a Benedictine monastery, and the Prior had the dual role of head of a religious brotherhood and governor of a prison used to incarcerate those arrested under *lettres de cachet*. Perhaps as a personal gesture of support for Sabatier, and certainly in defiance of the wishes of Louis Philippe Joseph, Madame de Genlis, on a tour of Normandy and Brittany in June 1788, insisted on visiting Mont St Michel accompanied by the young Orléans princes. The Duc de Chartres later, when King Louis Philippe, described their visit as a formative experience in his understanding of state terror. For it was here in the reign of Louis XIV that a Dutch journalist had been held in a cage for seventeen years for writing an article criticizing the Sun King. After dining with the monks the Orléans party toured the prison and met the inmates but were appalled by the iron cage that was later vividly described by Chartres:

> On one of the posts there was a flower that the wretched man had carved with a nail. The prior told us that the cage was scarcely ever used . . . He said he had toyed with the idea of demolishing it as a relic of barbaric times and we promptly asked him to do this to mark our visit. The prior cheerfully consented, to the great joy of the prisoners who were following.

In his *Memoirs* Louis Philippe Joseph claimed that this visit to Mont St Michel with Madame de Genlis and his brother was the origin of their 'ardour for the ideals of Revolution' and put in perspective their own lives of comfort and privilege.

II

LACLOS

B Y AUGUST 1788 the royal treasury was virtually empty
and the political vacuum of the past months had served
only to unite the three Estates against the King. Worn
out by the strain of office and the twin misfortunes of syphilis
and tuberculosis, de Brienne lacked the energy to continue,
and on 25 August he resigned. His successor was Geneva-
born banker Jacques Necker, who ten years earlier, as Director
rather than Controller of Finances – his foreign birth and
Protestant faith precluded him from the more imposing title –
had been more concerned with borrowing to fund the royal
debt than in raising taxes. Necker's first move now was to
persuade Louis XVI to recall the Estates General and the
opening session was arranged, surprisingly without any due
sense of urgency, for 1 January the following year. One of the
reasons for the delay was that the composition of the assembly
had changed little since 1614 although the political life of
France had witnessed a fundamental shift of influence away
from the clergy and aristocracy and towards the bourgeois of
the Third Estate.

In spite of his promise to the King to abstain from political
activity, the Duc d'Orléans remained president of the First
Estate and, whether he liked it or not, could not avoid involvement in the continuing political discussions at the Palais-Royal.
Unlike his fellow Princes of the Blood and the majority of the
aristocracy in the Assembly, he favoured a radical challenge to
the King's proposed reforms. His fellow notables, such as the
Maréchal de Beavau, the Marquis de Lafayette and the Ducs de
Mortemart and La Rochambeau, appeared more concerned
with preserving their historic privileges. When the Prince de
Conti presented Louis XVI with a document reminding him

of these rights Louis Philippe Joseph had refused to sign it, finding himself in the unlikely company of the Comte de Provence, the King's brother. Only a fundamental reform of the whole political system on the lines advocated by Brissot would now satisfy the Duc. His own account of his opinions at this time is revealing:

> For some time now, having mixed with different classes of society, I have been developing a taste for liberty. Furthermore my travels abroad have taken me to England, that homeland of liberty . . . although I have no detailed knowledge of the English constitution but I do know that it has produced a free and happy people.

What characterizes the period immediately before the revolution is the host of clubs and societies that sprang up to discuss and debate the new political opportunities that had appeared. The most important of these was the Club of Thirty, which Counsellor Duport established at his home in the rue Grand Chantier. Meeting several times a week, it included among its distinguished members the Comte de Mirabeau, the Marquis de Lafayette, the Duke of Dorset, British Ambassador to France, Talleyrand and Louis Philippe Joseph's old friend the Duc de Lauzun, now the Duc de Biron. Lawyers and businessmen too were among its members and able to openly debate the political future of France with their social superiors. At each meeting a series of issues was discussed and then voted upon in the democratic manner – a novelty in pre-revolutionary France. Some members espoused a new constitution for France based on the English system, others favoured that of America. All were agreed, however, that it must be characterized by transparency and fairness, otherwise a tyrannical parliament would merely replace an absolute monarchy. All agreed that the first step towards reform was to enlarge the structure of the old 1614 Estates General by doubling the number of members of the Third Estate.

Unable to contain himself further, on 5 December Louis Philippe Joseph broke his promise to the King and attended a meeting of the Club des Enragés at the Restaurant Masse in the arcades of the Palais-Royal. Furthermore he spoke enthusiastically in support of Emmanuel Sieyès' call for reform, and was cheered by the huge crowd that had gathered there. Within a few weeks Sieyès had his own club in the arcades, confirming the Palais-Royal as the most important centre for public debate in Paris. Most of the participants were already members of Masonic lodges and well used to debating the issues that were now coming into the public domain. All were clearly in favour of a peaceful revolution that would transform the whole system of government in France.

Finally on 27 December Louis XVI reluctantly announced that he would now agree to the doubling of the number of deputies in the Third Estate, but he still opposed the other fundamental demand of the reformers, that decisions be taken on a one-man, one-vote basis. Yet nothing could now stop the clamour for fundamental reform that was rapidly becoming a call for revolution. The actual word 'revolution' now began to appear in many of the titles of the political pamphlets that flowed from the presses. These tracts urged the reader to fight absolutism and privilege and to campaign to bring the finances of the state under the control and scrutiny of the people. It was an opportune message at a time when serious hunger again threatened thousands of lives and the very stability of the state, for bad weather throughout the spring and summer of 1788 had resulted in a meagre harvest and the price of bread had shot up alarmingly as it had done in the last years of Louis XV's reign. Many blamed Necker for the crisis, claiming that he was in league with ruthless speculators who were buying up grain and withholding it in order to make vast profits. The parlous state of the economy was also blamed on the incompetence of royal ministers who had entered into a commercial treaty with Britain two years earlier that had been detrimental to French interests, resulting in cheaper British goods flooding

the French market and putting hundreds of native manufacturing companies out of business. The privation and despair
that now harried the labouring poor made them eager, if less
eloquent, recruits to the cause of revolution. Grain convoys
were attacked in Brittany and Franche-Comté, and the agitation soon spread to every part of France. Ominous shouts of
'Wipe out all aristocrats and the bourgeoisie!' and 'Let's burn
Versailles!' were heard for the first time.

To his advisers at the Palais-Royal it seemed the opportune moment for the Duc d'Orléans to make his move and to
use the popular discontent to make himself the unequivocal
candidate for a reformed and liberal monarchy. What could
be more appropriate than that a Prince of the Blood who had
suffered at the hands of the absolute monarchy should lead
the people in a peaceful but fundamental revolution? Again
Louis Philippe Joseph procrastinated, unable to accept the
challenge of the moment and declare himself a candidate for
a reformed monarchy.

Among those now clamouring for him to fulfil his destiny
was a newcomer to the Palais-Royal, an ex-soldier and keen
disciple of Jean-Jacques Rousseau, Pierre Ambroise Choderlos
de Laclos. Born into a minor and impecunious noble family,
Laclos felt himself a victim of a system that offered little
advancement to a man, however great his abilities, who did not
have a powerful friend at court. As an officer, like Napoleon
Bonaparte after him, in the unfashionable artillery, Laclos
could expect only slow promotion with little prospect of
obtaining a significant command. Then in 1782 he poured all
his frustration and cynicism into one of the first great
modern novels, written in the form of an exchange of letters
between two aristocrats conspiring to seduce an innocent
bourgeoise. *Les Liaisons dangereuses* was a sensation from its
first edition, catching the imagination of French society and
being reprinted legally, and illegally, in fifty editions in the
next decade alone. Even Marie Antoinette possessed a copy
in a discreet plain binding, but Laclos' reward was a mere
1,600 livres from the first edition. Unprotected by law, he

became the victim of unscrupulous publishers who flooded the market with pirated editions. The effect of having his triumph snatched from him in this manner further embittered Laclos. His troubles were compounded in 1786 when, a few months after he had married, he unwisely published a pamphlet, without the permission of his superior officers, attacking the doyen of French military fortifications, Marshal Vauban. The Minister for War, the Marquis de Ségur, was furious, even recalling Laclos from leave and severely reprimanding him. He was assured that there would be little chance of even modest promotion in future. In desperation he attempted to resign his commission and find a command in the Turkish army. His unexpected saviour was the Vicomte de Ségur, son of his old enemy the War Minister, who admired his talents as a writer and immediately introduced him to the Duc d'Orléans.

Equally impressed by Laclos' obvious intelligence and ability, Louis Philippe Joseph decided in late 1788 to employ him at the Palais-Royal on a generous salary of 6,000 livres a year and with the use of an apartment near by. The timing was opportune, for Brissot had decided to leave France for America for a time and his absence would weaken the team of advisers at the Palais-Royal. Laclos accepted the post as a secretary with specific responsibilities for the political education of the fifteen-year-old Duc de Chartres. When told this startling news Madame de Genlis immediately resigned all responsibility for the education of the young prince, saying that she was shocked that the Duc d'Orléans would even consider appointing such an immoral man. 'You are worthy of consultation on anything to do with history or literature,' he replied coldly, 'but not on politics.' Félicité remained convinced, however, that she exerted a virtuous influence on her master while Laclos' effect was malign. The contrast was amusingly described by the historian Michelet, who wrote: 'As you pass the Palais-Royal, look up at the windows. In one you will see a man in white, at another a man in black. They represent virtue and vice, the twin counsellors of the Duc d'Orléans.'

From the moment of his arrival Laclos became indispensable to his master, working closely with Brissot and Ducrest
and involved in every political move. As Talleyrand wrote: 'To
have such a clever man as Laclos in his camp with his ruthless
ambition and bad reputation would have greatly appealed to
the Duc d'Orléans.' Laclos had arrived in Paris at an opportune moment and like a good soldier realized that any
campaign, military or political, must be supported by good
intelligence. This, for Laclos, meant planting spies at Versailles and throughout the political clubs to report events in
the fast-changing political scene. Although committed to
both a just society and a constitutional monarchy, he had not
yet developed a detailed concept of how it would work. He
has rightly been described as a 'sorcerer's apprentice' to the
political ambitions of his master.

His first contribution to the cause was to ghost-write for
Louis Philippe Joseph a small, eight-page manifesto entitled
The Instructions, which purported to set out the seventeen
most important political precepts of the Duc d'Orléans.
These included his positive attitude towards the new
Assembly and his implacable opposition to any royal interference in its composition. Most importantly, it demanded a
society that guarded the liberty of the individual, guaranteed
freedom of expression, made sure that all correspondence
was kept secret and affirmed an individual's right to own
property. On a personal note it also called for a fairer taxation
system but with compensation for those Princes of the Blood
who voluntarily gave up their privileges. Another of its most
socially radical demands, insisted on by Laclos, was an appeal
for divorce to be legalized in order to alleviate 'the scandal of
so many bad and ill-advised marriages'. These were revolutionary demands from Orléans, and all the more surprising
coming from a man who was among the leading beneficiaries
of the old system of noble privilege. Not surprisingly these
ideas went down well with such fellow radicals as the Abbé
Sieyès, Bishop of Chartres and a frequent guest along with
Louis Philippe Joseph at the home of the Duc de Biron,

another reprobate turned revolutionary. Emmanuel Sieyès was yet another talented man, born into near poverty, who found advancement by cultivating the aristocratic intelligentsia. No less a person than Madame de Staël found him 'an unusual and gifted individual driven by a desire for reform and prepared to sacrifice himself for noble ideals'. His first contribution to the debate, a pamphlet, *What Then is the Third Estate?* had recently elevated him into the first rank of the potential revolutionaries.

Working in collaboration with Sieyès, Laclos next produced for Orléans another more substantial, sixty-seven-page manifesto, *Deliberations,* that proposed in detail how the Assembly would work and the kind of just and liberal society that would emerge under its aegis. This was the most fundamental and important political manifesto yet produced, and its success was astonishing. More than 100,000 copies were printed and distributed through the network of Masonic lodges and, with Sieyès assistance, to parish priests throughout France. Considered by many of the aristocracy as an appalling example of class betrayal and near seditious in content, the *Deliberations* provoked a bitter attack in print from half a dozen fellow nobles. The controversy delighted and amused the Duc, who admitted that he basked in both the adulation of his friends and the hatred of his enemies. Spurred on by the success of these pamphlets, he then announced that he would stand in the coming elections for the Estates General as a candidate not only in Orléans, Villers-Cotterêts and Crépy-en-Valois but in Paris too. Louis XVI was appalled at the news, realizing that his cousin intended to renege on any promises he had made to renounce politics and to resume his place in the ranks of the opposition.

As winter approached the weather became bitterly cold, the Seine froze from November to January, and hunger returned. True to the family tradition of public charity, the Duc d'Orléans ordered that bread be distributed throughout his estates and that the old and infirm be given a warm refuge in every available building. In Paris, 1,000 livres' worth of bread was given each day to the poor of the parish of Saint-Eustache. Even his confirmed enemy the historian Montjoie was forced to admire Louis Philippe Joseph's compassion. He told of the Duc traversing the Faubourg Saint-Germain in his carriage and being so appalled by the misery there that he ordered his driver to stop. Seeing an empty coach-house to rent, he sent for the owner and gave him three months' rent in advance. A few hours later servants dressed in the Orléans livery arrived and set up a temporary kitchen in the coach-house before proceeding to roast large quantities of meat and to distribute it along with bread to the starving people of the area. Such examples of timely benevolence by one of their greatest critics naturally annoyed the court at Versailles. Yet the Marquis de Bombelles, recently returned as French Ambassador to Portugal, also wrote admiringly of the Duc d'Orléans' 'magnificent generosity'. Another diplomat, the American Benjamin Franklin, a regular customer at Café Foy in the gardens of the Palais-Royal, was equally impressed by this unequivocal display of social responsibility:

> There is a man here of exalted rank, great wealth and with an admirable social conscience who is worthy of the times. I speak of the Duc d'Orléans. Yes, he has some faults but all are outweighed by his many virtues that he has displayed in these difficult times. He has true character, original if eccentric, but he is driven by a desire for vengeance against oppression and the need to attain freedom for himself and his people.

This zeal for reform was also being encouraged in Louis Philippe Joseph's young sons, the Ducs de Chartres and Montpensier. A new instructor in political theory, the lawyer Gaultier de Biauzat, had been hired for this very purpose. Under Biauzat they studied the works of Rousseau, civil law and the constitutions of other societies. As Chartres the future King Louis Philippe later wrote, 'we drew the conclusion that the constitutions of the American states came nearest to perfection'. When he came to the throne in 1830 he was better prepared and better educated than any previous monarch in European history thanks to the tutelage of Madame de Genlis and such expert instructors as Biauzat. Although it was a hotbed of political ideas the Palais-Royal continued to attract the most fashionable and cultivated people of the age. Their presence at the weekly dinners and assemblies added a social dimension to the education of the young princes, for their father, no matter how radical his ideas, insisted that the strictest manners and protocol continue to be observed at the palace.

In January 1789 few could have predicted the momentous events that would occur that summer, least of all Louis Philippe Joseph who continued to hunt and go to the opera in spite of the misery and destitution around him. Having failed, in the face of Marie Antoinette's hostility, to bring about reconciliation between the two branches of the Bourbons by marrying the Duc de Chartres to Madame, the King's daughter, he tried again. This time his offer, the engagement of his daughter, the eleven-year-old Mademoiselle Orléans, to the fourteen-year-old Duc d'Angoulême, son of the Comte d'Artois, was at first accepted, perhaps because of the growing desperation at Versailles. It appeared that this concession to the Palais-Royal might help to unite the divided family in troubled times, but the proposed union would be swept away, like much else, by the coming revolution.

12

THE ESTATES GENERAL

O N 13 JULY 1788 France had experienced the most violent and sustained hailstorm in its history which devastated the most fertile land and ruined the harvest. There were persistent rumours at the time, related in great detail by the historian Montjoie, that the Duc d'Orléans had taken full advantage of this natural calamity to acquire the remaining grain and ship it to England. This had been made possible under the calamitous free-trade agreement signed a year earlier by the Finance Minister, de Brienne. The plan appears to have been devised by Laclos and to have been executed by the Marquis Ducrest. The intention was to hold the grain in England until famine forced the King to abdicate and then ship it back to a grateful France. This was certainly a dangerous and callous scheme to inflict on starving people and reflects Laclos' ruthless approach to politics. It is hard to understand why Louis Philippe Joseph, with his sincere and well-established reputation for charity and concern for the poor, agreed to it.

The misery and starvation that had characterized the terrible winter of 1788 continued into the following spring when melting ice flooded the fields. Grain prices rose even higher, and the poor, kept alive by the four-pound loaf of bread, now found even that debased with cheap additives. As the preliminary meetings of the Estates General were taking place the hunger of the people exploded into serious riots in Flanders and Brittany. But the most dangerous of all occurred in Paris, provoked by a rumour that Jean-Baptiste Réveillon, a self-made paper manufacturer in the Faubourg Saint-Antoine, was threatening to cut the wages of his already desperately poor workforce. In reality he had merely said that the price of bread was too high and should be allowed to find its correct level in the open market rather than be controlled by the state, but this innocent remark was seized upon by the crowd that gathered in the street leading to the Réveillon factory, and the resentment that had festered throughout the long winter months of hunger now exploded into violence that struck Paris like a thunderclap. Armed with sticks and cudgels, the mob began shouting, 'Death to the rich! Death to the aristocrats! Death to the capitalists!' Soon there were over 500 people marching towards the factory, at their head a mock gallows bearing a dummy of Réveillon himself. Two respected members of the local community courageously offered to speak to the crowd and with great difficulty managed to persuade them that Réveillon should not be hanged from the nearest lamp-post.

The following day the mob returned, its numbers swollen by the many unemployed dockers, tanners and brewery workers from the Saint-Marcel and Saint-Antoine districts. Now numbering over 10,000 it was opposed by only a small detachment of the newly raised gendarmerie, the *gardes françaises*, standing at a barrier with fixed bayonets. As each side hesitated, a carriage suddenly appeared carrying the Duc d'Orléans and his guests along the Faubourg Saint-Antoine on their way to the races at Vincennes. The mob at once broke into cheers and shouts of 'Long live King Orléans! Long live the only true friend of the people!', words that would later give credence to the suspicion that the riots had been organized and instigated by the Palais-Royal. When the carriage stopped Louis Philippe Joseph dismounted and delivered a short exhortation urging his audience to stay calm and put its trust in the growing power of the Third Estate. His servants then distributed a considerable number of écus to the crowd, the Duc remounted and with a careless wave was off. It was like watching a general review his troops, commented a cynical bystander.

The impasse between troops and rioters continued for a few hours more until a second carriage, again bearing the

Orléans livery, appeared. This time it was the Duchesse, travelling back in the opposite direction. Rather than avoiding the mob, it proceeded straight down the rue de Montreuil towards the barriers, where the Duchesse leant out of the window and demanded to be let through. It is impossible to believe that she would have taken such a route other than at the express instructions of her husband, who saw it as another opportunity to demonstrate the popularity of his family. There was now a vast sea of unwashed humanity gathered near the Réveillon works, composed, as the *Mercury de France* newspaper described it, of 'every type of barbarian known to man, Huns, Vandals and Goths from the north of Norway to the Black sea'. Again the crowd cheered the Orléans livery as her carriage passed through their ranks and then, following in her wake, proceeded to attack the Réveillon premises, smashing windows, breaking doors and forcing their way into every corner of the building. Those on the roof began pelting the soldiers below with tiles and large chunks of stone dislodged from the upper walls, provoking them to fire their muskets in response, so that 'the unhappy creatures fell from the roofs, the walls dripped with blood, the pavement was covered with mutilated limbs'. Two more companies of soldiers including the Swiss Guard were urgently summoned from barracks. Such a concentration of troops had never been seen on the streets of Paris in modern times.

Soon the entire Réveillon works was ablaze and the crowd battled desperately with the troops, who continued firing volleys of live ammunition into them. That day between twenty-five and thirty rioters were killed before the remainder were driven out of what was left of the Réveillon works. The proprietor himself had escaped earlier and taken refuge in the Bastille near by. Punishment was swift. Within a few days several of the assumed ringleaders were arrested, tried and executed, but the riots in the Faubourg Saint-Antoine left a bitter legacy for they were but the first of many that would transform Paris from a tranquil to a violent city where issues would be decided not in the debating chambers but on the streets.

But who was to blame for this violence? Some thought it was the English who had paid the mob, taking long-awaited revenge for French involvement in the American War of Independence a decade earlier; others were convinced that it was the court at Versailles acting to discredit the Duc d'Orléans and the opponents of absolute rule. Yet there can be little doubt that the Réveillon riots had been orchestrated by Choderlos de Laclos on behalf of his master, or that what was meant to be a minor civil disturbance got out of hand and became a full-scale assault on the bourgeoisie rather than the aristocracy. It was also known that in a recent preliminary election for the Third Estate Réveillon had stood against and defeated a protégé of Laclos'. Convincing evidence exists to show that at least some of the ringleaders had been paid by Laclos to foment trouble. When Montjoie visited the wounded a few days later he found one dying rioter who groaned to him, 'My God, my God, must one be treated in this way for just twelve miserable francs?' Montjoie claimed that the same sum of money, twelve francs wrapped in paper, was found, as if for distribution, in the pockets of many of the dead, leading to the assumption that these were the wages paid by the Palais-Royal. Naturally Montjoie was quick to believe such stories, being one of the first proponents of a 'Palais-Royal conspiracy'. Later he weakened his credibility by the ludicrous assertion that the Duc d'Orléans communicated with his aides by using the height of the fountains in the gardens as a primitive form of Morse code. Nevertheless a more objective witness, the British ambassador in Paris, the Duke of Dorset, reported to his minister in London that he was convinced that the Duc d'Orléans was behind the riots, having heard with his own ears the mob calling for 'King Orléans'. Many contemporaries, including Talleyrand, agreed that the violence had indeed been instigated by Orléans and his *éminence grise*, Choderlos de Laclos. An Orléanist supporter, Sebastien de Chamfort, was even supposed to have confessed to the Academician Marmontel that the riots were indeed financed by the Palais-Royal:

> Money and plunder are all powerful with the people. We just made the experiment in the Faubourg St Antoine and you would not believe how little it cost the Duc d'Orléans to get them to sack the manufactory of the honest Réveillon, who amidst these same people was the means of livelihood for a hundred families. Mirabeau cheerfully asserts that with 100 louis one can make quite a good riot.

What is undeniable is that many of the rioters were from outside the area. Some were swarthy and brigand-like in appearance, leading to rumours that they had been drafted in from other parts to act as *agents provocateurs*. Baron de Besenval, who commanded the Swiss Guards that day, reported unequivocally that he had seen 'strangers' distributing money and that many of the rioters had come from as far away as Lyon and Marseille. Yet an inquiry held a few weeks later found no such evidence of bribes being distributed or of outsiders being drafted in. Such conspiracy theories often manifest at times of civil disorder. What is beyond doubt is that the local people required neither bribes nor rewards to vent their desperation on the streets. Driven beyond endurance by months of starvation and privation, they were being paid just fifteen sous a day by Réveillon at a time when a single loaf of bread cost over fourteen. These were the dispossessed who stood to gain little or nothing from political reform, and they would soon become the shock troops of the French Revolution.

Less than a month later the first full session of the Estates General opened at Versailles. It was a gloriously sunny day as church bells pealed and the 1,200 deputies of the Three Estates marched from the Notre Dame church in solemn procession to the Palace of Versailles. Crowds thronged the streets and every window overlooking the route had been let to spectators for a high price. Master of Ceremonies for the day was the young Marquis de Dreux-Brézé who had ordered the design of the nobles' costumes to be based on those of the era of Henri IV and to include large plumed hats. But as the nobles moved off, each carrying a lighted candle, it was noticed that one of their number was missing. Perversely the Duc d'Orléans had chosen to walk, not directly behind the King at the head of his fellow aristocrats, but symbolically with the bourgeoisie of the Third Estate. When urged by Dreux-Brézé to return to his proper place with the Princes of the Blood, Orléans replied dismissively that he preferred to walk with his fellow deputies from the Crépy region. His presence again drew loud cheers from the crowd and cries of 'Long live Orléans!' This contrasted tellingly with the silence that greeted the arrival of Marie Antoinette, who was dressed entirely in mauve. Louis Philippe Joseph was seen to smile broadly at her reception. In an archaic ritual, one side of the salon door was held open to admit the nobility and then both sides for the clergy. Deputies of the Third Estate, however, were received by the King in a separate room. They had been asked to wear barristers' gowns to give them a form of corporate identity but some found this instruction offensive, and one farmer from Brittany, Old Gérard, ignored the instructive completely and arrived in a peasant's smock, his hair cut short and unpowdered. It was a highly effective protest that rivalled that of Louis Philippe Joseph earlier in the day.

As the session ended, Marie Antoinette, incensed by the way the Duc d'Orléans had behaved that morning, petulantly summoned his wife to her and in a voice shaking with fury accused her of neglecting her duties as a lady-in-waiting. 'Madame,' she said, 'it is over half an hour since you attended to my needs. It is your duty to be available whenever I need you.' The Duchesse, who had no involvement in the matter, was deeply hurt and turned and walked quickly away. The following morning Dreux-Brézé informed the King that the Duc d'Orléans had now asked to sit with the ordinary deputies of the Third Estate rather than among the Princes of the Blood. The King, nearly apoplectic with rage, immediately ordered his cousin to take his proper place, with the nobles. Still furious from this new provocation, the King entered the Assembly and doffed his hat, specially made for the occasion in black fur and decorated with white plumes, to the delegates. They in turn doffed their more modest ones. Then, according to custom, the clergy and nobility returned them to their heads. Unfortunately the Third Estate did the same, forgetting that wearing a hat in the presence of the King was a serious breach of protocol. Realizing their mistake, some then hastily removed their hats again. In the confusion that followed the King removed his own hat and placed it beside him. An eyewitness, Gouverneur Morris, coming from the relaxed social milieu of the American democracy, thought it all a hilarious fiasco.

When the King delivered his opening speech it was brief and to the point. The Estates General had been recalled to put the national finances in order. He warned the delegates neither to be distracted by debating 'innovations' nor to waste time by discussing the Constitution. Necker's speech was similar in content, dealing only with fiscal policy and failing to mention the long-anticipated constitutional reforms. Two days later Necker spoke again, this time to urge the three Estates to vote separately on the issues. However, a group of the more liberal nobles objected to Necker's interference, and their spokesman, the Comte de Crillon, rose to challenge him, supported by the Duc de la Rochefoucauld-Liancourt, the Marquis de Lafayette and the Duc d'Orléans. When a vote was taken the liberals lost by a sizeable majority, but the very idea of the nobility combining with the Third Estate and voting as one body had seriously alarmed Versailles. On 17 June Louis Philippe Joseph gave added weight to the cause by speaking out in favour of unity. It was a very hot day, and a few minutes after he began to speak his supporters noticed that he appeared about to faint. Windows were opened and he was urged to sit down and recover. Smelling salts were waved under his nose, but when his coat was unbuttoned it revealed, to the surprise of those around him, layer upon layer of leather waistcoats. These, it appeared, were a form of body armour, a primitive protection against some anticipated attempt at assassination. Whatever his numerous faults Louis Philippe Joseph was not a physical coward and this curious attempt at self-protection had been provoked by rumours that someone at Versailles had ordered his death.

The suspicion among members of the Third Estate was that the majority of the nobility refused to unite with them because they were more concerned with retaining their traditional privileges. The greatest orator in the Estates, the Marquis de Mirabeau, launched an angry diatribe against this reactionary faction, demanding to know why they thought themselves the only people capable of making laws and regulating the finances of France. As the Marquis de Ferrières wrote wearily to his wife, 'Whether we vote by head or by order, it's all the same to me. I have no opinion on how we should debate either, but I will not abandon my order in these critical times.' Yet a new social and political climate was fast evolving. The possibility of closer unity intrigued both the nobility and the emergent middle classes who were becoming more closely acquainted in Masonic lodges and political clubs throughout the country.

No less important in reforming social attitudes were the fashionable salons of such hostesses as the Duchesse de Luynes and Mesdames de Castellane, de Tessé, de Coigny and de Genlis. In these gatherings politics had replaced gallantry, and the most sought-after guests were no longer the higher nobility but people of talent and ability such as the young painter Jacques-Louis David and the political intriguer the Vicomte de Beauharnais, husband of Napoleon's future empress, Josephine.

Although a regular guest at Madame de Genlis' salons, Louis Philippe Joseph maintained a curiously low profile in society, attending few of the sessions of the Assembly and leaving the Abbé Sieyès to act as his representative there. His behaviour towards Versailles was ambiguous too, for in spite of his declared hostility he continued to entertain some

The coat of arms of the Duc d'Orléans: the three gold
fleurs de lys on a blue background are differentiated by
a silver label to denote the Orléans branch of the family.

Louis Philippe Joseph, Duc d'Orléans, in 1789;
engraving by Philbert Louis Debucourt

Louis Philippe Joseph's cousin, Louis XVI, whose absolutist policies provoked national opposition; painting by Joseph Siffred Duplessis

Louis XVI's wife Marie Antoinette, who never hid her dislike of Louis Philippe Joseph; painting by Alexander Roslin

Pierre Choderlos de Laclos, political secretary to Louis
Philippe Joseph and author of *Les Liaisons dangereuses*

The galleries of the Palais-Royal, the Paris seat of the
Orléans family that rivalled in splendour the Palace of
the Louvre, *c.* 1785

Historic descent of Louis Philippe Joseph in the Robert brothers'
balloon in December 1783; engraving

Gardens of the Palais-Royal after the great renovation scheme of
Louis Philippe Joseph and his architect Victor Louis; engraving by
Le Chevalier de Lespinasse

The courtesan Rosalie Duthé, first of Louis Philippe
Joseph's many mistresses; painting by Antoine Vestier

Louise Marie Adélaïde de Bourbon, Duchesse de
Chartres and Louis Philippe Joseph's wife; painting by
Joseph Siffred Duplessis

Louis Philippe Joseph with his children and their
governess Madame de Genlis, *c.* 1774; drawing by
F. Stone

Félicité de Genlis, Louis Philippe Joseph's mistress and the
leading educationist of her age

The little school at Belle Chasse near Paris founded by Madame de Genlis in 1777 to educate Louis Philippe Joseph's children with her own

Harp lesson given by Madame de Genlis to Mademoiselle d'Orléans, Louis Philippe Joseph's daughter; painting by Jean Baptiste Mauzaisse, 1842

The Réveillon riots that broke out in Paris in April 1789,
three months before the storming of the Bastille

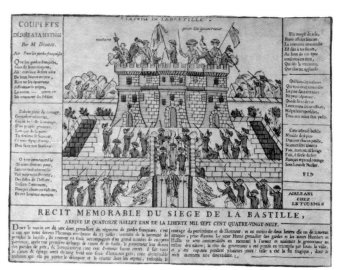

A contemporary newspaper account of the storming of the
Bastille prison that marked the start of the French Revolution
on 14 July 1789

'To Versailles!' The women of Paris lead the march to the
Palace of Versailles to bring the Royal Family back to Paris;
contemporary engraving

French troops uniting with the Paris mob in
revolutionary fervour at the overthrow of the King

Left and facing page:
Illustrations from a contemporary
pack of playing cards depicting
revolutionary values

The VICTIM of EQUALITY.

Louis Philippe Joseph brandishing the head of Louis XVI on
the steps of the scaffold; contemporary English print blaming
Philippe Égalité for his part in his cousin's trial and execution

Last known image of Louis Phillipe Joseph in
prison before his summary trial and execution
in 1793; drawing by Angelika Kauffmann

A coin issued by
Louis Philippe Joseph's
supporters to
commemorate his
execution on
6 November 1793

Louis Philippe Joseph's eldest son, General Louis
Philippe, future King of the French, in officer's
uniform, 1792; engraving by A. Lefevre after a
painting by Léon Cogniet

of the most reactionary members of court. On 13 May he had even dined with his supposed arch enemy the Duchesse de Polignac, and assured his fellow guest, the Comte d'Artois, that there was no question of him supporting a motion to merge the Three Estates. Yet when the seven-year-old Dauphin, already crippled by consumption, suddenly died a few days later on 14 June he excused himself from attending the funeral at the Val-de-Grâce, claiming implausibly that his duties at the Assembly prevented him from attending. He sent only a formal letter of condolence to the grieving parents but ordered his eldest son to attend in his place. This callous behaviour caused such offence that the proposed marriage between his daughter and Artois' son, the Duc d'Angoulême, was instantly doomed.

13

THE PAYMASTER

A S THE ESTATES General wrangled over procedures, apparently incapable of agreeing long-overdue legal and financial reforms, the people were becoming dangerously militant. Stealing and burglary were now endemic throughout Paris. To counter the growing crime wave, three more regiments of troops were ordered into the capital to supplement the 6,000 soldiers already stationed there. Even the gardens of the Palais-Royal were becoming a dangerous place. Pierre Besenval, commander of the Swiss Guard, thought the ten men delegated to maintain law and order to be totally inadequate to deal with the hundreds of ruffians who now gathered there. The bookseller Siméon Hardy, ill at ease in his shop in the Palais-Royal arcades, wrote, 'An air of discord hangs over the city. All it needs is a single spark to ignite some terrible conflagration.'

As anarchy loomed, Louis XVI was urged by the Queen and his brothers to act decisively by dissolving the Estates General and regaining control himself. Realizing that this would be tantamount to declaring war on the Assembly, his more cautious ministers, Necker and Montmorin, advised him to address the delegates again instead. A *séance royal* was swiftly arranged and on 19 June workmen began preparing the Salle des Menus Plaisirs for the session. A large dais was still being assembled as the delegates arrived that morning; the door to the salon had been securely locked in the interests of safety and armed guards were placed at the entrance. Assuming that they were being deliberately excluded as the first step in dissolving the Assembly, the angry deputies marched out into the pouring rain. One of their number, Dr Guillotine, whose invention would forever be associated with the excesses of the revolution, then suggested they retire to a real tennis court he knew in a street nearby. There, sheltered from the rain, 600 deputies crowded round their president, Jean Sylvain Bailly, seated at a simple pine table. In a moment of inspiration, Bailly clambered on to the table and, striking a classical pose with outstretched arm, exhorted his colleagues to join him in a simple oath: 'To God and the Nation, never to be separated until we have formed a solid and equitable Constitution as our constituents have asked us to do'. The scene was later commemorated as a historic analogy by the painter David in his canvas *The Oath of the Horatii*.

On 23 June the King again appealed for the delegates to listen to reason but presented them with little more than a rehash of his familiar requests. This time, however, he warned them that should they again reject these perfectly reasonable demands he would be forced to 'proceed alone for the good of my people and I will consider myself to be their sole true representative'. His words were greeted by a total silence that continued as he walked slowly and mournfully from the room. Fearing a repeat of the events of four days previously, the Comte d'Artois had, as a pre-emptive strike, booked the Versailles tennis court for the whole day. However, the deputies remained seated even when workmen arrived and began dismantling the dais, and the young and dandishly dressed Marquis de Dreux-Brézé appeared to order them out. 'Go tell those who sent you that we are here by the will of the people and we will not be dispersed except at the point of a bayonet,' Mirabeau roared at him. When told of their refusal to leave, the King sighed wearily, shrugged his shoulders and said, 'Oh, very well. Let them remain.' It was apparent to all that the old Estates General had died that day, but a new National Assembly was yet to be born. To many, it was too late for compromise with the King and the nation must move forward, towards a constitutional monarchy or perhaps even a true republic. The only legitimate and acceptable system now would have to be a truly representative government of the people, for the people and by the people.

Although Louis Philippe Joseph had played little part in the everyday debates of the preceding weeks he now intervened decisively, standing up in the Assembly on 30 June and leading forty-seven of his fellow nobles across the floor to join the members of the Third Estate. Three days later the rest of his colleagues voted with their feet by joining them. When this news reached Paris, rioting began, and that evening between 3,000 and 4,000 people attacked the Abbaye prison to release fourteen members of the *gardes françaises* who had been imprisoned for refusing to fire on the crowd during the Réveillon disturbances. The rescued soldiers were then carried in triumph through the streets to the Palais-Royal. The commander of troops in the Paris region, Maréchal de Broglie, hastily assembled enough soldiers to storm the Palais and re-arrest the men once he had received the order from Versailles. Once again the King lacking the stomach for a confrontation did nothing and three days later announced a pardon, allowing the soldiers to emerge in triumph and the Duc d'Orléans to be seen as the hero of the people once again.

Never had Louis Philippe Joseph been more popular than at this moment, for he had not only defied the King in the Assembly but had also protected those heroic soldiers in his own house. What could be more natural, therefore, than for his fellow delegates to now elect him President of the new National Assembly? When the vote was taken an overwhelming majority of 553 out of the 660 delegates voted in his favour. For a man who had risked his position, his wealth and reputation to promote the birth of the first democratic assembly in France it seemed no more than a just reward. Yet in a move that was to astonish his adherents and confound historians ever after, he rejected the honour immediately, saying to the astonished Assembly:

> Gentlemen, if I believed that I was able to fill the place to which you have elected me, I would accept it with joy. But I would be unworthy of your goodness if I did accept, knowing how little I am fitted for it. Accept therefore my refusal and

see in it only the indubitable proof that I will always sacrifice
my personal interest to the good of the state.

The motive for his rejection has been much debated.
Never one to sacrifice lifestyle to duty and particularly the
observance of duty, Louis Philippe Joseph would not have
fulfilled the role of President of the Assembly with distinction. He was too much of a wild card to observe the rules of
debate or the bureaucratic procedures that were necessary to
the functioning of a democratic chamber. Perhaps if he had
been offered the the far grander Regency or the more martial
Lieutenant Generalship of the Kingdom, as Mirabeau had
suggested, he might well have accepted. But the Presidency
offered little to challenge his restless spirit, while imposing
on him the need for conformity. In the face of this categorical
refusal the Assembly immediately voted in Lefranc de Pom-
pignan, Archbishop of Vienne, as its first President.

Even the presence of a new and democratic Assembly did
little to calm unrest in the country. With the fiscal reforms
still unresolved, business and particularly banking remained
in crisis. Ever the centre of discontent, the Palais-Royal was
now seen by the people as an alternative court without a king.
Placards praising the many qualities of the Duc d'Orléans
were fixed daily to its railings. He was described as 'The
avenger of the people, the only Prince of the Blood worthy of
his ancestor, Henri IV'. Almost as much praise was showered
on Jacques Necker, 'the new Sully' of French democracy. If
Necker and Orléans were the heroes, then the Condés,
the Contis and the Polignacs were the undoubted villains.
Petitions were circulated demanding that they all be sent into
exile and Necker made supreme administrator of the kingdom.
On the evening that the Three Estates were reunited, a vast
firework display was given in the gardens of the Palais-Royal to
celebrate the triumph of democracy. The English traveller
Arthur Young was surprised by the vehemence of the crowd as
he listened to an impromptu debate outside the Café Foy and
observed:

expectant crowds listening open mouthed to certain orators who from chairs or tables harangue their audiences. The eagerness with which they are heard and the thunder of applause they receive for every sentiment of more than common hardiness or violence against the present government cannot easily be imagined.

Young thought this not the good-natured tumult of the English hustings but the pent-up fury of a dispossessed people ready to explode into violence.

Although he had openly rejected the Presidency of the Assembly Louis Philippe Joseph continued to be thought of by the royalists as a Machiavellian puppet-master using his minions to bring about the downfall of the monarchy. Antonio Capello, the Venetian Ambassador, believed that 'his intentions are suspect and all that passes in the Palais-Royal must be condemned by anyone of sense'. Capello was also convinced that the Duc was funding the agitators. The Parma envoy, the Baillie de Virieu, agreed, claiming that the trouble-makers were on the Duc's payroll and being paid between twenty and thirty sous a day to make mischief.

However, those modest sums would have been insufficient to meet the remorseless rise of the price of bread that had continued into the summer of 1789. Paris was clearly on the brink of a catastrophe as Mirabeau denounced the royal conspiracy to use troops to coerce the people. The King simply replied that they were needed to keep order. On 11 July the King finally lost patience with Necker and ordered him to lay down his office and leave the kingdom as swiftly and discreetly as possible. Other ministers, known liberals such as Montmorin and Saint-Priest, were also dismissed and the more conservative Baron de Breteuil appointed in Necker's place. There is little doubt that the King was preparing to move against his enemies as regiments of foreign troops in the service of France together with others known to be loyal to the crown were being moved closer to Paris. If the King had acted decisively and above all swiftly at that moment, he might well have been able to send 25,000 troops into Paris to arrest the ringleaders and suppress disorder before negotiating an agreement with the Assembly from a position of strength. His hesitation was to prove his downfall.

The following day, a Sunday, news of Necker's sudden departure reached the Palais-Royal and was interpreted as a prelude to more draconian royal action. A young lawyer, Camille Desmoulins, pistol in hand, leapt on to a table outside the Café Foy and delivered the most famous call to arms in modern history. 'To arms! To arms! There's not a moment to lose,' he cried. 'I've just come from Versailles. Necker has been dismissed. This will be another Feast of St Bartholomew, comrades. This evening the Swiss and German Guards will be marching along the Champs de Mars to massacre us. Come on, this is a call to arms!' Snatching a cluster of leaves from a nearby chestnut tree, he waved it in the air as he urged his listeners to take this green cockade as the symbol of their imminent liberty. Within a few minutes most of the chestnuts in the gardens of the Palais-Royal had been stripped of their leaves. Inspired by Desmoulins' words the crowd scattered, some to build barricades and others to occupy the theatres. Two busts, one of Necker, the other of the Duc d'Orléans, were looted from the premises of the sculptor Curtius, then draped in black crepe they were carried at the head of a procession of cheering people along the rue Saint-Martin. 'Don't you want the Prince as your king and this honest man as his minister?' a bemused bystander was asked. At the Place Vendôme they encountered a detachment of the Royal German Regiment under the command of the Prince de Lambesc who, seeing that dozens of the *gardes françaises* had joined the mob, ordered his men to hold their fire.

Meanwhile Louis Philippe Joseph, on this momentous of days, had decided to go fishing at Raincy where he was entertaining Grace Elliott and other friends. At eight o'clock the party returned to the house before setting off for Paris to attend a performance at the Comédie Italienne. As their carriages approached the city it became obvious that a full-scale riot was taking place. To calm her fears, Louis Philippe Joseph agreed to join Grace Elliott in her unmarked carriage and together they crossed the city from the Porte Saint-Martin through angry crowds, finally arriving safely at his house at Monceau. Here they were joined by the Duc de Biron and Agnès de Buffon. Unable to sleep because of the chaos she had witnessed, Grace persuaded her host to walk with her in the elaborate Chinese gardens. For two hours they discussed the situation and Grace persuaded her old lover to go at once to Versailles and try to bring about a *rapprochement* with the King.

Unusually for such a stubborn man, Louis Philippe Joseph agreed, and he arrived at Versailles the next morning just as the King was rising from his bed. Predictably Louis was disgusted to see the man he held largely responsible for the current turmoil and a divided country, and barely acknowledged him. At this blatant snub the Duc, convinced as ever that he was the injured party, left immediately for Paris, thereby denying the King an opportunity to use his cousin's popularity with the crowd to halt the violence in Paris. From this moment, Grace Elliott believed, the Duc's attitude to his cousin became even more violent and his involvement with the revolutionaries in his household even deeper.

As Louis Philippe Joseph travelled back to Paris a full-scale rebellion was taking place as armouries were plundered and buildings set alight. The monastery at Saint-Lazare, a storehouse for grain as well as a religious institution, was pillaged by the hungry people and several prisons broken into and their inhabitants released to join the growing mob. Terrified citizens in some areas of the city hastily formed committees to establish local militias to keep order. Many of these would later become the most important force in France, the National Guard. To give these units an identity, a green cockade was suggested until it was realized that this was the livery colour of the Comte d'Artois, and a more appropriate red and blue, the colours of the House of Orléans, was substituted. Meanwhile Mirabeau and his friends were touring the streets urging the local committees to demand the Duc d'Orléans act as intermediary between the King and the people and be made, by popular acclaim, Lieutenant General of France. That day Mirabeau told Laclos that if Orléans were thus elevated then he, Mirabeau, would assuredly be the Duc's First Minister. But the events of the past two days had radically changed the political agenda and the ordinary people in the street now realized that they wanted, not a reformed monarchy and aristocracy, but an end to both. There was also a growing recognition that in spite of his early leadership and undoubted courage, the Duc d'Orléans was not the man to lead the country into a new era.

14

REVOLUTION

THE FOLLOWING DAY, 14 July, the price of a four-pound loaf in Paris reached a record high as a rumour that the Royal German Regiment was marching on the city galvanized the Parisian mob into action. Thousands of angry citizens began scouring the city for weapons and gunpowder. First the Invalides was stormed and thousands of muskets seized, but there was insufficient gunpowder there to fire them with.

The largest supply in Paris was known to be kept at the Bastille, a modest enough fortress but symbolic of royal tyranny, where prisoners were held under the hated *lettres de cachet*. By ten in the morning a mob numbering a thousand people together with some deserters from the *garde française* garrison at the Invalides assembled outside the Bastille. Although alarmed by the size of the crowd, the governor, Bernard René, Marquis de Launay, remained calm and in a gesture of hospitality invited two of the ringleaders inside to join him for lunch and to discuss the problem in a civilized manner. Their demands were simple, that the drawbridge be lowered and that they be allowed to carry off the cannon and all the powder from the fortress. De Launay appeared sympathetic to their request but told them that this was impossible until Versailles first gave permission. This was an obvious ploy to buy time until relieving troops could arrive from outside the city. Had de Launay known that the Archbishop of Paris was at that very moment successfully pleading with the King not to order his troops to enter Paris and relieve the Bastille, he might well have surrendered the indefensible fortress immediately. Two hours later the mob's patience ran out and to cries of 'Give us the Bastille' a nimble ex-soldier climbed up and cut the chain holding the drawbridge. As it crashed to the ground the crowd swarmed over and took possession of the outer courtyard. After a brief skirmish in which many were killed, the attackers managed to drag a cannon into place in front of the last remaining door and threatened to blow it in. Realizing that all his men would inevitably perish, de Launay then agreed to surrender. Eighty-three of the mob had already been killed, compared to a mere three defenders. This imbalance was corrected by the brutality of de Launay's end as he was dragged through the streets to the accompaniment of catcalls and spittle, then butchered in the gutter. Finally his head was severed with a pocket-knife, placed with several others on pikes and paraded through the city in a gruesome ritual that would characterize the brutality of the revolutionaries.

At Monceau the Duc d'Orléans was entertaining to lunch two of his fellow deputies, the hero of the American War, the Marquis de Lafayette, and Jean-Sylvain Bailly, about to be elected the new Mayor of Paris. That both Lafayette and Bailly had gone to see him at this critical time has been taken as evidence that they had intended to discuss the royal succession with him and perhaps negotiate the conditions under which he would assume either the Lieutenant Generalship or the Regency. Although neither mentions the meeting in his memoirs, the Marquis de Ferrières was convinced that this was indeed the reason for their visit. As the three talked they could clearly hear the sound of cannon in Paris before a messenger arrived to tell them the startling news that the Bastille had fallen. The Duc's guests immediately departed, leaving Grace Elliott alone with her host. Once more she implored him to go to the King and offer to pacify the mob. But Orléans replied bitterly that even his worst enemy would not have given him such bad advice. Nevertheless he did go to Versailles the following day, only to suffer another rebuff when the King refused to see him. Such stubbornness in a crisis alarmed the Baron de Breteuil, who agreed to carry a message to the sovereign on Orléans' behalf.

This would indeed have been the ideal moment for Louis

Philippe Joseph, as Grace Elliott had suggested, to offer some form of mediation with the people in return for a position that would have allowed him to play an important role in the creation of a reformed monarchy. With Orléans' support the King could then have bought enough time to prepare a new constitution that might have reconciled his continuing rule with the evolution of a democratic monarchy on the British pattern. This would certainly have been acceptable to the Assembly at the time, and perhaps even to the people of France. Yet instead of making such an offer, Louis Philippe Joseph's note merely contained a plea that he be allowed to visit London to check his English interests. Even the King was shocked by the irrelevance of the request, having expected some fundamental and unpalatable political demand. Louis' reaction was simply to shrug his shoulders in total disbelief.

Orléans' behaviour that day has puzzled historians ever since. Had he lost his nerve, and was the trip to England merely an excuse to run away and avoid responsibility, as he had done when offered the Presidency of the Assembly? Lafayette, who was to play a dominant role in future events, thought differently, convinced that the Duc was merely biding his time and waiting for an even more opportune moment to make his play for the crown. Lafayette's opposition to the Orléanist cause would be the decisive factor in denying them power as the monarchy continued frozen in inaction, for he was convinced that the hand of the Palais-Royal was behind the recent murder of Joseph Foulon, one of the King's ex-ministers and his own son-in-law. Foulon had been an outspoken anti-Orléanist in the Assembly, urging the King to arrest the Duc and his followers. Mirabeau later claimed, but only when he had fallen out with the Orléanists, that the murder had indeed been carried out by agents of the Palais-Royal and had cost many thousands of livres.

As Louis Philippe Joseph returned to Paris that day the King again prepared to face the National Assembly. He now had little alternative but to agree to all its demands, including the dismissal of his hard-line ministers and the recall of Jacques Necker. All present knew that this was a complete humiliation which he attempted to alleviate by appealing to the delegates to assist him in peacefully restoring order and calm without the use of troops. Having made his plea, the King left the Assembly and accompanied by the exuberant deputies walked forlornly back to the Palace of Versailles. The following day, for their own safety, he ordered his brothers together with the Prince de Condé and both Polignacs into what he hoped would be temporary exile. Then, accompanied by another party of deputies, he reluctantly set off to take the news of his capitulation in the Assembly to Paris. When asked by Bailly why he had not gone with them, Louis Philippe Joseph replied that it was 'not convenient'. This proved to be a mistake, for the Parisian crowd greeted the King warmly, particularly when he agreed to wear a red, white and blue cockade in his hat. It almost appeared that he had regained much of his lost popularity as cries of 'Long live the King' arose spontaneously from the crowd lining the road back to Versailles that evening. If Louis XVI had lost his opportunity of retaining the throne by not sending in the troops on 14 July, then the Duc d'Orléans lost his the following day by not demanding at least the Lieutenant Generalship of the realm. It was a lesson that his son would take to heart when in July 1830 he unhesitatingly accepted the crown, ironically from an elderly Lafayette, to become King of the French.

The price of indecision was the almost universal execration that he now suffered from his fellow aristocrats and Princes of the Blood. Having brought the country and the monarchy, in their eyes, to the brink of an abyss, he had then stood back and done nothing. The society beauty Diane de Langeron spoke for many when she swore that she would have been delighted to strangle the Duc with her own hands. From this moment he came under threat from both royalists and revolutionaries. If one faction did not take revenge on him, the other probably would. His son, the Duc de Chartres, was told prophetically by his English tutor at the time:

You think this has saved your father but it will lead to his
ruin for the leaders of a popular revolution have never
derived any advantage from it and have always become its
victims. You are too young and I don't know what will
become of you but your father is too prominent to escape.

Those who had anticipated a return to peace following the
King's capitulation were soon disappointed. For it appeared
that anarchy had been loosed upon the land and rumours
circulated that brigands were marauding through every part
of France, destroying crops, attacking houses and burning
châteaux. In a land gripped by fear, such criminals were
easily confused with the thousands of mendicants that had
roamed the countryside for decades. The leading historian
of the period, Georges Lefebvre, has estimated that in 1789 a
staggering one in ten of rural French peasants was an unemployed beggar, wandering the countryside homeless and
dependent on his poverty-stricken neighbours for survival.
Yet the obvious explanation of events is seldom popular, and
many believed or wished to believe that behind this time of
'Great Fear' lay the hand of the counter-revolutionaries.
Their leaders were said to be the usual suspects, the Comte
d'Artois, the Prince de Condé and, of course, the she-devil
herself, Queen Marie Antoinette. In Colmar a rumour circulated that she had ordered the troops to march into Paris to
massacre the inhabitants and to place a mine under the
National Assembly and blow up all the delegates. At Dijon
they preferred to believe that Paris was to be burnt to the
ground and the Comte d'Artois installed as Regent. Royalists,
for their part, attributed the mayhem to the Palais-Royal and
its evil occupants who were taking advantage of the political
vacuum to foment further unrest that would then be blamed
on Versailles. In reality the unrest and château-burning were
the work of desperate peasants more concerned with settling
scores with the aristocracy than with establishing a peaceful
and democratic republic. Writing of this chaotic period forty
years later, the Duc de Chartres remained convinced that the

people were duped and the panic was deliberately instigated by Mirabeau and his friends in order to encourage recruitment to the National Guard. The new democracy would then have a credible military force to defend itself in the event of an attack by resurgent royalists.

On 4 August the Assembly moved to placate the people and calm the situation by abolishing the privileges of the aristocracy and all feudal duties and taxes in an attempt to create universal fiscal equality. It also, controversially, confirmed that the Bourbon monarchy would continue on the basis of primogeniture, with both the House of Orléans and that of Bourbon Spain excluded from inheriting the crown. This was seen as a dangerous threat to Orléanist interests. As the debate drew to a close the Marquis de Sillery, the former Comte de Genlis, leapt to his feet and cried angrily, 'I demand that it be written into the minutes that this decree has been passed in the absence of the Duc d'Orléans.' 'And I demand,' interrupted a royalist deputy, the Marquis de Mirepoix, 'that it be added that it was passed in the absence of the King of Spain.' The consequence of the Assembly's decision that day was that it was now impossible for the Duc d'Orléans to be democratically elected king of a new and democratic France. His supporters rightly concluded that such an elevation could now only be brought about by some form of direct action.

Whatever his constitutional position, Louis Philippe Joseph now had to deal with an even greater personal crisis. The Assembly, having already voted to sell off the whole of the church lands and the greater part of those belonging to the crown, now decided to do the same with the apanages or inheritances of the three leading Princes of the Blood, the King's two brothers, Provence and Artois, and the Duc d'Orléans. All three would be recompensed with an allowance of a million livres a year each. This appeared grossly unfair to Orléans as his apanage was worth more than double that of the other two combined. As his eldest son noted succinctly, 'My father's income was reduced to a quarter while his debts remained the same.' Even this relatively modest sum would never be paid in the coming years, effectively threatening to bankrupt the wealthiest man in France.

In spite of this misfortune Louis Philippe Joseph continued to regularly attend the National Assembly while his wife remained at Raincy and Madame de Genlis cared for the children at the nearby Château de Saint-Leu where she had taken refuge. Félicité was convinced that they were all in the greatest danger of attack by brigands or arrest by the King's troops. There was little evidence that the House of Orléans was becoming unpopular with the people, however; when the young Duc de Chartres returned to Paris and helped demolish the last remnants of the Bastille he was loudly cheered. Again on 25 August, when he accompanied his father to Versailles to celebrate the King's birthday, wearing a very large tricolour cockade in his hat, the people lining the street gave him an enthusiastic welcome. Although careful not to show disrespect to the King, Chartres had long been a committed democrat and was captivated by the workings of the new, democratic Assembly. He was also far more assiduous than his father in attending debates, often being accompanied by his present guardian, Gaultier de Biauzat. On 10 September he remained all day throughout a long debate that finally decided the question of whether or not the Assembly should be composed of two chambers on the British pattern. A single-chamber system was eventually agreed and prepared itself to deal with the long-expected challenge from foreign exiles determined to restore the monarchy to full power.

In spite of the debates at Versailles, the city of Paris remained the driving force behind the revolution and its people continued to see Orléans as their hero, a man who had courageously set the whole process of social change in motion. In spite of having rejected the Presidency of the Assembly he continued to receive unquestioning support from his closest allies. The monarchist deputy Pierre Malouet was convinced that he now detected a split in Orléanist ranks and that no more than a handful of supporters remained convinced that the Duc should be given the responsibility of either the Regency or the Lieutenant Generalship, but Mirabeau, a remarkable weather vane of political change, continued his vociferous support while hedging his bets by becoming clandestinely involved in several alternative plots. Another unlikely supporter, given his future career as a violent Jacobin, was Georges Danton. This young lawyer, who was President of the Cordeliers, the most militant of all the Parisian political clubs, was destined to play a leading role in future events.

Hopes that the power of the fledgling Assembly would soon be challenged were encouraged in the royalists by the persistent unrest in Paris. At Versailles the King again considered the options open to him and debated whether or not he should encourage the royalist exiles to intervene on his behalf. One suggestion was that they send a military force to rescue the royal family and take them to safety in Champagne, from where Louis could order the dissolution of the Assembly. The idea of moving the court was discussed by Necker and Montmorin and supported by the rest of their colleagues. Finally it was decided that either Compiègne or Soissons would be the most advantageous location as both were close enough to Paris to maintain communications but too far for the mob to reach easily. To the consternation of his advisers the King categorically refused to even consider leaving Versailles, wary lest his abandonment of the palace leave the door open for Cousin Orléans to be ushered in as Lieutenant General. This, according to the Vicomte de Clermont-Gallerande, would not have been a bad move at all, for with Orléans in control there was still hope that the monarchy would not be abolished. In the chaos that would inevitably ensue the King could move to a border town like Metz and plan his return or, if all else failed, be easily rescued by Austrian troops.

15

VERSAILLES

I
N AN ATTEMPT to head off the supposed Orléans conspiracy, Montmorin, the King's increasingly exasperated Minister of Foreign Affairs, suggested at the end of September that the great hero of the American War, the Marquis de Lafayette, be made Lieutenant General of the Realm as well as retaining command of the National Guard. When the idea was put to Lafayette he replied haughtily that he had no need of such inducements to do his duty in defending the King against the Duc d'Orléans. What was evident to all was that the uneasy status quo could not last and that any new explosion of violence would favour the Orléanist cause. Throughout September the orators in the gardens of the Palais-Royal continued to harangue their audiences with calls to action, inciting their listeners to force both the King and the Assembly to accede to the wishes of the people and produce a more open and radical constitution. With growing confidence one such group had the audacity to send a letter to the Marquis de Clermont-Tonnerre stating that the self-proclaimed 'Patriotic Assembly of the Palais-Royal' had the honour to inform him that 'if the ignorant and corrupt members of the clergy and aristocracy continue their tactics, fifteen thousand men are ready to burn their châteaux and their houses, and yours in particular, Monsieur'. Equally out-spoken were the Cordelier party, based in a part of Paris that was home to many clerks, attorneys, students, teachers and printers and close to the most violent slums of the city. Since the Réveillon riots the Cordeliers led by Danton and Marat had become the leaders and strategists of the Paris mob. Their mouthpiece was Marat's journal, the *Ami du peuple*, in which he repeatedly claimed that the revolution could never

be completed until the nation had rid itself of the 200,000 enemies working against it.

In the first week of October there was yet another increase in the price of bread and consequently increased hatred of suspected grain speculators. Clearly what France needed now was not more wrangling over principles in the Assembly but cheaper bread and practical reforms to help the poor whose misery had continued unabated even after the fall of the Bastille. The people's anger was further aggravated by the news from Versailles that the Flanders Regiment, known to be unshakably loyal to the crown, had arrived there and been given a lavish banquet by the Queen at which the drunken troops were said to have mocked their tricolour cockades and trampled them underfoot. They had then fastened black or white cockades – the colours of the Queen and King respectively – to their caps in an ominous and provocative gesture. Reports of this drunken 'orgy' appeared the next morning in the *Ami du peuple*, causing outrage in Paris where the tricolour cockade had already become an almost sacred emblem of the revolution.

To avenge the supposed insult, a large mob began to gather on Saturday 4 October, its numbers swollen by the thousands of jobless servants in the city, their aristocratic masters having fled into exile. Having been persuaded by Danton, Marat and Desmoulins that the entire royal family was about to escape their clutches and flee to Metz, a huge crowd, led by women, many of them fishwives from the market area, assembled in the Faubourg Saint-Antoine. They declared that they were determined to go to Versailles and bring the King back to Paris for safekeeping. Led by a woman beating a drum and shouting 'When will we have bread?', the title of a recent pamphlet, the long column set off. The presence of so many angry and armed females was extraordinary – perhaps the first time in history that a revolutionary event was controlled and dominated by women. Their first objective was to get arms from the Hôtel de Ville, Lafayette's headquarters and the nearest symbol of authority. After overwhelming the small garrison the mob ransacked the building and freed several prisoners. Their most important acquisitions were 700 muskets from the armoury and two cannon. Armed with this small arsenal, they set off for Versailles at five the following morning. An hour later Louis Philippe Joseph was standing on a balcony at the Palais-Royal dressed in a grey riding coat and round hat watching the crowd stream past. After a leisurely breakfast he sent his aides, Clarke and Shée, to make sure that the mob had cleared the road from Paris, and then he set off for Versailles himself.

The main events of that controversial day are indisputable. Lafayette, arriving too late to save the Hôtel de Ville, had followed the marchers, bringing with him a large contingent of his National Guard, and was clearly determined to keep control of his troops and prevent them from joining forces with the mob. When the vanguard reached the outskirts of Versailles in pouring rain around midday, they were astonished to be greeted with cries of 'We are with you' from troops of the Flanders Regiment and to be given food and drink by a reception committee of the local National Guard. When a small delegation was allowed to enter the palace to see the King, one poor woman was so overcome by the grandeur of it all that she fainted. Louis promised them that any grain available in the area would be delivered to Paris the following day. Although the noisy mob took up residence in the grounds, all seemed relatively peaceful.

However, the situation changed dramatically in the early hours of the following morning when a section of the crowd managed to break into the royal apartments. As the royal bodyguard attempted to drive them back they were overwhelmed by the mob and eight of their number slaughtered and decapitated, their heads being placed on pikes and paraded around. Lafayette's prompt arrival undoubtedly saved the lives of the remaining soldiers, who would have been overcome by the sheer weight of numbers. The mob continued to rampage through the palace in search of their principal quarry, the Queen. If found she would undoubtedly have been murdered, but one of her servants had managed to lock the final door leading to her bedroom, buying time for her to escape along a corridor to the protection of the National Guard. An hour later, as the situation became ever more desperate, Lafayette insisted that the royal couple appear with him on a balcony overlooking the huge mob assembled in the courtyard below. In a moment of inspiration he bowed to the King and then turned and kissed the Queen's hand. This dramatic and impromptu gesture stunned the hostile crowd into silence and turned the mood of the moment, so that cries of 'Long live the King' and even 'Long live the Queen' then broke out. Lafayette's quick thinking had probably saved the lives of the entire royal family that day, although he was unable to influence what happened next, for the women insisted on taking their royal captives back to Paris as living trophies. Later that morning the mob reassembled and set off for the city with the royal family driving in a carriage among them. It was a strange cavalcade, with two women riding astride a cannon rather than sitting side-saddle in the feminine manner, a clear assertion of their right to participate in a revolution. Many of the marchers were loaded down with loaves of bread and other provisions looted from the royal kitchens. Ironically, the remnants of the Flanders Regiment, whose behaviour had originally provoked the march, had thrown in their lot with the rioters and were marching alongside them.

Although he had little choice in the matter, the King later told his Minister of the Marine, Bertrand de Moleville, that he was happy enough to go with them to Paris, where he would at least be safe from the machinations of the Duc d'Orléans who was surely behind this latest act of terrorism. But de Moleville, although a confirmed royalist himself, was unconvinced. If the Orléanists really were that powerful, he wrote, surely they could have seized power at this most opportune of moments? To their dismay the Assembly members were also forced to accompany the mob to Paris where the royal family was imprisoned in the Tuileries Palace, their arrival discreetly observed by the entire Orléans family from the terrace of the Maison Boulainvilliers nearby. Significantly for those who suspected an Orléanist involvement in the events at Versailles, the severed heads of the two bodyguards were paraded through the city and then erected as trophies in the gardens of the Palais-Royal.

Although the storming of the Bastille is remembered as heralding the start of the French Revolution it was the march to Versailles and the capture of the royal family that was the more fundamental event. From that moment the King's room for manoeuvre was virtually nullified. He was in every sense a hostage to fortune, his movements curtailed and his ability to communicate with royalist sympathizers abroad all but eliminated. All politicians, whatever their persuasion, were shocked by the events at Versailles and the prospect that, if left unchecked, mob rule would overwhelm democratic debate. Within a few weeks the Assembly had unanimously decided that the events of 5 October must be thoroughly investigated and the culprits punished. The Châtelet court of Paris was accordingly asked to sit in judgement and to give particular attention to the actions of both Lafayette and the Duc d'Orléans that day. Hundreds of witnesses, of varying degrees of reliability, were then summoned to give evidence. One sworn anti-Orléanist, Jean Gabriel Pelletier, editor of a royalist journal, claimed to have seen the Duc lurking in the Bois de Boulogne that morning surrounded by retainers and mounted messengers who set off at regular intervals to take his orders to the mob. Another hostile witness claimed that the Duc had paid Versailles café owners in advance to provide refreshments for the rioters when they arrived from Paris. A clergyman also claimed that he knew Orléans had given two assassins a large sum of money to attack the royal guards. Dozens of witnesses claimed to have seen him early that morning striding about dressed in a grey riding coat and brandishing a whip. Some even insisted that he used the whip to point the way to the Queen's apartments as the frenzied mob pushed past him on the staircase. At all times, they claimed, he was laughing and smiling demonically. From numerous reports he also appeared to change his headgear at regular intervals. In one sighting he was described as bare headed, in another wearing a two-cornered hat, in yet another a tricorne, and finally he was glimpsed in a round hat adorned with a tricolour cockade. Much of the evidence was clearly absurd, with Orléans portrayed as a kind of demon king popping up from time to time throughout the day to provoke more mischief. Writing long after the event, his eldest son insisted that his father had not visited Versailles at all that day. Although intending to attend the Assembly he had decided to stay away when he heard that the mob was converging on the town and went to Mousseaux instead where he spent the entire day. Chartres also remained convinced throughout his life that his father had sought neither the Lieutenant Generalship nor the crown:

> Whatever the stories about him that were circulated, I am convinced that he was devoid of ambition. Deep down all he wanted before the Revolution, was to be safe from the capricious ill will of the court, and afterwards a guarantee against persecution and vengeance from it.

But this is a son writing near the end of his own life, defending the reputation of a father he considered had died a martyr to democracy. But Louis Philippe Joseph did indeed go to Versailles on the day that the guards were killed, although he played no part in events there. He had been woken at six in the morning by Lebrun, one of his old retainers, and told that a large crowd was marching on Versailles. Later that morning he dressed and called for his carriage. Near Auteuil the coach and four was stopped by a detachment of sixty soldiers under the command of an officer named Bisseau. As they were talking, the vanguard of the crowd returning from Versailles passed by bearing the heads of the two murdered royal bodyguards on pikes. Further along the road the Duc encountered wagons crammed with grain looted from the palace. A detachment of the National Guard then appeared, their officer offering two mounted soldiers to escort him the rest of the way. Arriving at Versailles, Orléans fell into conversation with two deputies who told him that the King was soon to depart for Paris. Then as he approached the palace itself many in the huge crowd that thronged the Place d'Armes began shouting the now familiar cry of 'Long live King Orléans'. Their hero is reported to have smiled but said nothing. A far different reception awaited him inside for both the King and Queen refused to speak to him, turning their backs to him instead.

Although Orléans was considered by many as the villain of the piece that day, Lafayette's role was also ambiguous. One of the many characters to briefly take centre stage in the revolution before being swept aside by events, Lafayette appears to have seen himself as an honest broker bridging the gap between King and people, and he might well have anticipated high office from his bold intervention that day. What is certain is that he was convinced that the Orléanists posed a significant threat to his own ambitions. This was his motivation, a few days after the return from Versailles, in asking Louis Philippe Joseph to meet him secretly at the house of a mutual friend, Madame de Coigny, to discuss the situation. Lafayette told the Duc that although he considered him innocent of the charges being made against him, many did not. Moreover there were troublemakers using his name to threaten further unrest, and as head of the National Guard he, Lafayette, now had responsibility for restoring law and order, and it was essential that a period of calm prevail. Orléans must therefore remove himself from France and remain in England for a period so that his supporters could no longer claim they were merely carrying out his orders. If possible, he should take Biron, Laclos, Latouche Tréville and his other troublesome friends along with him. His absence would be explained by claiming that Montmorin, the Minister of Foreign Affairs, had sent him as a special representative to the English court to discuss the instability in the Austrian

Lowlands. Lafayette even hinted that the King would try again to persuade other European powers that Orléans be made Duke of Brabant and become the first ruler of the emergent Belgian state. It was a tempting offer for Louis Philippe Joseph to consider, for not only could he reacquaint himself with the pleasures of English society but he would also avoid the predictable turmoil that was about to occur in Paris. When told of Lafayette's proposal, Mirabeau laughed scornfully and advised total rejection, adding that he would denounce Lafayette to the Assembly for interfering in foreign policy and attempting to ingratiate himself with the King. But Orléans had already been seduced by the prospect of this new role of diplomat, and on 11 October he agreed to Lafayette's request that he discuss the matter face to face with the King.

The next morning he was at the Tuileries, where an unaccustomed reception awaited him. Instead of the usual hostility he was now received warmly by the King and spent ten minutes with him, seeking to excuse himself from any involvement in the riot and murders at Versailles. Although courteous, Louis listened to his cousin's protestations in silence. Two days later they met again, this time in the presence of Lafayette, and the King appealed personally to his cousin to accept the mission and to leave France. This appeared to be a sincere request and not, as in the past, written in the form of a dismissive order resulting from some assumed transgression. Arriving back at the Palais-Royal, Orléans wrote a long letter couched in the most unctuous terms accepting the mission and praising the King for his devotion to duty and commitment to the best interests of the nation. It was as if a prodigal son had returned, for what the Duc d'Orléans had always desired was the approval of the man who had become the figure of authority in his life. The emotional austerity of his childhood and the strict regime of the Comte de Pons had produced a dichotomy in his personality, for he was both rebellious and eager to please. If Louis had been perceptive enough to understand this psychological need, perhaps he could, when he came to the throne, have transformed a potential enemy into a genuine friend by allowing his cousin more participation in the affairs of state.

Certainly Louis Philippe Joseph was flattered at being asked to undertake a diplomatic mission that might allow him to prove himself in a European context. His supporters disagreed, seeing his decision to leave for England as a disastrous move as the Châtelet hearings were at a critical stage and by quitting France he would not be present to refute the damaging testimony of some of the witnesses. Among those imploring him to stay was his old friend the Duc de Biron, who wrote: 'If you go it will look as if you are running away. Ask to be judged, and say that until you have been you will leave neither the Assembly nor France, but that afterwards you will undertake anything that the King sees fit to entrust you with.' But the King's personal appeal carried more weight than the considered advice of his own supporters.

At five the next morning – for the King was clearly eager to be rid of him – a messenger arrived at the Palais-Royal with his official instructions. He was to proceed immediately to England and, having made a personal assessment, report back on the reactions of King George III and of the British Parliament to recent events in France. He should also ascertain Britain's attitude to the problem of Brabant and the British government's preference for a new head of state there.

When news of his departure reached the Assembly, Mirabeau, about to enter the Assembly, was disgusted at this political cowardice and, turning to a fellow delegate, said dismissively, 'He thinks I'm one of his most ardent supporters but I wouldn't even hire him as my valet.' Yet this new-found contempt for his patron did not stop Mirabeau launching a devastating attack on Lafayette in a debate later that day. Orléans' departure, he told the Assembly, was a disaster for France as it left Lafayette without a rival, and that would make it far easier for him to seize power. Lafayette had condemned the Duc d'Orléans out of hand and had driven him abroad, outside the protection of the National Assembly. Moreover the general was now using the police to harry his rivals more ruthlessly than any French monarch had ever done.

Events were to prove that Orléans' decision to leave France at this critical time was a major error of judgement. His son, the Duc de Chartres, remained convinced that the diplomatic mission was merely a ploy devised to remove his father from the country so that the royalist faction could destroy his reputation unopposed. In his absence he could then easily be portrayed as the villain behind the events of 5 and 6 October, a scoundrel who rather than face his political responsibilities had chosen to run away.

16

THE DIPLOMAT

THE CONTINUING DEBATE in the Assembly was now of little concern to Louis Philippe Joseph as he hurried off to London accompanied by Laclos and Clarke and with Madame de Buffon as his intimate companion. They were not travelling on a passport granted by the King, as in the past, but on one authorized by the new Assembly. They arrived at Boulogne on 16 October, and as testimony to the Duc d'Orléans' lasting popularity with the ordinary people three sailors on their ship at first refused to sail, believing that their hero was being forcibly sent into exile. Only after Clarke had been sent back to Paris to obtain a written guarantee from the Assembly that the Duc d'Orléans would be allowed back into France did the sailors rejoin the ship.

Significantly, within hours of the Duc's leaving port, Lafayette summoned the Russian and Swedish ambassadors and told them categorically that Orléans was indeed the author of a dangerous conspiracy that had attempted to overthrow the monarchy and seize power. He also made the alarming claim that the police had discovered that agents from the Palais-Royal had gone round Paris marking the doors of royalist supporters for attack and clandestinely distributing pikes to the mob, ready for the next attack. There is no doubt that Lafayette was preparing the way for a propaganda campaign against the Orléanists. As the Palais-Royal had once flooded Paris with scurrilous pamphlets attacking the King and Marie Antoinette, so now the royalist propagandists released theirs, blaming the Orléanists for the bloody events of October. With the Duc absent and unable to defend himself it was a highly effective campaign, reducing the Palais-Royal to silence and prompting Mirabeau to complete his own volte-face by striding into the Assembly and praising Lafayette for his responsibility and statesmanship.

Unaware of the controversy that his departure had caused, Louis Philippe Joseph arrived in London full of optimism for his new career as diplomat and took up residence at a new house secured for him by Nathaniel Parker Forth, 3 Chapel Street, Park Lane. Once settled in, he sought an audience with King George in order to provide him with a personal and authoritative account of recent events in Paris. On the day of his visit the *Gentleman's Magazine* carried the following report:

> This morning the Duke of Orléans, the French Ambassador and another French Nobleman went to Windsor to visit the King. On the Duke's return to town he gave a grand dinner to several of the nobility from France at his house in Park Lane. The reports of his errand to England are various; nothing, however, has yet transpired to justify even conjecture. It is certainly no trivial business: nor is he here merely at his own wish.

The reception at Windsor was again far from welcoming. George III was dismayed by what he had heard of the violence in France and by the misfortunes that had overtaken the royal family there. He did little to disguise from his guest his extreme displeasure. Nor was the tension helped by his guest arriving half an hour late for the meeting. Once they were seated King George immediately launched into a eulogy praising King Louis XVI as a good and moral person who had shown commendable bravery in the face of mortal danger. He also, pointedly, condemned those of rank and privilege in France who had ignored their duty and deserted the unfortunate monarch in his hour of need. His guest was assured of the indignation and abhorrence that the British people shared in hearing of these dreadful events. It was also clear that the royalist émigrés who had begun to arrive from France had linked the name of Orléans to the capture and humiliation of their King. They had done their job well, for wherever Louis Philippe Joseph went in England he now found cold reserve where there had once been open friendship.

With his customary disregard for public opinion he ignored his detractors and lived quietly at Chapel Street, his consolations being the presence of Agnès de Buffon, the convivial atmosphere of his old club and the continuing friendship of the Prince of Wales. Indeed his welcome at Carlton House was particularly warm, for Prince George was being vigorously pursued by his creditors and saw the arrival of his guest as an opportunity to escape their clutches. As the wealthiest man in Europe, the Duc d'Orléans might well provide a substantial loan to the Prince that could restore his fortunes. When the suggestion was made Louis Philippe Joseph responded positively, for the Prince's friendship would be invaluable if ever he was forced to leave France himself and settle permanently in England. A secret deal, with Nathaniel Parker Forth as the middleman, was proposed by which Orléans agreed to lend his host the then colossal sum of £300,000, to be divided between the Prince and his equally spendthrift brother, the Duke of York. The loan would be secured on the revenues of the Duchy of Cornwall and would be redeemed once George came to the throne. This was tantamount to an act of treason by the Prince as such security would have needed the permission of the ruling sovereign. Negotiations dragged on for months, only to be abandoned as events in France made the transfer of such a large sum impossible.

The diplomatic mission was proving equally frustrating, for Montmorin barely bothered to reply to Louis Philippe Joseph's regular dispatches, although he ordered French agents in London to keep a careful eye on 3 Chapel Street after hearing that ex-minister Calonne had become a regular visitor there. Calonne would often arrive suspiciously late in the evening, and the assumption was that he was acting as a royal negotiator. Yet his presence at Chapel Street had more to do with money than with politics, for as an experienced financier Calonne had been asked to help transfer Orléans' funds discreetly out of France and by circuitous routes into London. Perhaps this had to do with providing the loan promised to the Prince of Wales, or it may have been an indication of the increasing desperation of Louis Philippe Joseph to preserve whatever he could from inevitable confiscation. As Talleyrand wrote: 'It was from this time that his immense wealth began to disappear, all passed to London by round-about ways and by secret agents who because of their anonymity were able to be unfaithful and enjoy the fruits of their swindling.'

There was also the embarrassing matter of the vast quantities of French grain that had been bought up in France and were now held in the Channel Islands. This had been done on Laclos' advice, not as profiteering but in order to put pressure on the government at a time of famine. When news of the operation leaked out it had provoked universal condemnation and seemed at variance with the Orléans' long-established charitable reputation. Even Louis XVI had been embarrassed by the affair and had urged his cousin while in London to discreetly arrange the return of the missing grain. This was now done, and within a month of the Duc's arrival convoys of grain wagons were leaving the Normandy ports for Paris and the provinces. The amounts involved must have been enormous, for by Christmas the famine that had plagued France for the past two years had ended.

Yet there was always time for pleasure, and in November Louis Philippe Joseph took Agnès, a stranger to England, for a tour of the country, attending race meetings and staying with friends. Returning to London he attended the trial of Warren Hastings, the Governor General of Bengal, who had been impeached on a bewilderingly complex series of charges ranging from extortion to condoning torture and waging unjust wars in order to advance British interests in India. For Louis Philippe Joseph it was another heartening example of British democracy in action, demonstrating that no minister or government official was above the law. Here was a society that had long resolved the problems that now plagued France. America too appeared, in little more than a decade, to have successfully evolved a system of government that guaranteed liberty and opportunity to its citizens. Might not this new American republic offer a suitable refuge for France's most famous democrat if the situation in France deteriorated further? Indeed Orléans appears to have briefly considered the idea of abandoning France altogether at this time and emigrating to America. When he suggested the idea to Madame de Buffon, however, she refused outright to accompany him, claiming that she could not face living there with a man who would inevitably regret having abandoned his friends and his country.

Faced with hostility or at best indifference in both London and Paris, Louis Philippe Joseph struggled to complete his diplomatic mission. His intention was to help bring about a quadruple alliance between France, Britain, Prussia and Holland that would see the emergence of a new state out of the Austrian Lowlands. Vainly he tried to open discussions with the British Foreign Secretary, the Duke of Leeds, hoping that this would lead initially to a new free-trade agreement between their two countries. But Leeds remained aloof, refusing to even discuss such matters with anyone other than the official French Ambassador to the Court of St James. In spite of this snub Louis Philippe Joseph continued his efforts by requesting a meeting with the Prime Minister, William Pitt. This was granted, and Pitt and his cabinet received him on 3 November. Although the discussions were friendly enough, little of any consequence was achieved. Meanwhile the situation in the Austrian Lowlands had deteriorated further after the nationalist leader, Van der Noot, began encouraging his supporters to rebel against their Austrian overlords. The countries most sympathetic to the nationalist cause, Prussia and Holland, could offer little practical help without the agreement of Britain. Although Pitt favoured the establishment of a free Belgian state, he was careful to assure Orléans that Britain had not the least intention of meddling in the affairs of the Austrian Lowlands. Finding the British government's position so evasive, Orléans wrote to Montmarin in Paris suggesting that approaches be made independently to Prussia but that the French government should persist in acting as an honest broker in the establishment of the new Belgian state. He also wrote to Biron saying that he thought the Belgians did not much care whether their titular ruler was himself or one of the Prince of Wales' brothers as long as they gained independence.

The Duc d'Orléans' enthusiasm for his new role as a roving diplomat appears to have annoyed Montmorin, who became embarrassed by the constant flow of dispatches from London filled with ideas and suggestions. Both the Minister and Lafayette were determined to keep Orléans in London while the Châtelet hearings continued. Consequently Montmorin sought to distract the Duc by sending a new set of instructions to London, urging him to sound out British ministers on a whole range of subjects. In Paris, the King showed little enthusiasm for the cause of the Austrian Lowlanders, having enough problems with a rebellious people of his own. Nor would his marriage to the sister of the Emperor have allowed him to publicly support any measure that threatened to remove the last possession of the Austrian Empire in northern Europe. Fully aware of this, Orléans reminded Montmorin sharply that, because of the King's fear of offending Austria and the Queen's influence over her supine husband, France would miss the opportunity of being involved in the establishment of the new state and choice of first ruler.

A growing confidence in his own abilities as a diplomat characterizes all Louis Philippe Joseph's subsequent letters to Montmorin. To the King and Queen, however, he sent a far more personal letter on 31 December 1789 combining warm greetings from London with an assurance of his high regard for them both and insisting that he was working in their best interests. There were now promising signs of a change of the political atmosphere in London, for with the serious illness of George III his son had been made Regent of Great Britain.

The hostility of the father had been replaced with the warm friendship of the son, and Orléans was convinced that the shift in power would be to his benefit. He was also showing renewed interest in the possibility that he might, after all, become the titular head of a new Belgian state. This ambition was encouraged by a friend, the Comte de la Marck, who had returned to Brussels and was sending him glowing reports of the commitment of Orléanist sympathizers in Belgium. Their efforts culminated on 25 February 1790 when during mass at the Cathedral of Sainte-Gudule in Brussels hundreds of red, white and blue Orléanist cockades were released to drift down on to the heads of the congregation below while shouts of 'Long live the Duc d'Orléans!' rang out. The ringleaders then attempted to incite the crowd, with little success, to march on the Town Hall. This mini-uprising had been organized by the Comte de Proly and paid for by the banker Walckiers, both of whom would have gained substantially had Orléans come to power.

In London Louis Philippe Joseph continued to be frustrated by the lack of support he was receiving from Montmorin, and on 3 April he wrote him a report containing the following passage:

> Although the business of the Austrian Lowlands was the principal subject of my mission I now believe it is impossible to treat it in isolation. Circumstances have changed and there is need for a wider and more embracing agreement between the European nations and between Britain and France in particular. I am well placed to be able to offer my services in brokering such an arrangement.

This was the last thing that Montmorin wanted, although he assured the Duc de Biron that he was giving serious consideration to the offer. On 4 June the ambassador, Chevalier de la Luzerne, returned to Paris leaving Orléans as the *de facto* French representative in London. Louis Philippe Joseph was delighted to see the back of him, clearly expecting to have himself confirmed as acting ambassador by Montmorin. The Minister, however, soon found a way to avoid this by pointing out that a territorial wrangle over Nootka Bay on the Pacific coast of Canada had led to a confrontation between Britain and Spain. Should Spain go to war with Britain then she would undoubtedly seek the aid of France. To conclude a treaty with Britain at this moment would be most unwise as France might soon be facing her new ally on the battlefield. The Duc should put aside his attempts to bring about such an alliance for the moment, yet he must stay on in London, for if he were to return to Paris now it would be seen by the English as an indication that France was about to go to war with them.

For Louis Philippe Joseph this was the final straw. Furious at the rejection of his advice, he realized that all his efforts had been in vain. Writing angrily to Montmorin he accused him of favouring the interests of Spain over those of France, adding, 'What is the point of me remaining in London when I am in charge of nothing?' Further exchanges with the Minister failed to change his attitude, causing Orléans to lose patience and to announce that he was abandoning his mission altogether and returning to Paris forthwith. He then wrote formally to the King on 25 June, informing him of his decision and regretting that he had been unable to be of more use to 'the interests of my country and to the glory of Your Majesty'. Four days later two envoys hurriedly dispatched from Paris arrived with a letter from the King, telling him that on Lafayette's advice he should remain in London and resume his mission.

A more perceptive observer of human nature than Louis XVI would have realized that such a directive would only produce in Louis Philippe Joseph an immediate hostility combined with a resolve to disobey. It was the drama of the strict father and the recalcitrant son all over again. On the evening of 10 July 1790 Orléans arrived back in Paris unannounced, ready to challenge his detractors and confront the King.

17

Strained Relationships

A S WAS CUSTOMARY for a returning Prince of the Blood, the day after his arrival back in Paris Louis Philippe Joseph went early to the Tuileries to attend the King at his rising. Nothing of any consequence was discussed, Louis virtually ignoring his cousin and the Queen greeting him with curt hostility. Worse was to come, for as he was leaving the royal apartments he encountered several courtiers waiting for him, obviously consumed with hatred at his presence. 'You are nothing more than a miserable bastard,' one of them shouted as he passed. 'Sir, you appear to insult me,' replied the Duc. 'Of course I do,' retorted his antagonist, 'and no doubt you are quite capable of having me assassinated, but I warn you, there are forty people in Paris ready to avenge my death.' Only the arrival of Lafayette with his aides averted physical violence. Then as Orléans, accompanied by guards, continued on past the sullen courtiers a gobbet of spit landed on his back. This encounter with the King was all the more unfortunate for Orléans had arrived with the best of intentions, ready to tell the King that he was prepared to return to London and complete his mission. A letter to that effect, posted in London, was handed to Louis the following day.

Still smarting from this encounter, Orléans returned to the Palais-Royal, where a serious domestic crisis had arisen in his absence. When he had left Paris the previous year he had given the control of his children to Félicité de Genlis. This high-handed assignment of what she considered to be her own inalienable rights had infuriated Marie Adélaïde, who had for some time been hurt and perplexed by her daughter's near infatuation with the governess and her insistence on spending much of the time with her. Her sons, too, openly displayed the warmest affection for Félicité and had been encouraged by her, to their mother's great distress, to address her as 'maman'. As if this was not sufficient reason for the Duchesse's misery she was then confronted by her new lady-in-waiting, Madame de Chastellux, who revealed the true nature of her husband's former relationship with Madame de Genlis. Marie Adélaïde was deeply wounded, and her resentment ignited into open hostility towards the governess; moreover, abandoning her natural submissiveness, she bombarded her husband with angry letters and accusations. Oddly, she appears to have borne little resentment towards her husband's current mistress, Agnès de Buffon, who was living openly with him in London. Her warm feelings towards the present incumbent were expressed in a curious letter to Louis Philippe Joseph written when he was in London:

> I confess that at the beginning of your liaison with her I was in despair. Accustomed as I was to your phantasies, I was frightened and profoundly affected when I saw you form a tie which could take away your confidence from me. Mme de Buffon's behaviour since you have formed the connection with her has made me reconsider the prejudices which I had against her. I have recognized that she has so true and so disinterested an attachment for you, and that her feeling for me is so perfect, that I cannot help being interested in her.

Marie Adélaïde's resentment of Madame de Genlis arose not from the mere fact that she was her husband's mistress but that she did not know how to behave and had blatantly suborned the affections of another woman's children. Moreover she had encouraged the Orléans boys to dress up in the uniform of the National Guard and had even taken Chartres to debates at the Jacobin Club where he would encounter 'the kind of people who are certainly able to mislead the opinions of a young man of seventeen'. The result was that he had now begun to sign his letters provocatively 'Louis

Philippe, French prince and a Jacobin to his fingertips'. It is true that Chartres was a passionate disciple of the revolution, applauding the decree of 19 June 1790 which abolished the titles of the nobility, including his own, and publishing an article in Marat's *Ami du peuple* that infuriated his mother. The relationship between mother and son further deteriorated when as a response to her criticisms of his republican enthusiasms he announced that he would in future dine with her no more than once a week. Madame de Genlis, too, had sent her own tirade of letters to London complaining to her ex-lover, almost as vehemently, that her work as governess was being undermined by the Duchesse and that the education of the young Orléans was suffering as a result. The relationship between the two women had become so acrimonious that compromise appeared impossible, and it was agreed that Madame de Genlis, while retaining her educational responsibilities, would no longer visit the Palais-Royal. Deeply unhappy and knowing that she had finally lost her husband's affections over the matter, Marie Adélaïde found consolation in her close friendship with Madame de Chastellux, who may well have encouraged her to form a relationship with Choderlos de Laclos' earlier patron, the Vicomte de Ségur.

It was a year since the storming of the Bastille, and Louis Philippe Joseph's return to Paris coincided with the celebrations marking the anniversary. The Festival of the Federation, a carefully planned propaganda exercise, was to be held at the Champ de Mars where a vast arena was prepared with an 'Altar of the Fatherland' at which a sacred oath would be administered. Thousands of people, including priests and monks, were drafted into Paris to complete the work, and on 14 July 1790 in pouring rain the great spectacle began. As the military parade consisting of the National Guard and many units of the regular army entered the arena, 400,000 spectators cheered and artillery salvoes sounded. A mass was then celebrated by Talleyrand in his current role as Bishop of Autun. 'Sing and weep tears of joy,' he told his audience, 'for this day France has been made anew.' Lafayette played a prominent part, too, mounting his white charger and riding through the massed ranks of the National Guard to where the King was seated. Then, having asked permission of the sovereign to proceed, he raised his sword in his right hand, placing it on the altar in the manner of the old Crusader oath, and read the pledge of allegiance to the new constitution. When the volleys of cannon had ceased the King stepped forward and, using his new title of 'King of the French', he too swore to uphold the constitution. Showing little emotion, the Queen lifted the little Dauphin, dressed in a miniature uniform of the National Guard, and presented him to the cheering crowd. The celebrations continued for a week, causing an English visitor, Helen Maria Williams, to describe those July days as the most sublime spectacle that she had ever witnessed.

In spite of his cold reception at the Tuileries, Louis Philippe Joseph, who had marched happily with his fellow deputies, felt moved to write to the King expressing his delight at this 'memorable day for France and offering my love and respect to this best and most wise of Kings'. Unable to accept that the Duc's sudden return from London was anything other than an act of defiance that would only encourage further mayhem, the royal couple ignored his letter. Mirabeau too thought the reappearance of the Duc 'a bad move', although he assured the King that there was now no danger of an Orléanist party emerging and that the Duc was now little more than a political 'phantom'. Nor, in Mirabeau's opinion, would the newly emergent Jacobin party welcome such a dissolute and spent force to their ranks. Yet Mirabeau himself played an ambiguous role, keeping all his options open, for as Jean Joseph Mounier, who had helped administer the tennis court oath, wrote of this elusive political animal:

The restless ambition of Mirabeau, his excessive desire of increasing his own celebrity, and of acquiring riches and power, disposed him to serve all parties. I have myself seen

him go from the nocturnal committees held by the friends of
the Duke of Orléans to those of the enthusiastic republicans,
and from their secret conferences to the cabinets of the
King's Ministers: but if in the first months the ministers had
agreed to treat with him, he would have preferred supporting
the royal authority to joining with men whom he despised.

The Jacobins were at this time just one of three con-
tending parties in the National Assembly. Their seating
positions in the Assembly would later be used to define the
political allegiance of party factions. On the right of the
President sat the 'black' or aristocratic party, mainly comprised of the clergy and the nobility. On the left wing sat
deputies who were members of the 1789 Club and other
independents including Lafayette, Bailly, Talleyrand, de
Crillon, Thouret and others. To their left were the smallest
party, the more radical Jacobins led by Lameth, Barnave,
Pétion and Beauharnais. The Duc de Chartres, who to his
mother's distress had become a member of this group, agreed
with Mirabeau that there had never been and never was an
Orléanist party as such:

> Every party that existed in France during the Revolution was,
> in turn, accused without distinction of being the Orléanist
> party. But the less foundation there was in this accusation,
> the more it terrified those against whom it was levelled, and
> there is no doubt that from the very beginning the court pos-
> sessed in this trite accusation a gorgon's head that turned its
> enemies to stone, sowed dissent among them and impeded
> all their activities. It was precisely because no one wanted to
> elevate the Duc d'Orléans to the throne that everyone feared
> such an accusation.

Chartres, introduced into the Jacobin Club by the
Marquis de Sillery, also chronicled the growing friction that
would eventually lead to a split into two opposed factions,
the Girondins and Robespierreists. His father adhered to the

latter, he believed, because he sought protection from the machinations of the royalists and their allies in the Assembly.

By late 1790 the Châtelet court appeared ready to deliver its verdict on the killings at Versailles the previous October and to either clear or condemn those rumoured to have been responsible for the riots. The President of the Court, Boucher d'Argis, declared that he had been determined to discover not only the identities of the perpetrators but also those who had ordered and controlled their actions. He was also distressed, he told the Assembly, to see two of the accused, namely Orléans and Mirabeau, sitting in front of him as members 'of this august body', for there appeared to be sufficient proof to have them both arrested. At this Mirabeau rose and in his customary declamatory manner reminded the deputies that all of them shared inviolability from prosecution and that the matter should not be decided by the Châtelet but by the Assembly itself. The remaining royalists in the Assembly responded by repeating the old accusations against Orléans, that he had personally planned the attack on the royal family and that he had been seen at the door of the Queen's apartments, sword in hand. Again this was too much for Mirabeau, who responded by mocking the speaker as well as the whole questionable apparatus of the Châtelet court and its archaic procedures. Then, rounding on Lafayette, he accused him again of having persuaded the King to get the Duc d'Orléans out of the country so that he could enjoy power himself. Under this man, Mirabeau repeated, the secret police were far more active than they had ever been under the old regime.

In spite of Mirabeau's bluster the Assembly was unconvinced, and both he and Louis Philippe Joseph remained under threat of arrest. The Assembly then decided that one of its members, Jean-Baptiste Chabroud, should examine the Châtelet evidence in detail and report back to his colleagues on whether or not a prosecution should take place. This he did two months later, declaring that there was no case for further action: 'There has not been and never has been a plot, unless you consider the Châtelet report itself a plot against the Revolution. Just look at the names involved. They appear to be a league formed from the debris of the old regime to attack the new.' More importantly, in spite of the lurid witness accounts the court had found no firm evidence on which either Orléans or Mirabeau could be convicted. The terrible events of last October, Chabroud believed, had their origins in the social chaos and deprivation that existed at the time and were not the responsibility of any single individual.

Chabroud's report appeared to satisfy the great majority of the deputies. 'The Duc d'Orléans and Mirabeau have been found as pure as the driven snow,' wrote the Marquis de Ferrières sarcastically to his wife. Predictably, the verdict was denounced as a whitewash by the royalists in the Assembly, for Orléans' absence in England so soon after the murders at Versailles still mystified many. It was left to the Duc de Biron to defend the honour of his old friend and explain to the Assembly the valid reasons for that departure.

Nor was Louis Philippe Joseph himself wholly satisfied with a verdict which, although exonerating him, failed to fully explain his actions. On 29 October he published his own version of events, pointing out that if he had intended to usurp the throne there would have been no better time than immediately after the King's removal to Paris. Instead he had gone to London, and his absence, he explained, was solely out of duty to his country for he had been called upon to conduct a diplomatic mission on behalf of France, and this he had done, even at a cost to himself. The document then goes on to examine and explain in great detail all the events of the previous October and the Duc's own thoughts and reactions to them. To the people of Paris this lengthy apologia was of little concern, for they remained convinced that he had long ago proved his credentials as a champion of liberty and an implacable enemy of royal tyranny. Having read it, Marie Antoinette is reported to have turned to her husband and said, 'If you really want to see who is the real King of the French, just take a drive to the Palais-Royal.'

That same month saw a further deterioration in the already acrimonious relationship between Madame de Genlis and Marie Adélaïde when the latter refused either to receive the governess at the Palais-Royal or to visit her at Bellechasse. The tug of war for the affections of the Orléans children could now only be resolved by the intervention of the Duc himself. Distracted by the conclusions of the Châtelet inquiry, he nevertheless managed to persuade the Duchesse to accept a compromise by which the children would spend part of each month with her and the rest at Bellechasse. This arrangement suited the Duc de Chartres, who maintained his profound affection for Félicité although he would soon be leaving to commence his military career. His younger brother, the Duc de Montpensier, remained at Bellechasse to continue his studies, as did the eleven-year-old Duc de Beaujolais, reputedly his father's favourite son. In spite of his own disappointing experiences at sea, Louis Philippe Joseph was keen for Beaujolais to embark on a naval career and had hired no less than three instructors to teach him navigation and the other maritime skills. Their mother, however, continued in the misery that had plagued her past few years, jealous of Madame de Genlis and loathing her husband's dangerous involvement in the fast-changing revolution. Finally, when he insisted on dismissing her closest confidante, Madame de Chastellux, the Duchesse could bear it no longer and summoned Madame de Genlis to her apartment and then, as Félicité records in her memoirs:

> She came in brusquely, sat down, told me to be silent and took a paper out of her pocket, telling me in a very imperious tone that she was going to declare her intentions to me. She then proceeded to read in a loud voice the most surprising document in the world. She signified to me in this statement that, considering the difference of opinion, I had no other course to take if I were an honourable woman but to go away without further delay.

Banished from the Palais-Royal, Madame de Genlis departed for Lyon a fortnight later, taking her beautiful adopted daughter, Pamela, with her. 'I have been treated', she wrote to Mademoiselle Orléans, 'as they would not treat a servant girl. The Duchesse has forbidden me ever to go to the Palais-Royal again.' The departure of someone who had become a mother in all but name proved catastrophic for Adélaïde d'Orléans. Always a nervous and highly strung girl, she collapsed in a nervous breakdown that was only relieved when Madame de Genlis was urgently recalled, albeit temporarily, to Paris.

Even the defeat and departure of her rival was insufficient to placate the Duchesse, for on 5 April 1791, the twentieth anniversary of her marriage, she announced that she was leaving the Palais-Royal and going to live at one of her father's houses, the beautiful Château d'Eu in Normandy. Refusing to accept that her action was anything other than a temporary aberration, her husband blamed her abrupt departure on an attack of nerves and continued his life as if nothing had happened. Her father, the Duc de Penthièvre, however, realized that the separation would be permanent unless something was done, and he wrote to his son-in-law pleading with him to attempt a reconciliation. A gentle and pious man, Penthièvre shared his daughter's distaste for revolutionary politics and was particularly shocked when told that his grandsons had taken holy communion at Easter from the hands of a celebrant newly appointed by the Assembly rather than from a traditional priest. The difficulties of being a traditionalist married to a radical were all too apparent in the marriage. When Marie Adélaïde reproached Chartres for his anti-royalist sentiments and disdain for the Catholic religion, Louis Philippe Joseph was furious and wrote accusing her of interfering in the education of his children and pointing out that it was essential they be encouraged to keep an open mind on such matters.

All attempts at a *rapprochement* failed, and the separation between the Duc and his wife was now formalized, with the

Princesse de Lamballe acting as honest broker between them. The strain of the past months now proved too much for Marie Adélaïde, and she appears in May 1791 to have suffered from a nervous breakdown. With his wife indisposed and unable to play any role in the care of the children, her husband felt he had no alternative but to recall Madame de Genlis. A triumphant Félicité accepted his offer with alacrity. A few days after her arrival back in Paris Louis Philippe Joseph called his children together and informed them of the irreconcilable separation between their parents. The Duchesse's departure from the Palais-Royal brought about a fundamental change in the atmosphere there that was later sadly described by Chartres. 'Once this separation had taken place there could no longer be any reception there, any social gathering, or even any open table or open house.' The great palace now became a neglected relic of the past, the only new visitors being the hordes of creditors clutching outstanding bills.

18

FLIGHT TO VARENNE

IN THE SPRING of 1791 Louis Philippe Joseph told the Duc de Biron that he was 'sick of being the object of every scandal and the pawn of every rogue that comes along'. Consequently he again sought to take refuge in a military career by asking the Minister for War, Antoine Duportail, to be put on the active service list as a general officer. When the King predictably blocked the appointment, Orléans demanded to know the reason for this rejection: 'I know that in the eyes of many around him I am guilty of being a zealous partisan of the constitution and the Revolution – but this cannot be wrong, either in the King's eyes or in yours. Pray give me the explanation I ask for as soon as possible.' Knowing that his master was implacable, Duportail gave an evasive reply, only to receive a further appeal from Orléans pointing out that he was prepared to serve in a position subordinate to either of the present commanders Bouillé or Rochambeau, and that he had personally canvassed every member of the military committee of the Assembly and had found no opposition to his serving in the army. Moreover, he pointed out, such appointments were no longer the responsibility of the King. 'You, sir, at this moment, alone choose the general officers. I persist in demanding to be employed as such. I await your reply with impatience.' By now Duportail had grown weary of the correspondence and replied dismissively that such an appointment at this time was 'inconvenient'.

That Louis Philippe Joseph should have chosen this moment to attempt to return to a military career is extraordinary, given that his supporters were still insistent that he could and should be made either Lieutenant General or Regent of France. This illustrates the continuing divergence between his personal ambitions and those wished upon him by such as Laclos, Sillery and Marat. This dream of a new military career at the age of forty-four certainly seems unrealistic, yet it may have been inspired by the rapid promotion of his two eldest sons to the general staff of the new French army. More likely it was an attempt to opt out of the increasingly complicated and dangerous world of politics that had come to dominate his life. He had seen a series of doors closed in his face as promising naval and diplomatic careers had ended in near ignominy, and the path to further participation in the evolution of the new France was blocked by the implacable opposition of Lafayette and the royalists. There was also the incessant hostility and suspicion emanating from Versailles, for when an angry crowd prevented Louis XVI from leaving the Tuileries and travelling to Saint-Cloud on 18 April 1791 the malign hand of the Duc d'Orléans was again seen at work, desperate to destroy the sovereign and to take his place. Certainly his supporters kept the Orléanist cause alive, as was seen in a placard fixed to the gates of the Palais-Royal six days later:

> The King is a traitor. Lafayette a counter-revolutionary. The Assembly is corrupt and bureaucratic. The municipality is despotic. The National Guard is a flat-footed mob. Name Monsieur d'Orléans as Regent. Then we can all be free!

This call to action might well have been written by Laclos himself, who remained totally committed to the cause of making his master the dominant figure in the new France. Laclos' dream was of a Duc d'Orléans who would be a more enlightened version of William of Orange or even a new Cromwell, a man of unimpeachable integrity leading his people to democracy and liberty in a manner that no hereditary monarch had ever achieved in France. Already a member of the Jacobin Club, Laclos now promulgated his ideas through his new publication, the *Journal of the Friends of the Constitution*. His simple message was a warning, reiterated almost daily, that the royal family was about to make an escape and, backed by Prussian gold, return and unleash a war of revenge on the people of France. If this did happen, he insisted, then the departure of the King should be taken as proof of his abdication, leaving the way clear for the Duc d'Orléans to be declared Regent. An anecdote of the time has Louis Philippe Joseph on the road to Vincennes meeting a very large carriage, a *Berline*, carrying the Swedish-born Count Fersen, an ardent royalist and rumoured to be the Queen's lover. 'Where are you going in that?' asked the Duc. 'It's big enough to carry a whole choir to the opera.' The implication was that the carriage was large enough for the whole royal family to escape in.

Three days after this event, on 21 June, Laclos' suspicions proved well grounded when Paris awoke to discover that the King and Queen, the Dauphin and his sister, together with the King's sister, Madame Elizabeth, had all escaped the previous night in the very *Berline* that Fersen had been seen driving. The King's brother, the Comte de Provence, and his wife had also made off by a separate route. The only remaining figures of authority in Paris were Lafayette as Commander of the National Guard and Jean-Sylvain Bailly as Mayor of Paris.

It was apparent to everyone that the King had finally succumbed to the siren voices of ex-minister Breteuil in Switzerland and Calonne in London urging him to escape while he still had the chance. If the royal family could reach Metz, close to the border and the Austrian army's camp, their safety would be assured as Lafayette's cousin, the Marquis de Bouillé, was in command of the garrison there and his troops remained loyal to the crown. Although the border was nearly 200 miles from Paris the road to Metz was a fast one, and normally the journey would take only two days. The problem was that the cumbersome *Berline*, which the Queen had insisted on using, was extremely slow and capable of no more than seven miles an hour. The royal party were all in disguise, with the King playing the role of 'Durand', a valet. At two o'clock on a moonless night the carriage, accompanied by the mounted Count Fersen, passed out through the Porte Saint-Martin, heading north-east into the open country. As they proceeded towards Montmédy, where a military escort awaited them, an accident to the *Berline* slowed their progress, causing them to fall seriously behind schedule. By the time they reached Sainte-Ménehould the news of their escape from Paris had reached the small garrison there, but it was not a soldier but the local postmaster, Drouet, who proved to be their nemesis. Recognizing the Queen, whom he had once seen in Paris, he then compared the face of the 'valet' against the royal image on a fifty-livre banknote in his pocket. Although the royal party moved quickly on to Varenne, Drouet followed on horseback and managed to rouse enough of the local guardsman to arrest them. Poignantly the local mayor fell instinctively to his knees when he recognized the King.

In the Jacobin Club back in Paris Robespierre warned Lafayette that he could pay with his head for his incompetence in allowing the escape. The reaction in the Assembly was equally hysterical, the journalist Louis Fréron condemning Lafayette and calling for the King's immediate execution in the most lurid terms: 'He has gone, this imbecile King, this perjured King. That scoundrel Queen who combines the lustfulness of Messalina with the bloodthirstiness of the Medicis. Execrable woman, Fury of France, it is you who were the soul of the conspiracy!' His words provoked the crowd to search out and destroy any remaining insignia still displayed in Paris showing either the King's head or the fleur-de-lis, and a placard was hung on the gates of the Tuileries bearing the words 'To Let'. Far more significant was the reaction of even the more moderate politicians, who were shocked by the King's perfidy and resolved to have no further dealings with him. The nation appeared so united in condemnation that when the royal family set out from Varenne to return to Paris they were surrounded by 6,000 armed citizens and guardsmen, making any attempt at rescue by the loyalist troops stationed near by impossible. When the elderly Comte du Val de Dampierre ill-advisedly attempted to ride up to the royal carriage and salute the King he was dragged from his horse and hacked to death by a crowd of peasants. The King returned to Paris to a reception of almost unanimous hostility, although the Assembly was determined to maintain law and order in a city that appeared about to be overwhelmed by mob violence. An order was issued that stated quite unambiguously: 'Anyone who applauds the King will be beaten. Anyone who insults him will be hanged.' Louis Philippe Joseph stood in silence on the terrace of the Tuileries to watch the arrival. Beside him Grace Elliott was appalled to witness 'the insolence of the people' and was shocked to see that the Queen's hair had turned completely white.

France now appeared to face a dilemma, the unpleasant choice between a discredited monarchy with the near certainty of invasion by foreign troops seeking to restore the King to power, or a leap into the unknown with a whole-hearted commitment to further revolution and the concomitant violence that it would certainly entail. To Laclos it appeared that his time had come, for only a regency offered a sensible alternative to these two unpalatable choices. No evidence remains of Laclos' specific advice to his master, but on 21 June the Duc d'Orléans appeared, in the best of humour, riding in an open carriage and driving around central Paris acknowledging the plaudits of the people. 'What a wonderful occasion for the Duc,' wrote the publisher Nicholas Ruault sarcastically. 'Here's what you get for having neither talent, courage nor even virtue.' As he continued his progress through the city Louis Philippe Joseph reached the Tuileries to find his second son, the Duc de Montpensier, in command of a detachment of troops mounting guard there. These public appearances continued, and two days later he was seen at the Jacobin Club applying for membership, where his sponsor was, as could be expected, Pierre Choderlos de Laclos. In the debate that followed there was a heated discussion on the future of the monarchy, with the majority of members appearing to favour its retention but under the most stringent controls. To Laclos' consternation no one appeared ready to suggest a regency, not even Georges Danton, who argued ambiguously for a temporary Council of State to be established, the inference being that such a council would soon be followed by a permanent regency, an idea that appeared to alarm the more extreme republicans. Only two of the many political publications that flooded the streets that month called unequivocally for the immediate establishment of a regency. The rest remained uncommitted, although Marat's idiosyncratic *Ami du peuple* proposed the appointment of a 'dictator', presumably Marat himself or one of his close associates. Finally on 28 June Laclos' ambitions took a step closer to realization when the Abbé d'Anjou rose formally in the Assembly to propose that the Duc d'Orléans be elected to the position of Regent of France during the minority of Louis XVII and that he preside over a new Council of State. Louis Philippe Joseph was absent from the chamber that day, but the following morning a statement from him appeared, without Laclos' knowledge, in the much-respected *Journal de Perlet*:

> I am ready to serve my country on land or sea or as a diplomat, in other words in any position where my zeal and commitment to the people can be of use. But as for the Regency I renounce the offer formally and finally, preferring to humbly continue my work for the liberty and freedom of the common people. I repeat, I seek neither high office nor reward. I trust that this statement will finally silence my detractors who have sought for years to condemn my actions, which were only taken in the best interests of the people.

This comprehensive rejection of the Regency was as devastating as it was unexpected, a blow to Laclos and the hopes and ambitions of all the Orléans supporters at the Palais-Royal. Many were convinced that the high moral tone of the statement came from the pen of Madame de Genlis.

Back in control at the Palais-Royal, having defeated the Duchesse d'Orléans in the domestic arena, Félicité had now routed her old enemy, Choderlos de Laclos, in the political sphere, ending his long-held ambition to make his master Regent of France. At a stroke Laclos was deprived of the whole *raison d'être* for both his political and his journalistic campaign. The repercussions were immediate. The following day the Assembly ordered an investigation into the relationship between the activities of the Palais-Royal and the continuing unrest in Paris. Summoned before the deputies, Louis Philippe Joseph was forced to admit that Laclos was no longer in his service and that he had no idea of his whereabouts, having not seen him for days.

A jubilant Félicité de Genlis now wrote to the Duc de Chartres assuring him that, although many had wanted his father to become Regent, he had displayed honesty and purity of purpose by refusing the post even before it could be formally offered. She also urged Chartres to follow this noble example and, if he were ever offered the throne of France himself, to refuse it. Her return to the Palais-Royal had certainly restored the governess's self-confidence, for she now produced a book, *A Discourse on the Education of Monsieur the Dauphin*, in which she advocated a practical and patriotic system of education for the young prince very like her own at Bellechasse. Some observers thought that she might even have written it in order to be offered the position of royal governor herself. It was even suggested, given her constant references in the book to the Romans Trajan and Marcus Aurelius, who were both adopted, that she intended to float the possibility that the Duc de Chartres might be adopted by Louis XVI and eventually become the untainted and democratic king of a new France.

As the debate on the constitutional position of Louis XVI continued, in early July the Assembly passed a decree proclaiming the King's 'inviolability', which was tantamount to pardoning him for the flight to Varenne. Laclos, who had emerged from hiding still resolute, was furious at this leniency and took the occasion as an opportunity for a last throw of the Orléans dice. Perhaps a popular petition demanding that the young Dauphin be declared King with the Duc d'Orléans as Regent could be the covert means to produce a situation in which his master would be unable to continue his refusal to accept the position. On the morning of 16 July Laclos was addressing a meeting at the Jacobin Club on the merits of such a petition when a mob, by his prior arrangement, burst into the room demanding that the petition be drawn up immediately and then taken to the Champ de Mars the following day where the people could sign it. When the crowd had departed a heated debate on its merits ensued, continuing later in the Assembly where the deputies grew increasingly suspicious that it was merely a ruse to help the Jacobins seize power. After much discussion it was decided to have nothing more to do with it, but this rejection meant little to the mob, who ignored the Assembly and urged Laclos and his colleagues to produce a new and even more radical document. The next morning, accompanied by an angry mob, Laclos, Danton and four of their colleagues set off for the Champ de Mars with a more fundamental petition demanding that Louis XVI abdicate immediately, that he be put on trial for treason and that his replacement by constitutional means should be sought. This was a serious challenge both to the authority of the Assembly and to the fragile rule of law and order. Bailly, the Mayor of Paris, responded firmly, declaring immediate martial law and ordering a large detachment of the National Guard under Lafayette to march forthwith to the Champ de Mars.

By then the crowd had already murdered two men who were discovered hiding beneath the Altar of the Fatherland, which had remained in place since the Feast of the Federation the previous year. One was a wig-maker, the other an old soldier; both were rumoured to have hidden there in order to look up the women's skirts as they signed the petition. If this was true, they paid a high price for their titillation as they were assumed to be royalist spies and were promptly lynched. Then, turning on the National Guard, the mob began bombarding them with stones and other missiles. Riding up on his white charger, Lafayette ordered the crowd to disperse as Bailly raised the large red flag of martial law. When pistol shots began to follow the stones, the troops did not wait for further orders but fired a series of volleys into the crowd, causing dozens of deaths. Fearing arrest, Marat joined the fleeing mob and went into hiding while Danton made his way to Calais and then on to England. The remaining Jacobins, now led by Robespierre, swiftly distanced themselves from their disgraced colleagues by producing a placatory address of loyalty which they rushed round to the Assembly. Within days Laclos, Orléans and the Marquis de Sillery were forced to resign from the Jacobin Club. Sillery in particular was furious at the way the Orléanist cause had been all but destroyed by Laclos' mismanagement, even denouncing his erstwhile colleague before the Assembly as the cause of the massacre at the Champ de Mars.

Although he was not directly involved with the events of 15 July, Louis Philippe Joseph had lost much of his remaining political credibility. In August he formally clarified his constitutional position before the Assembly after the committee on the constitution had proposed depriving members of the royal family of their civic rights to vote and to stand for office. The Duc protested that this was contrary to equality before the law and asserted that if it was adopted he would renounce his rights as a member of the reigning dynasty and insist upon having the same legal status as an ordinary French citizen. As he left the podium there was much applause before a deputy, Dandré, stood up and suggested that the Duc did not have the right to renounce the throne on behalf of himself or his children. This provoked Sillery to take the podium and give an eloquent tribute to the Orléans princes, who had not fled abroad like others but had willingly renounced their titles and were playing a full part in the defence of the new France. They had earned far worthier accolades than any title, he suggested – those of patriot and true citizen.

No longer a Prince of the Blood or even a duke, Orléans was now known simply as Louis Philippe Joseph d'Orléans, in which style he now signed his letters until a further decree ordained that he should have no family name at all other than his given names together with the title 'Prince Français'. Accepting this new nomenclature with resignation, he asked his sons to write to their mother addressing her as Madame Louis Philippe Joseph and to their sister as simply Mademoiselle Adèle.

19

ÉGALITÉ

I N A DESPERATE attempt at a *rapprochement* with his estranged cousin or possibly in an attempt to regain his lost popularity with the public, the King in September 1791 suddenly decided to make Louis Philippe Joseph an Admiral of France. The news was brought to the Duc by the new Minister of the Marine, Bertrand de Moleville. Ironically the office mattered far more to the recipient than any of the hereditary titles he had just lost, and it seemed a belated recompense for the humiliation he had suffered fourteen years earlier after Ushant. The new admiral was touched by the honour and particularly by the pleasant and open-minded manner with which de Moleville addressed him. Having seen himself as the victim of much unjustified calumny over the years, Orléans was grateful to meet a man who was prepared to judge him purely by his actions rather than by the word of others and told him:

> A thousand atrocities have been laid to my charge of which I am completely innocent. I have been supposed guilty by many merely because I have disdained to absolve myself from crimes of which I have a real horror. You are the first minister to whom I have ever said as much, because you are the only one whose character ever inspired me with confidence.

De Moleville further recommended himself by suggesting that they go together to the Tuileries for an audience with the King. The meeting proved amicable, and the King later told de Moleville that his cousin 'had sincerely promised to do all in his power to right the wrongs of the past'. Heartened by his reception, Orléans repeated his visit again the following

Sunday, only to find his path blocked by a group of belligerent courtiers who refused to let him pass.

Louis Philippe Joseph's attempt at domestic reconciliation fared little better. Marie Adélaïde still refused to return to the Palais-Royal, insisting that there must be a legal separation between them. To resolve the matter it was agreed that a family tribunal should decide the terms of their parting. Still in nominal control of the Orléans children, Madame de Genlis was increasingly concerned for their and her own safety and requested permission to take Mademoiselle Orléans and Pamela over to England with her. She vowed that they would return within a month – a promise she had no intention of keeping, having taken a temporary house in Bath and reserved another in Bury St Edmunds for the whole year. Scarcely had they departed when a new decree was published by the Assembly ordering émigrés to return to France or face confiscation of their property. This was another serious threat to the Orléans finances. Already the family treasure of precious stones and medallions had been sold to the Hermitage in St Petersburg. Now the incomparable art collection had to go too, with the reliable Nathaniel Parker Forth acting as agent by selling the paintings and sculptures through the firm of the rising young London art dealer James Christie. Some believed that the Orléans' financial embarrassment was as much the product of the Duc hoarding funds in England as it was of debt in France. Dark rumours continued to circulate that his constant visits to England had more to do with political intrigue than with finance.

Since late 1791 the other European powers had followed events in France with growing alarm as they witnessed the marginalization and humiliation of Louis XVI. Should the ideas that fuelled the French Revolution spread throughout Europe then long-established dynasties would be under a similar threat. Consequently an anti-revolutionary alliance led by Prussia and Saxony began to emerge, causing the Assembly in Paris to introduce ever more draconian measures to discourage any attempt at a counter-revolution. On 20 April 1792 Austria declared war on France and the new Minister for War, Charles Dumouriez, was faced with having to challenge a powerful enemy with a force that had lost the greater part of its officer corps. These men, mainly from aristocratic families, had either resigned their commissions or gone into exile with the royalists. Desperately short of skilled leaders, he now eagerly welcomed both Louis Philippe – the Duc de Chartres – and his younger brother Montpensier on to his general staff and encouraged their rapid promotion. Their father, meanwhile, remained an admiral without a fleet. Anxious to play his part in the inevitable conflict, Louis Philippe Joseph wrote to the King asking if he could inspect the port of Lorient. It was an odd request and curtly refused. Ignoring the rebuff he made his way there regardless and put up at the Hôtel Henri IV. The reason for his interest in Lorient soon became apparent, for staying at the same hotel equally incognito was the King's brother, the Comte d'Artois, who had slipped over clandestinely from Dover. The reason for his visit is unknown, yet their simultaneous arrival at such a place could hardy have been a coincidence. In the past they had been involved in the purchase of English racehorses together, and it is quite possible that this was a planned meeting to discuss the management of their mutual interests in the London money market.

As the Austrian army advanced, so the demoralized French fell back in disorder on Valenciennes and then Lille, where the troops managed to hold the line while the government in Paris debated whether or not to sue for peace. Rather than face the consequences of a humiliating treaty with the enemy, the Assembly eventually united in a determination to fight on, knowing that any agreement would inevitably involve the restoration of the monarchy and imprisonment or worse for themselves. Robespierre expressed their anger and frustration in a speech that accused the King of being in traitorous contact with the Austrian invaders. New decrees were issued ordering the deportation of recalcitrant priests, the abolition of the royal bodyguard and rapid recruitment of a 20,000-strong militia to protect Paris against any attempt at a royalist coup. To demonstrate their resolve the Assembly further decreed that 20 June be declared a day of National Salvation, and thousands of armed Parisians were encouraged to demonstrate outside the Tulieries. This display of unity was watched by Louis Philippe Joseph, now returned from Lorient, who with his customary persistence appealed again to the new navy minister, Lacoste, for active service as an admiral. Lacoste appeared no more enthusiastic for his services than Louis XVI had been. In desperation Louis Philippe Joseph abandoned the attempt to resurrect his naval career and wrote instead to his eldest son requesting him to ask Dumouriez to find him a post, regardless of rank, under his command. 'I have decided to join him as a simple amateur volunteer,' he told his friend Biron, then without even waiting for a reply he left Paris and arrived at Valenciennes on 3 May in the company of Madame de Buffon to discover that his son had leased a country house for him and another for his mistress in a small town near by. Although anxious to be seen as a simple soldier resolutely defending his country, he still managed to bring with him the accoutrements of his old lifestyle: his cook, his secretary and his personal physician as well as numerous other servants.

On 16 June General Luckner managed to turn the tide, driving the invaders back across the border and capturing the town of Courtrai. He then pointedly wrote to the King assuring him of his loyalty and condemning the faction-fighting among the politicians in Paris. Lafayette, too, took the opportunity of this French victory to resign his command of the National Guard and to pledge his personal loyalty to the King. When the news reached the streets of Paris, Lafayette was seen by the mob as a traitor to the revolution and immediately burnt in effigy.

Suspicion of all foreigners now produced a national paranoia that led the Assembly to declare the fatherland in danger. Although the King had opposed the recruitment of the new militia, thousands converged on Paris to join up. In a desperate move to maintain law and order the Assembly appealed, unsuccessfully, to the King to abdicate in favour of his son. Nor was the paranoia confined to the revolutionaries. The King, alarmed by new rumours of an Orléanist conspiracy, persuaded Luckner to order Louis Philippe Joseph to leave the army camp forthwith, and his close ally Biron was instructed not to rejoin the Army of the Rhine at Strasbourg. None of this much helped the hard-pressed French army under Dumouriez, which again fell back before a rapid Austrian advance. With the invaders now at Orchies and Bavay, within striking distance of Paris, a previously obscure deputy, Ribès, made a violent and declamatory speech attacking what he called the new Orléanist conspiracy and accusing Dumouriez of being party to it. What was the real purpose of Louis Philippe Joseph's visits to England, he asked, other than to plot with Britain the seizure of all the French colonies throughout the world? But he then undermined his credibility by further accusing the so-called Austrian Committee of Marie Antoinette, the Comte de Mercy-Argenteau, Montmorin and even Bertrand de Moleville of being Orléanists in disguise. As crazy as Ribès' diatribe appeared, it showed that such accusations, however preposterous, could produce fear and discomfort among the increasingly paranoid deputies and would set a precedent for Robespierre and his cohorts in the future. It was left to Gaudet, a Girondin deputy, to discredit Ribès' wild denunciations and to point out that Britain, at that very moment, was discussing the prospect of a treaty of alliance with France rather than plotting to rob her of her colonies.

As the Austrian army threatened to advance on Paris the increasingly powerful federal militia petitioned the Assembly to depose the King immediately and arrest all the remaining officers of aristocratic descent still in the army. All were aware of the ominous statement issued by the Austrian Emperor that had been read to the Assembly a few months earlier:

> The Emperor believes he owes it to the well-being of France and the whole of Europe, as well as being authorized thereto by the provocations and the dangerous intrigues of the Jacobin party, to unmask and denounce publicly this pernicious sect as the enemies of the Most Christian King and of the fundamental laws of the present constitution and as disturbers of the peace.

On 10 July the King left the Tuileries to cheers from his Swiss Guards and shouts of 'No more veto!' from the National Guard, and walked to the Salle du Manège to hear the final decision on the fate of the monarchy. As they were forbidden to be present during debates, the King and Queen were placed in a small room used by reporters. Unable to even hear the debate, they were later curtly informed that the French monarchy had been totally abolished. Outside a large crowd had gathered, and at the news that the King was deposed a large section including thousands of National Guards and militia began to attack the Tuileries. Totally outnumbered, the Swiss Guards attempted to stem the invasion by firing volleys of shot into the advancing crowd but were soon overwhelmed by weight of numbers. Those who could threw away their arms, stripped off their uniforms and escaped. The rest were simply butchered on the spot, shot, stabbed and mutilated by the mob and their bodies burnt. Six hundred soldiers perished that day, the greatest massacre so far in the revolution. Two days later the King and the royal family together with the Princesse de Lamballe were taken from the relative comfort of the Tuileries and incarcerated in the dank Temple prison. France was now without a constitutional figurehead of any sort and riven with disagreement on who or what should replace the King.

At the Palais-Royal Louis Philippe Joseph kept a low profile with his mistress, attended by a mere handful of servants. His carriage was still one of the few that could travel around the city without hindrance. The kind-hearted Agnès wrote to Biron of her great sadness at the plight of the poor Princesse de Lamballe, locked up in the Temple without a single servant: 'For a woman of such sensibilities who once fainted when shown a painting of a lobster this is a terrible ordeal.' Her sole concern, she told his old friend, was that Louis Philippe Joseph should remain well and content and that she shared his dread of some 'horrible conspiracy' following the massacre of the Swiss Guards that might suddenly erupt and destroy their happiness together. Fear of the counter-revolutionaries appeared to be of more concern to the ex-Duc d'Orléans, for on 29 August, with the Paris prisons full of suspected royal sympathizers, he warned the journalist Louis Marie Prud-homme that 'we could all have our throats cut if these aristocrats with their pistols and daggers ever get out of prison'. Prudhomme thought him an idiot. From his letters to his family it was clear that Louis Philippe Joseph really did believe that his life and those of every patriot were in danger, either from a counter-revolution or from the invading Austrians. He fully shared the hysteria that now gripped Paris and endorsed the demand for action to be taken against this fifth column of imprisoned aristocrats to stop them breaking out and joining forces with the invaders. That such a normally gentle and conciliatory person as Agnès de Buffon shared these fears is indicative of the climate of fear that gripped Paris in early September 1792. Marat in the *Ami du peuple* urged his readers to act while there was still time and seize the priests, the remaining officers of the Swiss Guard and their accomplices and to run a sword through them. Danton too joined the chorus for pre-emptive revenge, dramatically expressed in the words of his friend Fabre d'Eglantine:

Once more, citizens, to arms! May all France bristle with pikes, bayonets, cannon and daggers. Everyone must become a soldier. Let us clear our ranks of those vile slaves of tyranny. Let the blood of traitors be the first holocaust to Liberty, so that in advancing to meet the common enemy we leave nothing behind to disquiet us.

News that Verdun had fallen reached Paris on 2 September and finally ignited threat into action, leading to the most appalling massacre of the whole revolutionary period. The slaughter of over 1,400 defenceless prisoners was justified by the use of terminology similar to that later used by the Nazis against the Jews. They were 'gilded aristocrats, venial priests, diseased whores or court lackeys' and therefore sub-humans who must be cleansed from the face of society. The authorities showed little concern; the Minister of the Interior, Roland, ignored what was about to happen, and Danton, having just made an inspirational speech to the Assembly that galvanized the nation into defending France against the invaders, dismissed an appeal to save the prisoners with the words, 'I don't give a damn about them. Let them fend for themselves.'

The slaughter began at the Abbaye prison, where twenty-four priests were hacked to death with knives and axes, before spreading to the other prisons. The next day the killings continued and included the Bishops of Arles, Saintes and Beauvais and ex-minister Montmorin. Particularly shocking was the massacre of adolescents: almost half those killed at the Bicêtre were under the age of eighteen, and one was a twelve-year-old boy. The most celebrated of the murders, if such a word can be used in this context, was that of the Princesse de Lamballe, who had bravely opted to accompany the Queen into captivity. At a brief hearing she was required to swear an oath of hatred against the King and Queen. She refused and was pushed out into a yard where she was butchered and her head struck off, fixed to a pike and carried around the streets. At the Palais-Royal Louis Philippe Joseph was breakfasting with Madame de Buffon when they heard a commotion outside. Going to the window he saw the head of his ex-lover being brandished on a pike by a baying mob. He is said to have contemplated it coldly while Agnès half fainted and cried, 'My head will be paraded like that one day.' Blame for this particular atrocity was even attributed by some to the ex-Duc himself as an act of revenge for the support the

Princesse had given his wife. Yet Grace Elliott witnessed the shocking effect the murder of the Princesse had upon him and the conclusions he drew from it:

> He spoke of this abominable murder. He seemed much shocked at her fate and said that he had done everything in his power to save her. It made him so sad to witness such terrible events even though our children would benefit from the revolution in the long run. He assured me that he had always envied the life of an English country gentleman, and that although his enemies taxed him with wishing to be king he would willingly change his lot and all his fortune for a small estate in England, and all the privileges of that delightful country which he hoped to see once more.

Grace urged him to abandon his revolutionary colleagues but he assured her, sadly, that it was already too late. He was poised on the edge of a raging torrent and must either cling to them or risk falling in alone. In other words, his personal safety depended upon his remaining close to the more extremist elements in the Assembly, a further explanation of his increasing adherence to the Jacobins.

Through no fault of her own Grace was also in great danger. On the night of 2 September she had hidden, at risk of her own life, the Marquis de Chansenets, Governor of the Tuileries. Chansenets been wounded and left for dead during the slaughter of the Swiss Guards. He was discovered by a sympathetic soldier who gave him his own coat and helped him escape from the palace. Given help but not shelter by several friends, including the British Ambassador, Lord Gower, Chansenets eventually arrived at Grace Elliott's door. Knowing that she risked instant execution for aiding an enemy of the state she unhesitatingly took him in and even hid him in her own bed when a National Guard patrol insisted on searching the house. The irony was that Chansenets had been among the nobles who had insulted and derided Orléans when he had last attempted to visit the King at the Tuileries. For this reason Grace hesitated to tell her friend what she had done, fearing that he would insist on the fugitive being handed over to the authorities. Her fear seemed justified when, two days later, Louis Philippe Joseph arrived for breakfast and replied to her concerns about the royal family by saying that he was sure they would not be worrying about him if their roles were reversed. Plucking up courage she eventually admitted that Chansenets was at that very moment hidden in the house. To her surprise Orléans did not appear angry but warned her, as she recalled, 'That I had exposed my life for a very bad purpose for that Chansenets was a good-for-nothing creature; that many better people had been taken up and executed: that he wished I had saved anybody else and that it would be cruel if I were to lose my life for such a poor, miserable being.' He refused to see Chansenets, who was hiding close by and over-heard the conversation, but the following day he returned and having thought the matter over agreed to see the fugitive. Chansenets was admitted to the drawing room and, shaking with fear, tried to explain his past conduct. But Orléans silenced him with a wave of his hand, saying, 'We will neither talk of the past nor on any other subject but the situation of this good person who is trying to save your life at the expense of her own.' Eventually Grace managed to take Chansenets by carriage to her house at Meudon outside Paris, from where he was smuggled, at Orléans' suggestion, in a mail cart to England.

On the political front the situation had become even more confused for on 19 August Lafayette, who had proved a useful bridge between the royalists and the revolutionaries, finally despaired and left France for good. Still discussions con-tinued over the merits of installing the Dauphin as King. There was even a counter-suggestion by the influential journalist Jean Louis Carra that the English Duke of York, once mooted as a husband for Marie Adélaïde d'Orléans, be invited to accept the throne of France. Carra argued that the emergent France was not yet sufficiently mature to be a republic and that some form of monarchy under a strong but

constitutional king would be more suitable. It was not surprising that the very idea of asking France's traditional enemy
to provide her next head of state caused derision. Undeterred,
Carra immediately proposed the German Duke of Brunswick
instead. This was an equally fatuous suggestion as the Duke
was currently commanding enemy troops poised to march on
Paris. The very idea of a foreign-born head of state had little
appeal for the great majority of the deputies and was ruthlessly
mocked by the Jacobins Billaud-Varenne and Robespierre.

The question was again asked that if only a true-born
Frenchman would do as a democratic sovereign why should
it not be the proven patriot, the ex-Duc d'Orléans? Although
he had rejected the Regency could he not be finally tempted
by the offer of the throne itself? What is certain is that
Louis Philippe Joseph had become disillusioned with the
way the revolution was evolving into a faction fight between
Girondins, Jacobins and the right-wing Feuillants. He was
also disgusted that his personal sacrifice of wealth and
position had been virtually ignored and that he and his
household had been blamed for all that had gone wrong in
the revolution. The hatred of the royalists was acceptable,
being mutual, but the danger of losing his natural con-
stituency, the people of Paris, was hard to bear. Moreover he
had seen his daughter and Madame de Genlis threatened
by the new regime, and his sons, although risking their lives
in the army of the new France, treated with suspicion. Those
whom he helped, such as Brissot, Laclos and Danton,
seemed happy to abandon him although he had financially
and politically supported them in the early years of opposition to the throne. His disconsolate mood was echoed in
the inactivity that now characterized life in the Palais-Royal.
Returning on leave Chartres found his father withdrawn and
motiveless:

He had adopted a very withdrawn and even monotonous
style of life. The theatre was a sort of compulsion for him: he
went nearly every night. Since he never had a taste for work

or had become accustomed to it, he did not know how to fill his day. He was fully aware that he could expect little support from the partisans of the revolution.

This sense of lost identity was not helped by the changes that had occurred in his nomenclature, culminating in his own commune in Paris referring to him as 'the nameless citizen' and threatening to exclude him from voting in the forthcoming local elections. On 15 September he wrote to them protesting that he had been registered in the electoral rolls under the name d'Orléans, which he claimed not to be using. Furthermore he now had no family name, a situation that he found deeply embarrassing. He therefore asked the authorities to advise him and to find a more appropriate family name. On 15 September he was invited to the commune offices to discuss his predicament with Louis Pierre Manuel, President of the Commune. During the conversation Manuel suddenly turned and glanced at the statues adorning his office. His eye came to rest on one in particular, that of the nymph Equality. Turning back to Louis Philippe Joseph with a smile, Manuel suggested that 'Égalité' would be the perfect choice. At this his visitor merely shrugged his shoulders and nodded in agreement, later claiming that he had no alternative but to agree. 'I had come to plead for my daughter, who was about to be declared an émigré, and I had to sacrifice to that my repugnance at taking this burlesque name.' A few days later he put his new name to use, signing an announcement that was hung on the gates of the equally democratized Palais-Royal, now the Garden of the Revolution, informing anyone receiving a pension or sinecure from him that in future five sols a day would be retained to support the wives of the soldiers at the front.

When he was returned on 19 September as representative in the new National Convention for Saint-Roch, his local district of Paris, a rumour circulated that the name change had simply been a ploy to ensure that he was elected and to further ingratiate himself with the Jacobins. Although in public he appeared satisfied with his new name, his sons accepted theirs reluctantly, Chartres becoming General Égalité, Montpensier Antoine Égalité and Beaujolais Léodgard Égalité. They all now addressed their letters home to Maison Égalité, rue Honoré, the postman often adding the words 'To the Palais-Royal' on the envelopes to remind himself of their true destination.

20

DILEMMAS

HIS NEW NAME did little to reinvigorate Louis Philippe Joseph's declining enthusiasm for the revolution and the path it was taking. He told a fellow deputy, Louis-Michel Lepeletier de Saint-Fargeau, enigmatically that when one had 600,000 livres a year in rent there were only two places to be, with the exiles at Coblenz or up on the 'Mountain' at the Convention with the Jacobins. The Mountain was the high area of seats that had become the preserve of Robespierre and his colleagues. Ironically, as he told his son Montpensier, it was here among the more extreme revolutionaries that he felt safest. For he was now a man surrounded by enemies, not least the supposedly more moderate Girondins. Whereas they favoured a republic based on the libertarian American system, the Jacobins espoused one on the more authoritarian, Roman model. These opportunists were of a different breed from the members of the old Assembly who had risen by their own efforts, he told his eldest son Chartres, fresh from the Battle of Valmy where he had distinguished himself commanding a division. The French artillery had driven off a half-hearted infantry attack by the Prussians, but this relatively trivial engagement proved to be the turning point of the campaign, for within ten days, without firing another shot, the invading army began to retreat.

Although he was treated as a hero by the regime Chartres was becoming as disillusioned as his father with the politicians. Still on leave from the army he encountered Danton who warned him that the émigrés were determined to return and exterminate all their enemies, beginning with his father. When Chartres protested at the September atrocities, Danton was quick to defend these extreme measures and was, to Chartres' surprise, quite willing to accept much of the blame for the gruesome killings, himself saying, 'Do you know who gave the orders for those massacres? It was me.' His justification was that the prisons were full of conspirators and wretches who were waiting for the foreign armies to arrive so that they could take their revenge. There was also a need, Danton claimed, to maintain a harsh regime, for the young men of Paris needed to be 'blooded' by taking part in such killings so that they would be bonded to the state and fight with determination when serving in the army. Danton then warned him that although his father's patriotism and political commitment to the revolution were appreciated throughout France, the Convention was a dangerous place and Chartres himself was far safer in the army, a sentiment the young man acknowledged, saying that he had no intention of exchanging his saddle for a padded bench in the Convention. This advice, he concluded, might well have been Danton ensuring that if the Austrians and Prussians successfully invaded France and restored some form of monarchy involving the Orléans, then they would be in his debt.

Returning to the front, Chartres found that the Prussians had approached the French commander, General Kellerman, with the offer of an armistice. Negotiations began on 22 September, with Chartres as a member of the French delegation. During these discussions he was after dinner taken to one side by General Heyman, formerly in the French service but now commanding a Prussian army. Heyman spoke admiringly of Chartres' father and their once close friendship before pressing into his hand a letter addressed to the new Philippe Égalité and saying:

> I should like the Prince, your father, to know that it perhaps rests with him to stop the scourge of the war. I know the intentions of the allied sovereigns; I know that they would desire to preserve France from anarchy, and as it was thought likely that you would come here, I have been authorized to

tell you and your father that they would be reassured if they saw him at the head of a French government.

Without hesitation Chartres rebuffed the suggestion, pointing out that his father had declared on numerous occasions that he would never accept such a role, least of all if it came as an imposition by a foreign power. Nevertheless he sent the letter on to Paris, where his father, having been told its contents, refused to open it, taking it immediately to the Convention, anxious that no one should accuse him of communicating with the enemy. The unopened letter was then ceremonially burnt at the table by the Convention's new secretary, Jacques-Pierre Brissot.

Whenever he was on leave, Chartres listened to the debates at the Convention, the first representative body in France elected by universal male suffrage, although he agreed with his father that the calibre of the new deputies was far inferior to that in the old Assembly. Many appeared ill dressed and shabby in appearance; in marked contrast his father had retained his smart clothes and noble countenance. Worst of them all was the macabre figure of Marat, 'a sickly little man with a pale and hideous visage shaking with convulsive movements, a dirty coloured handkerchief around his head'. On one occasion when called upon to speak Marat had leapt up and produced a small pistol from his pocket, placing it to his head in a gesture of mock suicide. He then embarked on yet another hysterical denunciation of Brissot, Gaudet, Vergniaud and the other Girondins. Having witnessed this farcical scene, Chartres succumbed to despair, and he turned his back on the bickering politicians for ever, seeking solace in his military duties. He despaired, too, of his father, whom he saw as a powerless marionette whose strings were increasingly pulled by the worst elements in the Convention. For the new Philippe Égalité the hostility he had endured at the hands of the royal family now seemed curiously feeble when compared with the provocation and bullying he received from his fellow deputies. What would he do, Chartres had asked his father, if ever the King were brought to trial? Égalité dismissed such a prospect, claiming that 'as no one really knows who will win the war it would be madness for anyone to suggest harming him'. Yet the threat to France had been significantly reduced and the King put in new danger when on 6 November the army won another decisive victory over the Austrians at Jemappes where the young General Égalité again distinguished himself. News of the victory reached Paris on the very day that the Convention announced that the King must be brought to trial and began assessing the charges against him.

For only the second time in European history a monarch stood to face judgement by his parliament. That the first had been Charles I of England, the sovereign of a country with a political system that he much admired, would have appealed to Philippe Égalité's Anglophilia. For the occasion he appeared on 11 December 1792 dressed in a set of his finest clothes. In contrast Louis XVI, a pathetic figure at the bar of the National Convention, arrived wearing a shabby olive-green silk coat and bearing three days' growth of beard. Peering myopically round the vast and bitterly cold Salle du Manège, once the royal riding school, the King would have been unable to see his cousin seated high up in the Mountain. Here under his new nomenclature, Philippe Égalite sat uneasily among his colleagues, the Jacobins. His obvious discomfiture was noted by the new Minister of Justice, Dominique Joseph Garat, who thought he would have looked far happier perched on a rock somewhere in distant Norway.

Yet the events of the past three months had ensured that Louis Philippe Joseph could not fail to be present. Driven by a desire to do the right thing and fearful of showing the least sympathy with either the royal family or the predicament of the émigrés, he increasingly sided in the Convention with the most extreme republicans. When Marat had appealed for him to fund his journal, the *Ami du peuple*, 'in the name of the people with whom you share the soul of the nation', he had promptly obliged. Although as diminished in wealth as he was in reputation, he knew that if ever the new republic foundered he retained the potential to play an important role in future events. This belief had been encouraged two months earlier by a second meeting that his eldest son had with Danton. After again congratulating the young man on his military achievements, Danton went on to praise his father for displaying impeccable republican credentials. Danton also hinted that although Philippe was now a simple deputy in the Convention he might still have an important role in the destiny of the nation if ever France's enemies proved victorious and a restored monarchy was forced on the nation. It would be far better, Danton suggested, to have a true democrat like Philippe Égalité on the throne than the Dauphin or one of Louis XVI's despised and discredited brothers. Although Danton's words were supportive, Chartres left the meeting convinced that his father was now fatally compromised, reviled by the monarchists on one side and by the extreme republicans on the other.

In spite of his past conflicts with the royal family, Louis Philippe Joseph tried discreetly to avoid any personal involvement in the forthcoming trial. He even appealed to a leading Girondin for help. Jérôme Pétion, the ex-mayor of Paris, had been dismissed by the King for supposedly displaying 'personal enmity' towards the sovereign. Now an influential voice in the Convention, he was sympathetic to Orléans' predicament and when General Égalité was next on leave from the army Pétion summoned him to his office to discuss the problem. He began like Danton, praising the Orléans family's undoubted commitment to the revolution but felt he could not guarantee that they would not be involved in the trial. They must, he said, like all good French citizens be loyal and do their duty to the new republic no matter how personally unpleasant that might be. That evening Chartres, now acutely aware of the imminent danger, pleaded with his father to avoid the trial and to go to America instead. In fact, they should take both their families and escape together and start a new life there. America was their only possible refuge given that no other European country would accept a family so closely associated with revolutionary France. 'Even England, which you so much admire, is now closed to you,' Chartres told his father. Had not his closest friend Biron, who had fought in the War of American Independence, been contemplating returning there himself and starting a new life? But his father now thought the suggestion ridiculous, saying that neither he nor Biron, quintessential libertines, could endure living in such a puritanical and unsophisticated society as America:

> Unless one worked with one's hands, the only form of enterprise that could be conducted there was running a commercial enterprise, of which he was not capable, or a Negro plantation like General Washington's, which did not suit at all. That in the towns there were neither congenial households, nor society, nor theatres; that everything was sad and mournful and calculated to make him die of boredom and melancholy.

Moreover, his father reminded him that as an elected deputy for Paris it was his duty, as Pétion had pointed out, to remain in France and attend the Convention, for to leave now would make the Orléans appear no better than those despised émigrés now gathered on the borders of France awaiting her downfall. This was the first manifestation of his anxiety to please or at least accord with those whom he considered to be the new masters of France. It would be a thankless task, for these men would prove to be implacable and as prepared to denounce and destroy each other as they were to eradicate the last vestiges of the nobility, even if that included a man who had played such an important role in challenging the King in the early stages of the revolution.

On 12 October Louis Philippe Joseph's worst fears were confirmed when the Convention passed a law ordering all émigrés to return to France within a month; those who ignored this order would be formally attainted and forbidden to re-enter the country on pain of death. This decree would be a particular disaster for him as Madame de Genlis, together with Mademoiselle d'Orléans and Pamela, had against his wishes lingered on in England. In desperation, in the first week of November he sent his friend the journalist Hugues-Bernard Maret, later the Duke of Bassano under Napoleon, to London with written instructions to bring Félicité and her party home before the act came into force. When Maret was delayed a worried Louis Philippe Joseph sent a second messenger with counter-instructions for them to remain in England rather than risk arrest on their return to France. He too was delayed and failed to reach them before they had sailed for Calais on 20 November. Following the group back across the Channel the messenger eventually caught up with them at Calais. There he handed Madame de Genlis a note warning her that if they had already crossed the Channel, to remain in the town of Calais and under no circumstances proceed on to Paris, where they could certainly be arrested and imprisoned.

Characteristically, the self-assured Félicité ignored the order and took it upon herself to set off at once for the Orléans château at Raincy, near Paris. Once there she then decided that they must all go on to the opera that evening where Pamela could renew her acquaintance with the Irish peer and future revolutionary, Lord Edward Fitzgerald, who had paid her much attention in London. It was a dangerous and irresponsible jaunt inspired by Madame de Genlis' predilection for matchmaking. But exchanging their travelling clothes for evening wear the ladies set off for Paris where they met Lord Edward and saw Cherubini's *Lodoiska* at the Opéra. The next morning Louis Philippe Joseph arrived at Raincy early and was soon ranting at his ex-mistress for having risked the life of his cherished daughter. His anger appeared fully justified, for the following day he was summoned to the Convention and asked why his daughter had arrived back in France and why she should not be classed as a returned émigré. He pleaded that Marie Adélaïde was an innocent girl in poor health and ignorant of politics who had merely gone to England to take the waters at Bath. After a heated debate the deputies decided that Madame Égalité must leave French soil until a decision on her status could be determined. As Madame de Genlis and her sad little party were preparing to depart from Raincy, Louis Philippe Joseph arrived in a sullen mood. Seizing the moment, Félicité begged him, as Chartres had earlier done, to escape immediately to America while there was still time. Galled by his curt dismissal of her plea, she then asked him why he had allowed the Orléans insignia of three fleur-de-lis to be retained in the plasterwork above the main fireplace of the salon they were standing in. Surely this was in flagrant contravention of the law banning all Bourbon insignia. He replied coldly, 'I have left them because it would be cowardly to remove them.' The next morning he stood disconsolately in the doorway apparently unable to say a word other than 'Adieu, Madame' to Félicité as he watched his ex-mistress depart with the daughter he would never see again.

While the Orléans ladies were leaving Raincy for temporary exile at Tournai in what is modern Belgium, the Convention in Paris was debating the introduction of two more decrees proposed by the Girondins that would have a profound effect on the future of the House of Orléans. François Buzot, colleague and lover of the firebrand Madame Roland, had introduced a bill proposing the death penalty for anyone seeking to re-establish the monarchy. This was clearly aimed at the Orléanists, for after the victory at Jemappes and the revelation of secret talks between the Prussians and the French commanders that included General Égalité, it was suspected that either Égalité or his son would make a last bid for the French throne.

On 16 December Buzot was more specific, demanding the exile of anyone connected with the House of Orléans, claiming that these troublemakers posed a dangerous and continuing threat to the new republic: 'Let them carry elsewhere the unhappiness of being burdened with a name that can serve as a rallying cry for factious people or to emissaries of other powers and with which the ear of a free man can no longer be wounded.' Were the Orléans not only Bourbons but also inextricably linked by blood and marriage to some of the most autocratic royal families of a hostile Europe? Their very name, Buzot continued, could serve as a rallying call to all the clandestine and malicious opponents of the new regime. At this, another Girondin, Jean-Baptiste Louvet, jumped up to support him, likening the threat that the Orléans posed to contemporary France to that of the Tarquins to the fledgling Roman republic. Every Bourbon, except those already in custody at the Temple prison, and their supporters such as Dumouriez, Biron and Valence, must be totally and ruthlessly expelled from the soil of France, he demanded. Merlin de Thionville also gave his support to the motion, claiming that they had been at the centre of every conspiracy to hijack the throne since the storming of the Bastille in 1789. Their very presence would always be a threat to the survival of the new republic. Perhaps he had forgotten or was unaware of Brissot's perceptive words, 'The Prince was rather fond of conspiracies that lasted only twenty-four hours – any longer and he grew frightened.'

21

THE REGICIDE

S UCH WAS THE increasingly fractious atmosphere in the Convention that the Jacobins could not allow such a seeming victory for the Girondins to pass unchallenged. Deputies from the Mountain rushed down to the podium to protest that the motion was a travesty of justice. They strongly defended their new colleague, Philippe Égalité, as a good republican, an honest citizen and an innocent man. More-over, Camille Desmoulins demanded, was it not scandalous for the Convention to demand the banishment of a fellow deputy, a man who, whatever his questionable antecedents, now honestly represented the ordinary people of Paris? If this man was banished today, could any deputy truly feel safe in the future? From every part of the hall voices shouted support for Égalité, praising his courage in remaining in Paris and playing his full part in the establishment of the new democracy. It was a powerful argument at a time when para-noia had begun to dominate the Convention. Robespierre added his formidable weight to the argument, albeit clandes-tinely. Determined to retain control of the Jacobin element, even if it meant a temporary concession to the Girondins, he ordered his acolyte, Louis Antoine de Saint-Just, to take the podium.

At twenty-five, Saint-Just was the youngest deputy in the Convention and, with his shoulder-length black hair and single gold earring, the most striking in appearance. In a brief but chilling address to the Convention, Saint-Just swung the argument back against the Orléanists. Giving his full support to Buzot's motion, he too raised the spectre of Tarquinian treachery and echoed the demand that every Bourbon be expelled and the King put immediately on trial for his life.

These harsh words from Saint-Just showed the ex-Duc d'Orléans that he would never be able to rely on the Mountain for support if he was ever fundamentally and comprehensively attacked again. Yet some remained faithful. That evening in the Jacobin Club, Camille Desmoulins, who had urged the mob to attack the Bastille four years earlier, condemned the debate in the Convention. Why should Philippe Égalité, a man who had contributed so much to the revolution, be sent into exile, he demanded? He would surely become the target for embittered émigrés who would attempt to assassinate him, to the delight of the King and royalists. His words opened the way for Robespierre, who had not spoken at the Convention earlier in the day, to launch another attack on the despised Girondins:

> We Jacobins have only appeared to defend Citizen Égalité because we believe the cause of principle is attached to the cause of Égalité, yet we have never had contact with the House of Orléans and those who provoked this decree have had the greatest possible contact with it. Was it not a Girondin who nominated him for a seat in the Convention in the first place and who spread the rumour that the Jacobins want to see him on the throne of France – none other than Jean-Baptiste Louvet, a Girondin deputy!

However he fully supported, Robespierre continued, the plan to send Philippe Égalité and every other Bourbon into exile. Let them take refuge with their friends in London if they wished – the French Republic was quite willing to pay all their bills. Their departure should be seen not as a punishment but as a response to the national request that they all go into voluntary and honourable exile. It was solely for this reason, he added with his customary deviousness, that he now fully supported Buzot's motion that the Bourbons be exiled. It was left to Marat, anxious to contain Robespierre's growing influence, to have the final word. Leaping to the rostrum he shouted:

I condemn what Robespierre has just said. Égalité must stay because he is a representative of the people. Today the criminal faction that wants to destroy the rights of the people in the person of Égalité would like to exile all the friends of the people, and you yourself, Robespierre, you will be at their head. Let Égalité remain among us!

Marat sat down to furious applause after this impassioned defence of principle rather than of the man himself, for he privately considered his patron to be 'an unworthy favourite of fortune without virtue, soul or guts'. There was little else to say on the issue; the Convention had grown weary of the endless debate, which was causing friction and division in every political faction. The next day the deputies agreed that the whole issue be set aside until after the King's trial.

The question of whether or not to try the King had dragged on throughout November and had almost been negated by another dramatic intervention from Saint-Just, who argued that the very act of putting the King on trial presupposed the possibility of his innocence, and this was clearly nonsense. For if Louis XVI was innocent then the revolution of 10 August was illegal. The deputies had a simple choice – the revolution or the King – therefore the King might have to die for the republic to continue to live. Saint-Just's powerful and ruthless speech stunned the Convention but it was openly supported by Robespierre, who agreed that there was no need for a trial as the King had already been judged by the events of 10 August. However, if there had to be one then it had best be swift and summary or the new republic would be endangered. As far as Robespierre was concerned, the King was an irrelevance and an embarrassment and the sooner he was disposed of by the guillotine or incarcerated in a prison cell for life, the better.

To Louis Philippe Joseph the prospect of the trial was almost too awful to contemplate for, as he told his eldest son, he was convinced that Louis was still conspiring with the enemies of France and if convicted might well be sentenced to death. He had no alternative, therefore, but to side with the Jacobins and their insistence on a trial because they were less his political enemies than were the Girondins. With luck, he told Chartres, he would be considered not impartial enough to vote on the fate of a man who had been his enemy for the past decade.

The King's predicament was not helped by the discovery at the Tuileries on 20 November, thanks to a dutiful republican locksmith, of the infamous *armoire de fer*, a metal casket stuffed with the most incriminating royal correspondence. Some of the letters in this Pandora's box were, Jean-Marie Roland announced to the Convention, between the King and his supporters and the Austrians. Among the more surprising of the correspondents was, to almost universal consternation, the late Marquis de Mirabeau. That one of the greatest champions of the revolution was revealed to have been discussing with Louis the possibility of restoring him to power was an alarming scandal. Although some suspected that Roland had infiltrated these particular letters into the casket for his own devious purposes, the revelation gave weight to Saint-Just's argument that now the simple choice was between the survival of the republic and the elimination of a dangerous and untrustworthy King.

France, like the Convention, remained divided over the fate of its monarch. Country areas in general and the Vendée in particular remained sympathetic to his predicament and appealed to their deputies to show mercy if not leniency. Messages of support for the Girondin position that the King, if convicted, should be imprisoned and not executed flowed into Paris from the rural *départements* of the south and west, but Paris, always the driving force of the revolution, remained loyal to the Jacobin hard-line insistence that Louis XVI be given a swift and summary trial and then executed. When the King appeared on 26 December for a second time, weary after four nights without sleep, he had at least the benefit of having seen all the relevant documents in the hands of the prosecution. He was also ably represented by a leading member of the Convention, the lawyer Romain de Sèze. After entering a plea of not guilty on behalf of his client, de Sèze spent the next three hours in a complicated legal argument claiming that Louis was no longer a monarch, nor was he an ordinary citizen, this anomaly making him the only man in France without the protection of the law.

The debate continued for the next two weeks until voting began on 15 January, with the Convention given just three issues to decide. Was the King guilty? If so, what punishment should he receive? If it was the death sentence, should he then have the right of appeal? The voting procedure was also unusual in that each deputy in turn was required to go to the bar of the house and openly declare his verdict. This process had been devised by Marat in order, as he claimed, to flush out the unseen traitors who lurked in the Convention and who would hide behind the anonymity of a secret ballot. It was a machination worthy of a paranoid twentieth-century dictator. For Louis Philippe Joseph it provided a terrible predicament: if he decided to vote for the conviction of his cousin, then he must now do it before the eyes of the world.

As he contemplated what action to take, his younger son, the ex-Duc de Montpensier, arrived at the Palais-Royal and pleaded with him not to condemn the King. 'I assure you', replied his father coolly, 'that I am incapable of such action.' Then an event occurred that almost certainly altered his intention not to vote. Early the following morning two deputies arrived at the Palais-Royal. They were Merlin de Douai and Jean-Baptiste Treilhard, both leading lawyers who sat with the Mountain. In the past both had acted as advisers to the Palais-Royal and still enjoyed the confidence of its owner. According to Montpensier, they had been sent by Robespierre to accompany Philippe to the Convention and to warn him that if he failed to attend or voted for the King's acquittal then certain unspecified troubles would descend on him, the least of which would be immediate exile for himself and his family. Their visit provoked an immediate volte-face for he broke his promise to Montpensier that he would not go to the Salle du Manège later that day and take part in the vote. Whatever his faults, Louis Philippe Joseph would have been almost incapable of such deceit had he not believed that in breaking his word he was saving his family from imminent disaster.

When the ballot began at noon each deputy, as his name was called, pushed his way through the crowded hall to vote. When his turn came, Philippe Égalité had no difficulty in finding his cousin guilty. Striding up to the tribune he uttered the single word, 'Yes'. The verdict on the first count, of the King's guilt, was overwhelmingly positive, with not a single deputy voting against. Curiously, the third issue, on the right to appeal against a possible death sentence, was decided next. To great rejoicing it was rejected by another large majority. Again Égalité voted with a single terse word, this time 'No'. As if exhausted by these momentous events, the deputies then agreed to adjourn the sitting until the following day when the last and most controversial issue would be decided. Returning to the Palais-Royal, Philippe found his entire household assembled and ready, with great humility, to urge him either not to attend the Convention, or at least to refrain from voting. He was said to have listened to their pleas in silence. To these appeals and those of his family was added an even more telling one, that of his closest companion in youthful debauchery and most faithful friend, Armand, Duc de Biron.

Biron was in Paris *en route* to taking command of a republican army in Nice. Some days earlier he had decided to call on their mutual friend, Grace Dalrymple Elliott, at her house at Meudon. Grace was appalled that Philippe could even think of taking part in what was little more than a show trial of his cousin. Biron shared her distaste but reassured her that in his opinion the King was in no immediate danger even though some deputies would undoubtedly vote for the death sentence. Grace Elliott replied that she prayed Philippe would stay at home and not become involved with 'such vile miscreants'. Knowing his stubbornness, they decided to confront him together and invited him to Meudon on what was to be the eve of the fatal vote. At first Égalité was evasive and tried to make light of the matter, but when Grace Elliott took his hand and appealed directly to him, his manner changed abruptly. Rising to his feet he told her brusquely that as a deputy he must do his duty and attend the Convention whatever the personal cost. 'Then, Monsiegneur,' she said, 'I hope that you will vote for the King's deliverance.' 'Certainly,' he replied, 'and for my own death.' There was a chilling silence before Biron attempted to calm the situation by assuring Grace, 'The Duc will not vote, even though the King has used him very ill all his life; but he is his cousin, therefore he will feign illness and stay at home.' Unconvinced, Grace again appealed to Philippe, saying, 'I am sure you will not go to the Convention on Saturday. Pray do not.' Perhaps in an attempt to placate her for the moment or because he was still genuinely undecided, he appeared to have been won over by her argument. Then with his next words Philippe began the process that was to blacken his reputation for posterity as a liar and a regicide. According to Grace's memoirs: 'He said that he certainly would not go; that he never intended to go; that though he thought the King had been guilty by forfeiting his word to the nation, yet nothing should induce him, being his relation, to vote against him.'

It was not until the following evening that the 721 deputies present began the fatal vote that would ensure Louis's martyrdom and the universal condemnation of Louis Philippe Joseph as a modern Judas. Grace Elliott had been asked to join Biron and General Dumouriez, Chartres' commanding officer, at the Hôtel St Marc near the Salle du Manège. She arrived at seven thirty to find the assembled party anxiously scanning the voting lists that were being sent hourly from the National Convention. At eight o'clock a messenger reported, to their consternation, that Philippe Égalité, in spite of his promise, had just arrived at the Convention and taken his customary place on the Mountain. As the voting proceeded it became apparent that the deputies were evenly divided on whether the King should suffer death or imprisonment. Grace Elliott told her companions that she remained convinced that even though Égalité was present his intention was still to vote for the lesser penalty.

At ten o'clock the name Philippe Égalité was called and the deputies fell silent as the ex-Duc d'Orléans, senior Prince of the Blood and cousin of Louis XVI, descended from the Mountain to make his way slowly to the bar where he declared in a quiet and unemotional voice: 'Motivated solely by my duty, and convinced that those who threatened or will threaten the sovereignty of the people deserve the ultimate punishment, I vote for death.' As he returned to his seat the room filled with boos and catcalls of derision. But a fellow deputy, Monsieur de Mailly, leant over and patted his arm and reassured him that he had voted like a true patriot. Égalité replied, 'I voted according to my conscience and with the love of liberty that must never be compromised.' Even though he had already suffered months of disappointment and humiliation, the effect of his cousin's condemnation on Louis XVI was devastating. When taken back to the Temple prison that night he said to his valet, Cléry, 'I did not expect any mercy but I am deeply shocked that my own kinsman, Monsieur Orléans, should vote for my death.'

When news of his vote reached the Hôtel St Marc a few minutes later, Grace Elliott collapsed into Biron's arms and they both wept openly. A young man present, one of Égalité's aides-de-camp, leapt to his feet and in a fury tore off the liveried coat he was wearing and threw it into the fire, saying that he would blush to wear it again. 'I never felt such horror for anybody in my life as I did at that moment at the Duke's conduct,' Grace later wrote. Arriving home that night she took every gift and trinket that Philippe had ever given her and, unable to bear even the presence of an object associated with him, threw them all away. By then Louis Philippe Joseph had returned to the Palais-Royal where Montpensier found him alone at his desk, his hands covering his eyes and weeping silently. When his son tried to comfort him his father pulled away, saying, 'Montpensier, I do not have the courage to look at you. No, I am too wretched. I cannot now imagine what could have led me to do what I did.' In Montpensier's memoirs, written years after the event, he shows an understanding of his father's failings while making a passionate defence of his actions:

> Perhaps you lacked the firmness that makes a man act in accordance with his own impulse; that, in addition, you lent your confidence too easily, and that scoundrels had found ways of gaining it in order to ruin you and sacrifice you to their atrocious schemes. Very well! Let them complete their defamation of the memory of this unfortunate being, this victim! But let it at least be known one day! Let the world know what I know! May I still be alive at the time!

Sadly this understanding was never to come, and Philippe Égalité is remembered not for his defence of liberty against an absolutist regime but as one of the great betrayers of history. Had he done it to save his own skin and the lives of his family by further ingratiating himself with the Jacobins, or should he be taken at his own word when he claimed in his brief memoirs, written in prison while awaiting trial, that he acted solely on principle? Certainly there was enormous pressure on him to attend the Convention that day, as Jérôme Pétion foretold and the presence of Merlin de Douai and Jean-Baptiste Treilhard had proved. Once in the Salle du Manège he could not have abstained from voting, for that would have shown cowardice, and for all his weaknesses he was not a coward. This was a man who had openly challenged the King in the Estates General and suffered internal exile for it, a man who had championed the cause of black slaves to the fury of his fellow aristocrats, and had shown astonishing physical courage in his pioneering ballooning exploit. Moreover his constant, if fruitless, attempts to be given a command of troops or serve at sea shows that he relished the thought of danger, if only as a relief from the constant ennui that plagued him.

Given his long and bitter relationship with Louis XVI and his firm conviction that the King was still intriguing with France's enemies, his assent to the conviction is understandable. Yet when voting for the punishment he could have opted for imprisonment rather than death, nor would he have been alone in showing the King mercy. For of the 721 deputies who had taken part that day, 360 voted for imprisonment, and it would have been perfectly safe and respectable for him to have been among their number. Among them was the deputy for Guérat, Jacques-Marie Rouzet, who ironically later became the lover and companion of Louis Philippe Joseph's widow. Yet Philippe Égalité deliberately chose to be among the 361 who opted for the death penalty, and his, it could truly be said, was the deciding vote. The howls of derision that greeted him as he descended from the tribune received after casting his vote clearly indicated that most of those present had expected him to show mercy to his cousin.

At least the score between the ruling Bourbons and the House of Orléans had now been settled. All his adult life Louis Philippe Joseph had smarted from what he considered the shabby treatment he had received from the ruling branch of the family. The King had treated him with suspicion and jealousy rather than as a kinsman. He had been mocked at court and refused the military commands that he thought he merited and which his eldest son, ironically, had now received from the new republic. The King's innate hostility had only increased with the arrival of Marie Antoinette, who, like her husband, found his relaxed Anglophilia particularly distasteful. Soon she had become his greatest enemy, combining personal dislike with the conviction that he was determined to oust her husband and seize the throne of France for himself. Yet he had repeatedly attempted to bring about a reconciliation between them, the last time as late as November 1792 when he had implored the Comte de Grave to intervene on his behalf. The Comte reported back that the King's actual words were, 'Never mention his name to me again. No reconciliation between him and me will ever be possible.'

Yet the underlying reason why he acted as he did was that he was determined to stick by the principles of the revolution he had wholeheartedly embraced, and he was convinced by Saint-Just's and Robespierre's argument that the King must die so that the republic could live. In voting as he did he hoped to show the world that he was indeed a committed and sincere republican who had sacrificed his social position, his vast wealth and even his personal happiness to the cause of the revolution. Only his affection for his sons and his daughter, now in vulnerable exile in Belgium, might have persuaded him to act otherwise that day. As it was, his fatal vote consigned him to universal obloquy among his contemporaries. Not only did he became a hated figure among the exiled aristocrats, he was soon also a figure of contempt for fellow republicans, who, whatever their political principles, retained a belief that blood was thicker than water.

To the rest of Europe his behaviour seemed incomprehensible. The reaction of his once close friend and fellow libertine, George, Prince of Wales, was typical. When George, at Carlton House in London, was told that Philippe had voted for his cousin's death, he leapt up from his chair, dragged down from the wall the portrait of Philippe that he had commissioned from Joshua Reynolds decades earlier and smashed it to pieces in the fireplace.

22

Death and Dishonour

T HE FIRST VICTIM of royalist revenge was not Philippe
Égalité but the deputy Louis-Michel Lepeletier de
Saint-Fargeau. On the evening of 20 January he went as
usual to the gardens of the Palais-Royal to dine alone at a café
in the Valois arcade. While he was eating two men entered
wearing bulky overcoats. One of them, a man of giant stature,
was clearly enraged and shouted aloud, 'We can't find that
bastard Égalité anywhere.' Saint-Fargeau completed his meal
quietly, but as he was about to pay the bill the giant leapt up
and shouted at him, 'I know your face. You are Deputy Saint-
Fargeau and you voted for the death of the King.' Then
drawing a short sword from beneath his coat he ran Saint-
Fargeau through with it and both men ran off. It was later
revealed that the murderer, an ex-member of the royal bodyguard named Pâris, had once worked at the Palais-Royal and
had almost certainly come there that evening to kill Louis
Philippe Joseph. Saint-Fargeau's death provoked the first of
several state funerals decreed by the Convention, a propaganda exercise designed and executed with great pageantry by
the painter Jacques-Louis David, portraying Saint-Fargeau as
a martyr to the cause of the revolution.

For Louis Philippe Joseph there was to be a more lingering
extinction, as the last of his allies abandoned him to political
and social isolation. Talleyrand, the archetypical survivor himself, remarked caustically, 'After the crime of his vote, he was
nothing, a non-being, a totally debased nonentity.'

Six weeks after the King's execution Grace Elliott invited
her old lover to visit her at Meudon. He appeared wearing a
plain black coat, and when she asked him if he was in
mourning for the King he smiled and replied, 'No, it is for my

father-in-law, the Duc de Penthièvre.' He explained that Penthièvre had never recovered from the atrocious murder of his daughter-in-law, the Princesse de Lamballe, and had shut himself away from the world at his château at Bizy. The conviction and death of the King was the last straw, and having seen the France that he had known swept away he succumbed to his grief on 4 March. Unable to contain her emotions, Grace burst into tears and castigated Égalité for voting for the King's death, provoking him to get up and prepare to leave. As he was climbing into his carriage he turned and gave her a brief explanation of his actions, saying, 'I could not avoid doing what I have done. I am perhaps more to be pitied than you can form an idea of. I am more a slave of faction than anyone in France.' He then pleaded with her to leave France for her own safety, assuring her that he would provide the bribe needed for her to acquire a passport. She felt she had that day seen a different Louis Philippe Joseph from the one she had known for many years. His whole demeanour had changed and he now had the aura of a man hunted by unseen but implacable forces, although strangely he retained his customary air of hauteur, nonchalance and indifference to fate. They were never to meet again; Grace was arrested a few days later and thrown into prison, narrowly escaping the guillotine herself.

On 8 March 1793 Danton mounted the tribune of the Convention and gave an impassioned speech saying that there was not a moment to lose. France was in the gravest danger, but thank God she had such an able soldier as General Dumouriez to defend her. Public safety was under threat from the invaders from without and the traitors within. A revolutionary tribunal with dictatorial powers was the only way to save the state. Only one voice spoke out against him, that of Jean Denis Lanjuinais, who denounced this attempted violation of 'all the principles of the rights of man'. His voice was unheeded and the rest of the Convention, including Philippe Égalité, voted for the establishment of a Committee of Public Safety that, ironically, would be the instrument of death for Égalité, Robespierre and even Danton himself.

One of the first actions undertaken by the new Committee was to send the Minister of War, Beurnonville, and two other commissioners to the war front to investigate conditions in the army and the cause of General Dumouriez' recent defeat at the Battle of Neerwinden. At Madame de Genlis' house at Tournai they met Dumouriez and the young General Égalité. At dinner Dumouriez launched into a violent attack on the Convention and the Jacobins, calling them regicides and tyrants. He mocked their decrees and insulted the revolutionary tribunals. Moreover he threatened that if the situation did not improve he would act himself and with his army march on Paris, close down the Jacobin Club and dissolve the Convention before restoring the constitution of 1791 and putting a king back on the throne. A more fundamental declaration of opposition to the existing regime is hard to imagine. He then arrested the three commissioners and handed them over to the Austrians. Clearly he had been planning to overthrow the Convention or to go over to the enemy himself. Perhaps Dumouriez saw himself as a latter-day General Monk, an honest soldier who would throw out the corrupt and incompetent politicians and restore the monarchy in France as Monk had done a century earlier in England. Detailed plans were later discovered that showed he had indeed intended to divide his troops into three sections. The first would arrest the members of the Convention, the second seize every member of the Jacobin Club and the third would rescue the royal family from the Temple prison. That same day the young Louis XVII would be proclaimed King and the Baron de Breteuil would perform the role of Regent with Dumouriez as Chief Minister.

When news of the commissioners' fate and Dumouriez' threats reached the Convention, ten days of hysterical debate ensued. Many believed that it was not the son of the late King that Dumouriez intended to place on the throne of France but the ex-Duc de Chartres. On 23 March orders for the arrest of Dumouriez, General Égalité and his aide-de-camp, Sillery, were issued together with those for Pamela – already safe in

Ireland with Lord Edward Fitzgerald – Laclos and the other Orléans sons, Montpensier and Beaujolais. At this point Dumouriez had intended to set off for Paris but his attempted coup turned to farce when his exhausted and demoralized troops ignored his orders and refused to march. Realizing that the game was up, Dumouriez mounted his horse and together with General Égalité crossed over to the Austrian lines. One of the young man's last acts was to write a letter to his father explaining his actions. It was intercepted and read out to the Convention a few days later, causing uproar:

> I see the Convention completely ruining France by forgetting all principles. I see civil war kindled. I see innumerable armies descending from all sides on our unhappy country, and I do not see the army to oppose them. Our line regiments are almost destroyed and volunteers desert and fly in all directions. The Convention believes that with troops it can wage war against all Europe. I assure you that they will all be disillusioned. Into what abyss are they hurling France?

The Girondin deputy, Barbaroux, knew exactly where the blame lay and began yet another tirade denouncing the Palais-Royal and all its works, accusing Citizen Égalité, or the Duc d'Orléans as he insisted on calling him, of coveting the Regency, and demanded his arrest. France, he declared, would never be safe while the Orléans were at liberty and able to continue their plotting against the state. Further orders for the arrest of anyone even marginally connected with the conspirators, including uncles, aunts and servants, were issued by the near-panic-stricken Convention. Even the estranged Marie Adélaïde was put under house arrest, as was the elderly Madame de Montesson. Louis Philippe Joseph naturally protested his innocence, declaring that if his eldest son were found guilty he would be among the first to condemn him in the Roman manner.

As the Convention went about its work of issuing the arrest warrants Louis Philippe Joseph was enjoying what was to be his last dinner at the Palais-Royal with a friend, de Moinville. As the fish course was being served Merlin de Douai rushed in and told the host that the Convention were about to destroy him. Philippe appeared shocked, and putting his hand to his head demanded to know what he had done to deserve this. De Moinville, who was carefully squeezing the juice of a lemon over his sole, shook his head sadly and said, 'Frightful business, Monseigneur, but what do you expect? They have taken everything they wanted from you and now that you are no more use to them they will do with you what I am about to do with this lemon,' and with that he threw it into the fireplace. Then, displaying an insouciance that would have appealed to his host, he remarked that sole is best eaten hot, and without another word resumed his meal.

Early on the morning of 7 April officials sent by the Committee of Public Safety arrived at the Palais-Royal to conduct its owner and his youngest son to the Hôtel de Ville for questioning. When shown the warrant ordering the arrest of every remaining member of the Bourbon family, Louis Philippe Joseph angrily protested and insisted on dispatching a note to the Convention pointing out that as a representative of the people he enjoyed immunity from prosecution, at least until a proper case had been made against him. But unknown to him a decree of 1 April had revoked this protection and his claim was rejected by the Committee of Public Safety. He was ordered to be taken immediately with his youngest son, the thirteen-year-old Beaujolais, to the Abbaye prison. Although Robespierre was eager that he be brought before the Committee of Public Safety without delay, the Convention disagreed and decided that together with his son, his sister and his cousin Conti he should be taken to a prison far away in Marseille. It appeared that his very presence posed such a threat to a paranoid regime that they feared, even at this late stage, that an attempt to restore the monarchy with Orléans as King would be made. Of the entire Orléans family only Marie Adélaïde was left in freedom although she was kept under surveillance by the authorities at her late father's château at Bizy in the heart of Normandy.

The journey to Marseille was arduous in the extreme, for the infrastructure of travel in France had all but collapsed. Post-horses were hard to find, food was scarce and the guards sullen and unpleasant. Everyone complained, and Louise Bathilde, Duchesse de Bourbon, soon lost her voice from shouting at the clumsiness of the guards. The weather had deteriorated too, and progress was slow, with the party travelling just a few miles every day. Through each village that they passed crowds of inquisitive peasants and artisans gathered to see the once all-powerful Duc d'Orléans now reduced to being a captive of the state. Should anyone have bothered with a rescue attempt it would have been a simple business. When they reached Vienne the guards and their captives boarded a boat and proceed down the River Rhône as far as Avignon where the trek along dusty roads continued. But as they moved further south the indifference of the spectators changed to outright hostility. At Orgon a large armed and drunken mob attempted to take over the role of guards themselves, and at Aix an even larger crowd surrounded the Hôtel de Ville baying for blood. When they finally reached Marseille on 23 April the vast crowds made it impossible to take the prisoners into the city by daylight and they were smuggled in at night and locked in the fort of Notre Dame de la Garde. It seemed as if Marseille, having missed the execution of the King in Paris, wanted now to compensate by executing one of his closest relatives in their own city.

Égalité and Beaujolais were incarcerated together in a single cell, with only the ailing Louise Bathilde shown any sympathy by being given the more comfortable Governor's room. To their dismay the prisoners found that the second of the Orléans brothers, Montpensier, was already in the Notre Dame, having been arrested a few days earlier. Montpensier later wrote a detailed memoir of their incarceration at Marseille in which he confesses himself astonished by his father's unfailing cheerfulness and unconcern. It appeared that this final resolution of his fate had lifted a burden from his mind. 'At least we are happier than if we had been separated,' he told his sons as they walked together on the ramparts of the fortress.

Dressed in a drab overcoat and wearing the battered riding boots that he retained since they had left Paris, the ex-Duc d'Orléans, with a week's growth of beard, looked more a beggar than a prince. Equally unkempt was the elderly Prince de Conti, dressed like a relic from the past in an old hunting coat from the time of Louis XV and constantly complaining about their fate. 'It is all very well for your brother to follow his sword into exile,' he complained to Montpensier, 'but he has left the rest of us as hostages to fortune.'

For the first few days of their captivity the prisoners were able to communicate with each other, but they were then ordered to be kept apart as the interrogation began. The Prince de Conti and the Duchesse de Bourbon were the first to be taken before the local prosecutor, Giraud. Then on 6 May Louis Philippe Joseph himself appeared and was subjected to an ill-prepared and vague string of accusations by Giraud. Responding with his customary *froideur*, Égalité angrily denied that he had ever had designs on the throne, nor had he plotted with Mirabeau, nor discussed with Lafayette a secret deal to make him Regent. Moreover he had never even met Dumouriez and had no knowledge of his plans to come to Paris and overthrow the Convention. As for his son, General Égalité, he regretted that the young man had been hounded from France by his enemies, but both he and Montpensier, who had been serving France on an entirely different front, were loyal to the new republic. His own record in the Convention was blameless. Had he not sat with the Mountain, whose opinions were indivisible from his own? Any attempt to condemn him for visiting England so frequently was equally foolish for visits there had been for a diplomatic purpose to further the interests of France, and the accusation that he had sent his daughter there in the hope that she would marry the Duke of York was too ridiculous to even answer. Frustrated by this stout defence, Giraud ended the interrogation by asking his prisoner why, if he was blameless, so many people suspected his motives. 'There are no doubts among true patriots,' he replied. When the thirteen-year-old Beaujolais was questioned he put up an equally impressive defence, claiming that he was glad to see the back of the old regime, that his father had always been in the vanguard of the revolution and that he was delighted to bear the title of Citizen rather than that of Prince.

No one present doubted that both Orléans had acquitted themselves well, but a few days later an official version of the hearing was published. This was such a travesty of the truth that Voidel, a deputy who had been present throughout, felt compelled to issue a personal and more objective version of the interrogation. He emphasized that Philippe Égalité had stood up to his accuser and had convincingly refuted the accusations against him. But in Paris few were convinced, preferring to believe that the ex-Duc d'Orléans must be the next victim to be sacrificed beneath the wheels of the juggernaut of the revolution.

On 27 May a large detachment of 1,200 guards arrived at the Notre Dame and announced that they had orders to take Citizen Égalité to a new prison. Calmly he embraced Beaujolais and asked him to embrace Montpensier when he next saw him. He was then escorted to the tower of the neighboring fortress of Saint-Jean and locked in a windowless dungeon. A week later his sons were taken to join him there, and they managed a brief conversation together before being locked in separate cells. After protests from his father, Beaujolais was allowed the privilege of a daily walk under close supervision in the courtyard of the fortress. Although he was outwardly calm and dignified, Louis Philippe Joseph's health was clearly declining and his only pleasure now was the letters from his family and Agnès de Buffon that he was allowed to receive.

For the next five months he endured these miserable conditions until on 15 October Montpensier was allowed to see him and tell him that he was to be taken to Paris to face his accusers in the Convention. Three commissioners had arrived and treated him, to his surprise, with great respect, explaining that he was not being taken to stand trial but merely to explain 'certain matters'. This raised his spirits, particularly when he was shown the list of charges against him, consisting of the now familiar generalities unsubstantiated by any specific detail.

On 2 November, accompanied by his valet Gamache, he was back in Paris and lodged in the Conciergerie prison from where, two weeks earlier, Marie Antoinette had been taken to the guillotine. Also executed that day had been Félicité's husband, the Marquis de Sillery, who had remained faithful to the Orléans cause to the end. That evening Voidel, who had been designated to defend him before the Committee of Public Safety, arrived at the Conciergerie to find his client perfectly calm and relaxed. Together they went over the case, both agreeing that the charges were so insubstantial that an acquittal should be a mere formality. But they had not yet seen Fouquier-Tinville, the public prosecutor, at work, nor had they realized that this would be a show trial with the verdict already determined by the political needs of the Convention. As George Orwell observed in *1984*, it is not enough that enemies of society be destroyed – they must go to their deaths utterly discredited even in their own eyes.

When the hearing began the central tenet of the prosecution's case was that Citizen Égalité had prior knowledge of Dumouriez' intention to overthrow the Convention and restore the monarchy and that he had continued to correspond with his son up to the minute of his desertion, and even since. Yet again the accusation that he had tried to marry his daughter off to an English prince in order to coerce the republic was repeated and again dismissed with the same coolness and nonchalance that he had exhibited in Marseille. But his words had little effect on his judges, and the inevitable verdict of guilty was pronounced on 6 November. He received the sentence of death with his customary sang-froid, requesting only that he not be kept waiting too long. At least this last wish was granted and he was told that he would be guillotined later that same day.

He dined quietly in his cell on eight oysters and lamb cutlets accompanied by a bottle of Bordeaux. At three o'clock in the afternoon one of the judges entered and asked if he had anything more to say to the court; he smiled but said nothing. At five o'clock, with his hair carefully powdered in the manner of the old regime and wearing a green frock coat carefully buttoned, he walked confidently from the prison and climbed into the tumbrel that was to take him to the place of execution. With him were his old aide-de-camp, General Coustard, and three other men. One of them, Monsieur de Laroque, is supposed to have suddenly recognized him and said bitterly, 'I don't mind dying for my country, but I object to sharing the same guillotine as you.' Louis Philippe Joseph merely turned his back on him. At least de Laroque was excused the ignominy of having to lie in Orléans' blood, for he was the first to die. He was then followed by the three others. Louis Philippe Joseph witnessed their deaths without the least sign of emotion. Then he took off his coat, handed it to his valet and advanced to the blood-drenched guillotine. As the executioner indicated that he should take off his boots first, his victim dismissed him with a wave of the hand. 'You can do that later,' he said. 'Come on, let's not waste time. Get on with it.'

BIBLIOGRAPHY

Aldington, Richard, *Choderlos de Laclos*, London: George Routledge, 1934

Allonville, Armand-François, comte d', *Mémoires secrets de 1770 à 1830*, Paris, 1838–41

Almeras, Henri d', *Marie-Antoinette et les pamphlets royalistes et révolutionnaires*, Paris: Librairie Mondiale, 1907

Antoine, Michel, *Louis XV*, Paris: Éditions Fayard, 1989

Antonetti, Guy, *Louis Philippe*, Paris: Éditions Fayard, 1994

Aulard, Alphonse, *Histoire politique de la Révolution française*, Paris: Armand Colin, 1901

Badinter, Élisabeth, *Les Remontrances de Malesherbes 1771–1775*, Paris: Éditions Tallandier, 1978

Baecque, Antoine de, *La Caricature révolutionnaire*, Paris: Solar, 1988

Bailly, Jean-Sylvain, *Mémoires*, Paris, 1804, (4 vols)

Barnave, Pierre Joseph Marie, *Introduction à la Révolution française*, Paris: Armand Colin, 1960

Bertrand de Molleville, A.F., *Mémoires secrets pour servir à l'histoire de la dernière année du règne de Louis XVI*, London, 1797 (3 vols)

Besenval, Pierre Victor, Baron de, *Mémoires du Baron de Besenval*, Ghislain de Diesbach (ed.), Paris: Mercure de France, 1987

Blanc, Olivier, *Les Hommes de Londres: histoire secrète de la Terreur*, Paris: Albin Michel, 1989

Bluche, Frédéric, *Danton*, Paris: Éditions Perrin, 1984

Bredin, Jean-Denis, *Sieyès, la clé de la Révolution française*, Paris: Éditions de Falois, 1988

Brissot, J.-P., *Correspondance et papiers*, Paris, 1912

Britsch, Amédée, *La Jeunesse de Philippe Égalité*, Paris: Éditions Payot, 1926

Broglie, Gabriel de, *Le Général de Valence*, Paris: Éditions Perrin, 1972

Carmontelle, *Le Jardin de Monceau*, Paris, 1779

Caron, P., *Les Massacres de septembre*, Paris: Maison du Livre Français, 1935

— *Paris pendant la Terreur*, Paris: Klincksieck, 1949 (6 vols)

Casanova, Giacomo *Memoirs*, New York: Putnam, 1953

Castelot, André, *Philippe Égalité, le prince rouge*, Paris: Librairie Académique Perrin, 1950

Castillon du Perron, Marguerite, *Louis Philippe et la Révolution française*, Paris: Éditions Grasset et Fasquelle, 1984

Chateaubriand, René, Vicomte de, *Mémoires d'outre-tombe*, Maurice Levaillant and Georges Moulinier (eds), Paris: Livre de Poche, 1949

Chevallier, Jean-Jacques, *Barnave ou les deux faces de la Révolution*, Paris: Éditions Payot, 1936

Dard, Émile, *Le Général Choderlos de Laclos*, Paris: Éditions Perrin, 1936

Darmon, Pierre, *La Longue Traque de la variole*, Paris: Éditions Fayard, 1986

Deffand, Marquise du, *Lettres à Horace Walpole*, Paris: Mercure de France, 1912 (3 vols)

Desmoulins, Camille, *Correspondance inédité*, Paris, 1836

Diesbach, Ghislain de, *Madame de Stael*, Paris: Éditions Perrin, 1983

Dumouriez, Charles-François, *Mémoires du Général Dumouriez, écrits par lui-même*, Paris, 1821

Elliott, Grace, *Journal of My Life During the French Revolution*, London: Rodale Press, 1953

Ellis, Lucy, *La Belle Pamela*, London: Herbert Jenkins, 1924

Faure, Edgar, *La Disgrace de Turgot*, Paris: Éditions Gallimard, 1961

Fayard, Jean-François, *La Justice révolutionnaire*, Paris: Éditions Robert Laffont, 1988

Fleischmann, Hector, *Les Maîtresses de Marie-Antoinette*, Paris: Broché, 1910

Franklin, Benjamin, *The Works of Benjamin Franklin*, Jared Sparks (ed.), Boston, 1840

Garat, Dominique Joseph, *Mémoire sur la Révolution*, Paris: Belin, 1862

Genlis, Felicité du Crest de Saint-Aubin, Comtesse de, *Mémoires sur le XVIII siècle*, Paris, 1825 (10 vols)

Godechot, Jacques, *The Counter-Revolution: Doctrine and Action, 1789–1804*, Princeton: Princeton University Press, 1961

Gottschalk, Louis, *The Letters of Lafayette to Washington, 1777–1790*, Chicago: University of Chicago Press, 1976

Gower, T., *The Despatches of Lord Gower* (June 1790 to August 1792), Cambridge: Cambridge University Press, 1885

Grimm, Friedrich Melchior, Freiherr von, *Correspondance, littéraire, philosophique et critique par Grimm, Diderot, Raynal, Meister, etc.*, Maurice Tourneux (ed.), Paris: Éditions Garnier Frères, 1877–82

Gruyer, François-Anatole, *Les Portraits de Carmontelle*, Paris: Librairie Plon, 1902

— *La Jeunesse de Louis Philippe*, Paris: Librairie Hachette et Cie, 1909

Guédé, Alain, *Monsieur de Saint-George*, New York: Picador, 2003

Guenot, J., *Les Orléans*, Paris: Bloch, 1886

Harmand, Jean, *Madame de Genlis*, London: Bell, 1912

Héron de Villefosse, Réné, *L'Anti-Versailles, ou le Palais-Royal de Philippe Égalité*, Paris: Jean Dullis, 1974

Hibbert, Christopher, *George IV: Prince of Wales*, London: Longman, 1973

Holland, Henry Richard Vassall, Lord, *Souvenirs diplomatiques publiés par son fils*, Paris, 1851

Howarth, T.E.B., *Citizen-King: The Life of Louis Philippe*, London: Eyre and Spottiswoode, 1961

Hyslop, Beatrice, *L'Apanage de Philippe d'Orléans*, Paris: Société d'Études Robespierreistes, 1965

Jordan, David, *The King's Trial: Louis XVI vs. the French Revolution*, Los Angeles: University of California Press, 1979

La Marck, Prince Auguste d'Arenberg, Comte de, *Correspondances et manuscripts*, Paris, 1851

La Marle, Hubert, *Philippe Égalité, Grand maître de la Révolution*, Paris: Nouvelles Éditions Latines, 1989

Labourdette, Jean-François, *Vergennes, ministre de Louis XVI*, Paris: Desjonquères, 1990

Laclos, Choderlos de, *Œuvres complètes*, Maurice Allem (ed.), Paris: Éditions Gallimard, 1959

Lafayette, Gilbert du Motier, Marquis de, *Mémoires*, Paris: Inventaire, 1869

Lauzun, Armand-Louis de Gontaut, Duc de Biron and Duc de, *Mémoires*, G. d'Heylli (ed.), Paris: Edouard Rouveyre, 1880

Lefebvre, Georges, *La Révolution française*, Paris: Presses Universitaires de France, 1963

— *The Great Fear of 1789*, London: Vintage Books, 1973

Lenotre, G., *Les fils de Philippe Égalité pendant la Terreur*, Paris: Éditions Perrin, 1932

Lever, Evelyne, *Louis XVI*, Paris: Éditions Fayard, 1985

— *Louis XVIII*, Paris: Hachette Livre, 1988

— *Marie-Antoinette*, Paris: Éditions Fayard, 1991

— *Philippe Égalité*, Paris: Éditions Fayard, 1996

Ligne, Charles-Joseph-Lamoral, Prince de, *Fragments de l'histoire de ma vie*, Paris: Librairie Plon, 1928

Louis Philippe, King, *Mémoires*, Paris: Librairie Plon, 1973 (2 vols)

Madame Élisabeth, *The Life and Letters of Madame Élisabeth de France*, Katharine Prescott (tr.), Boston: Hardy, Pratt and Co., 1902

Maricourt, André de, *Louise Marie Adélaïde de Bourbon-Penthièvre, Duchesse d'Orléans*, Paris: Émile Paul, 1913 (2 vols)

Marie Antoinette *Correspondance secrète entre Marie-Thèrése et le comte de Mercy-Argenteau*, Paris: Librairie de Firmin Didot Frères, 1874 (3 vols)

Marionneau, Charles, *Victor Louis, architecte du théâtre de Bordeaux*, Bordeaux: G. Gounouilhou, 1881

Marmontel, Jean-François, *Memoires*, Brigit Patmore (tr.), London: Routledge, 1930

Maugras, Gaston, *Le Duc de Lauzun et la cour intime de Louis XVI*, Paris: Plon-Nourrit et Cie, 1924

Montjoie, Christopher Félix Louis, Galart de, *Histoire de la conjuration de Louis Philippe Joseph d'Orléans*, Paris, 1796

Morris, Gouverneur, *Journal pendant les années 1789–1792*, Paris: Librairie Plon, 1901

Moustiers, Pierre, *Un aristocrate à la lanterne*, Paris: Éditions Gallimard, 1986

Necker, Jacques, *Œuvres de Necker*, Paris, 1820–21

Orléans, Louis Philippe Joseph, Duc d', *Correspondance de Louis Philippe Joseph, Duc d'Orléans, avec Louis XVI, la reine, Montmorin, Liancourt, Biron, etc.*, Paris, 1800

Piton, Camille, *Paris sous Louis XV (rapports des inspecteurs de police au roi)*, Paris: Mercure de France, 1890

Poisson, Georges, *Choderlos de Laclos ou l'obstination*, Paris: Éditions Grasset, 1985

Roland, Madame (Marie-Jeanne Phlipon), *Mémoires de Madame Roland*, Paris: Librairie de la Bibliothèque Nationale, 1863

Ruault, Nicolas, *Gazette d'un Parisien sous la Révolution: lettres à son frère, 1783–1796*, Paris: France Loisirs, 1975

Rude, Georges, *The Crowd in the French Revolution*, Oxford: Oxford University Press, 1959

Saint-Priest, Guillaume Emmanuel Guignard, Comte de, *Mémoires*, Paris: Mercure de France, 1929

Schama, Simon, *Citizens*, London: Penguin Books, 1989

Scudders, Evarts Seelye, *Prince of the Blood*, London: Collins, 1937

Soboul, Albert, *La Révolution française*, Paris: Éditions Gallimard, 1964 (2 vol)

Solnon, Jean-François, *La Cour de France*, Paris: Livre de Poche, 1987

Stael, Mme de, *Considérations sur les principaux événements de la Révolution française*, Paris, 1843

Sydenham, M.J., *The Girondins*, London: Athlone Press, 1961

Taillemite, Étienne, *Lafayette*, Paris: Éditions Fayard, 1989

Talleyrand-Périgord, Charles-Maurice, Duc de, *Mémoires*, Paris: Calmann-Lévy, 1891–2

Taylor, W. Cooke, *Memoirs of the House of Orléans*, London: Richard Bentley, 1849

Thomas, Chantal, *La Reine scélérate: Marie-Antoinette dans les pamphlets*, Paris: Seuil, 1989

Tilly, Alexandre, Comte de, *Mémoires*, Paris: Mercure de France, 1929 (2 vols)

Tour du Pin, Henriette Lucy Dillon, Marquise de la, *Memoirs of Madame de la Tour du Pin*, New York: Brentano's, 1985

Tronchin, H., *Un Médecin du XVIII siècle, Théodore Tronchin*, Paris: Plon-Nourrit et Cie, 1906

Verlet, Pierre, *Le Château de Versailles*, Paris: Éditions Fayard, 1985

Vinot, Bernard, *Saint-Just*, Paris: Éditions Fayard, 1985

Wallon, H., *Histoire du Tribunal révolutionnaire*, Paris: Librairie Hachette et Cie, 1880

Walpole, Horace, *Letters of Horace Walpole*, New York: Harper and Brothers, 1926

Walzer, Michael, *Régicide et révolution, le procés de Louis XVI*, Paris: Éditions Payot, 1989

Ward, Marion, *Forth*, Chichester: Phillimore and Co., 1982

Webster, Nesta, *The French Revolution*, London: Constable and Co., 1921

Welch, Oliver, *Mirabeau*, London: Jonathan Cape, 1951

Winock, Michel, *1789, l'année sans pareille*, Paris: Hachette Livres, 1988

Young, Arthur, *Travels in France During 1787, 1788 and 1789*, London: J.M. Dent, 1926

Index

Adhémar, Louis, Comte d', 94

Alembert, Jean le Rond d', 55

Allaire, Abbé, 26

Angoulême, Louis Antoine de
    Bourbon, Duc de, 133, 143

Argenson, René de Voyer de,
    22, 46

Arlandes, François Laurent,
    Marquis d', 97

Artois, Charles Philippe,
    Comte d', 33, 66, 72, 87, 96,
    100, 101, 114, 115, 123, 133,
    143, 146, 157, 158, 201

Bailly, Jean Sylvain, 61, 146,
    154, 156, 191, 196, 197

Barère de Vieuzac, Bertrand,
    109

Barthès, Joseph, 112

Baudeau, Abbé, 101

Beauharnais, Alexandre
    François Marie, Vicomte de,
    142

Beauvau, Charles Juste de,
    Maréchal de, 125

Berry, Charles de France, Duc
    de, 33

Besenval, Pierre Victor, 145

Billaud-Varenne, Jacques
    Nicholas, 209

Biron, Duc de, formerly
    Armand Louis, Duc de

Lauzun, 36, 58, 69, 108, 115,
    151, 167, 169, 176, 189, 202,
    218, 228, 230

Blot, Gilbert de Chauvigny, 114

Boissy, Louis de, 22

Bombelles, Marc Marie,
    Marquis de, 132

Bonaparte, Napoleon, 104, 128

Bonnard, Chevalier de, 80

Boucher d'Argis, 184

Bourbon, Louis Henri Joseph,
    Duc de, see Prince de Condé

Bourgogne, Louis Joseph
    Xavier de France, Duc de,
    33

Breteuil, Elisabeth Theodore le
    Tonnellier, Abbé de, 40, 41

Breteuil, Louis Auguste le
    Tonnellier, Baron de, 120,
    121, 149, 154, 237

Brienne, Étienne Charles de
    Loménie de, 116, 118, 121,
    122, 135

Brissault, Madame, 47

Brissault, Monsieur, 37

Brissot, Jacques Pierre, 109,
    112, 113, 117, 126, 209, 215

Britsch, Amédée, 17

Broglie, Victor François, Duc
    de, Maréchal de France, 147

Brunswick, Charles Guillaume
    Ferdinand, Duc de, 209

Buffon, Georges Louis Leclerc,
Comte de, 10, 225, 267–9
Buffon, Marie Marguerite de
Cepoy, Comtesse de, 107,
109, 121, 174, 175, 180, 202,
205, 206, 242
Buzot, François Nicolas, 220, 224

Calonne, Charles Alexandre de,
115, 116, 173, 174
Canillac, Mademoiselle de
Roncherolles, Madame de,
71, 72
Capello, Antonio, 149
Carlyle, Thomas, 11
Carmontelle, Louis Carrogis,
known as, 31–2
Carra, Jean Louis, 208
Carrache, Ludovico, 87
Casanova, Giacomo, 20
Castellane, Madame de, 142
Chabroud, Jean Baptiste, 184,
185
Chalmazel, Louis de Talaru,
Marquis de, 19
Chamfort, Sébastien Nicolas,
138
Chartres, Duc de, *see* Orléans
Chartres, Duchesse de, *see*
Orléans
Chastellux, Madame de, 160,
186
Chastenay, Victorine de, 84
Chesterfield, Lord, 37
Chevallier, Pierre, 284
Choiseul, Étienne François,
Duc de, 32, 41

Cholmondeley, Lord, 108
Christian VII, King of
Denmark, 39
Clarke, Henri, 112, 163, 171
Clarkson, Thomas, 113
Clermont-Tonnerre, Stanislas,
Comte de, 55, 161
Coigny, Louise Marthe de
Conflans, Marquise de, 142,
167
Collé, Charles, 44
Condé, Louis Joseph de
Bourbon, Prince de, 20, 49,
51, 56, 72, 156
Condorcet, Jean Antoine
Nicolas de Caritat, Marquis
de, 55
Conflans, Louis Gabriel,
Marquis de, 91
Conti, Louis Armand, Prince de,
111, 241
Conti, Louis François Joseph
de Bourbon, Comte de La
Marche, *later* Prince de, 44,
51, 52
Coustard, Guy, General, 244
Crillon, François Félix
Dorothée, Comte de, 141
Cumberland, William
Augustus, Duke of, 97

Dampierre, Chevalier de, 22
Danton, Georges Jacques, 161,
194, 196, 205, 214, 217, 236
David, Jacques Louis, 142, 235
Desmoulins, Camille, 8, 58,
109, 150, 162, 223

Devonshire, Georgiana,
    Duchess of, 94
Diderot, Denis, 46, 47
Dorset, John Frederick
    Sackville, Duke of, 126, 138
Dreux-Brézé, Henri Évrard,
    Marquis de, 140, 146
Dubuisson, 102
Ducrest, Charles Louis,
    Marquis de, 78, 91, 111, 118,
    121–2, 135
Ducrest, Pierre Cesar, Marquis
    de Saint-Aubin, 59
Dumouriez, Charles François,
    201, 202, 203, 229, 236, 237,
    243
Duport, Adrien Jean, 126
Duportail, Antoine, 189
Durfort, Emmanuel Félicité,
    Chevalier de, 36, 81
Duthé, Rosalie, 35–6, 95

Elliott, Grace Dalrymple, 10,
    108, 150, 154–5, 193, 207,
    208, 228–9, 230, 235–6

Ferrières de Marçay, Charles
    Élie, Marquis de, 142, 154,
    185
Fersen, Hans Axel, Comte de,
    191, 192
Fitzgerald, Lord Edward, 89,
    219, 238
Fitzjames, Jacques Charles,
    Duc de, 37, 47, 69, 91, 98
Foncemagne, Étienne
    Laureault de, 25–6,

Forth, Nathaniel Parker, 88–90,
    102, 172, 173, 200
Foulon, Joseph François, 155
Fouquier-Tinville, Antoine
    Quentin Fouquier, 243
Fox, Charles James, 94
Franklin, Benjamin, 55, 132
Fréteau de Saint-Just,
    Emmanuel, 118, 120, 121,
    122
Fronsart, Louis Antoine, Duc
    de, 36

Gainsborough, Thomas, 108
Gaultier de Biauzat, François,
    132, 159
Genlis, Charles Alexis Brulard
    Comte de, *later* Marquis de
    Sillery, 59, 75, 109, 158, 183,
    197, 243
Genlis, Félicité Ducrest de
    Saint Aubin, Comtesse de,
    9, 25, 48, 58–60, 82–5, 88–9,
    124, 129, 133, 159, 179, 181,
    186, 194–5, 200, 219, 220
George III, King of England,
    92, 169, 172, 176
George, Prince of Wales, *later*
    King George IV of England,
    10, 69, 92, 93, 108, 109, 173,
    176, 233
Giraud, Joseph, 241, 242
Gourdan, Alexandrine
    Ernestine, Madame, 47
Gower, Francis Leveson, Lord,
    207
Grave, Comte de, 232

Hastings, Warren, 174
Haussman, Georges Eugène, Baron, 92

Jousserand, 102

Keppel, Admiral, 73, 74
Kerpatry, Doctor, 28

La Chanterie, 23
La Luzerne, Anne César, Marquis de, 177
La Marck, Auguste Marie Raymond, Prince d'Arenberg, Comte de, 177
La Motte, Jeanne de, 110, 113
La Tour du Pin, Comte de, 36, 48
Laclos, Pierre Ambroise François Choderlos de, 8, 58, 128–9, 130, 131, 138, 171, 181, 190, 193, 195–6
Lacoste, Jean de, 202
Lafayette, Marie Joseph Paul Yves Gilbert Motier, Marquis de, 125, 126, 141, 154, 156, 163, 167, 168, 176, 182, 184
Lamballe, Marie Thérèse de Savoie-Carignan, Princesse de, 40, 66, 75, 77, 121, 188, 204, 206
Lamballe, Louis Alexandre de Bourbon, Prince de, 40
Lambesc, Charles Eugène de Lorraine, Prince de, 150
Lameth, Alexandre Théodore Victor de, 183

Lamoignon, Chrétien François, 119
Lanjuinais, Jean Denis, 236
Launay, Bernard René Jordan, Marquis de, 153–4
Lauzun, Armand Louis, Duc de, see Duc de Biron, 36, 58, 69, 108, 115
Le Peletier de Saint-Fargeau, Michel, 213
Leeds, Francis Osborn, Duke of, 175
Lefebvre, Georges, 157
Limon, Jérôme Geoffroi de, 112, 121
Louis XIII, 80
Louis XIV, 17, 19, 20, 23, 70, 80
Louis XV, 17, 20, 21, 23, 25, 32, 33, 41, 42, 43, 51, 52, 67
Louis XVI, 7, 10, 67–8, 72, 76, 104, 116, 119–20, 121, 123, 140, 146, 148, 155, 161, 164, 167, 168, 179, 192, 199, 204, 216, 225–6, 230
Louis, Victor, 79
Louvet, Jean Baptiste, 221
Luckner, Nicolas, Baron de, 202
Luynes, Charles Albert, Duc de, 21, 82
Luynes, Elisabeth de, Duchesse de, 142

Malesherbes, Chrétien Guillaume de Lamoignon de, 50, 51, 68
Malouet, Pierre Victor, 159
Manuel, Louis Pierre, 210

Marais, Louis, 36, 37, 40, 50
Marat, Jean Paul, 161, 162, 181,
  194, 205, 215, 224, 225, 227
Marie Antoinette, Archduchess
  of Austria, Dauphine, *later*
  Queen of France, 10, 49, 50,
  66, 72, 77, 100, 103, 104,
  109–10, 114, 120, 140, 157,
  162, 163–4, 182, 192, 243
Marmontel, Jean François, 139
Marquise, Étiennette Marie
  Perrine, *known as*, 30, 38
Maupeou, René Charles de, 51,
  56, 67, 72
Maurepas, Jean Frédéric
  Phélypeaux, Comte de, 67,
  75, 76
Melfort, Louis Hector
  Drummond, Comte de, 23,
  24,
Mercy-Argenteau, Florimond
  Claude, Comte de, 53, 203
Merlin de Douai, Philippe
  Antoine Merlin, *known as*,
  227, 239
Merlin de Thionville, Antoine
  Christophe Merlin, *known
  as*, 221
Mignard, Pierre, 17
Mirabeau, Honoré Gabriel
  Riqueti, Comte de, 112, 126,
  142, 146, 149, 152, 155, 158,
  160, 182, 184
Mirepoix, François Gaston de,
  Marquis de, 158
Miromesnil, Armand Thomas
  Hue de, 68

Moinville, Baron de, 239
Moleville, Bertrand de, 164,
  199, 203
Montagu, Lady Mary Wortley,
  28
Montaut-Vavailles, Josephine
  Louise de, 84
Montbarrey, Alexandre Leonor
  Marie de Saint-Maurice,
  Comte, *later* Prince de, 25, 76
Montesquieu, Charles Louis, 55
Montesson, Charlotte de la
  Haie de Riou, Marquise de,
  39, 47, 58, 60, 78, 103, 104,
  113, 121, 238
Montgolfier, Joseph and
  Étienne de, 58
Montjoie, Christophe Felix
  Louis Ventre de la
  Touloubre, 56–7, 98, 132,
  135, 138
Montmorin, Armand Marc, 145,
  149, 160, 173, 176, 178
Morris, Gouverneur, 141
Mounier, Jean Joseph, 182
Moustiers, Comte de, 92

Necker, Jacques, 125, 127, 141,
  145, 149, 160

Orléans, Adélaïde Louise,
  Mademoiselle de Chartres,
  later Mademoiselle
  d'Orléans, *later* Madame
  Adélaïde (daughter of
  Philippe Égalité,
  1775–1847), 133

Orléans, Louis Antoine
    Philippe d', Duc de
    Montpensier (son of
    Philippe Égalité,
    1775–1807), 123, 132, 186,
    187, 201, 227, 229, 240–41,
    242
Orléans, Louis Charles d',
    Comte de Beaujolais (son of
    Philippe Égalité,
    1779–1808), 123, 186, 240,
    242
Orléans, Louis Philippe Joseph
    d', Duc de Montpensier,
    later Duc de Chartres,
    known as Philippe Égalité
    (1747–1793)
    birth, 7, 21
    childhood, 24
    education, 25–7, 31
    smallpox vaccination, 27–9
    early affairs, 35–40, 107
    marriage, 41–4
    finances, 42, 78, 95, 101, 111
    and Palais Royal, 46–7, 4,
        78–80, 101–2
    relations with Versailles,
        51, 52, 163, 165, 166, 232
    Freemasonry, 53, 55, 131
    relations with Madame de
        Genlis, 60–62, 82, 117,
        129, 179, 219, 220
    naval career, 65–6, 68,
        70–71, 72–6, 199
    balloonist, 90–100
    love of and visits to
        England, 87, 88–9, 172
    opposition to King, 10,
        117–21, 120, 125, 147,
        158
    relationship with Madame
        de Buffon, 108, 109, 121
    charity to the people,
        131–2
    quarrels with Marie
        Antoinette, 14, 232
    relationship with Grace
        Dalrymple Elliot, 150–51,
        155, 192, 229–30, 235–6
    trial and death, 241–4
Orléans, Louis Philippe, Duc
    de Chartres, then Duc d'
    (father of Philippe Égalité,
    1725–1785), 18, 22, 30, 33,
    38–9, 47, 79
Orléans, Louis Philippe, Duc de
    Valois, Duc de Chartres,
    later Duc d', later Louis
    Philippe I, King of the
    French (eldest son of
    Philippe Égalité, 1773–1850),
    7, 62, 84, 124, 132, 166, 170,
    201, 213–15, 218
Orléans, Louis, Duc de
    Chartres, later Duc d'
    (grandfather of Philippe
    Égalité, 1703–1752), 18
Orléans, Louise Henriette de
    Bourbon-Conti, Duchesse
    de Chartres (mother of
    Philippe Égalité), 20, 23
Orléans, Louise Marie Adélaïde
    de Bourbon Penthièvre,
    Duchesse de Chartres, later

Duchesse d' (wife of
Philippe Égalité, 1755–1821),
20, 23, 40–44, 48–9, 60, 69,
100, 109, 137, 179, 238
Orléans, Mademoiselle d'
(daughter of Philippe
Égalité, 1777–1782), 23, 29,
30–31, 39
Orléans, Philippe de France,
Duc de Chartres, *later* Duc
d', The Regent, 17
Orléans, Philippe de France
(brother of Louis XIV), Duc
d', 'sMonsieur', 4, 17
Orvilliers, Louis Jacques
Honoré Guillouet, Comte
d', 66, 73–4
Orwell, George, 243

Pamela (Samuel Richardson),
88–9, 187
Paulmy, Marquis d', 22, 46
Pelletier, Jean Gabriel, 165
Penthièvre, Louis Jean Marie
de Bourbon, Duc de, 40, 44,
65–6, 78, 122, 236
Penthièvre, Louise Marie
Adélaïde de Bourbon (wife
of Philippe Égalité),
Duchesse de Chartres, *later*
Duchesse d'Orléans, *see*
Duchesse d'Orléans
Pétion, Jérome, 109, 114, 217,
218, 231
Pilâtre de Rozier, Jean
François, 97, 216, 217, 225,
226

Pitt, William, 93, 175
Polignac, Yolande Martine
Gabrielle de Polastron,
Comtesse, *later* Duchesse
de, 48, 75, 78, 143
Pompadour, Jeanne Antoinette
Poisson, Marquise de, 21,
22, 32, 67
Pons Saint-Maurice, Charles
Philippe, Comte de, 25–7,
31, 42, 50, 168
Provence, Louis Stanislas
Xavier de France, Comte de,
33, 42, 96, 126, 158, 191

Réveillon, Jean Baptiste, 135–8
Reynolds, Sir Joshua, 232, 233
Richardson, Samuel, 202
Richelieu, Amand du Plessis,
Cardinal de, 45
Richelieu, Louis François
Armand du Plessis, Duc de,
Maréchal de France, 36, 80
Robert brothers, Jacques
Charles and Marie Noël, 98–9
Robespierre, Maximilien Marie
Isidore de, 9, 183, 209, 224,
225, 233
Rochambeau, Mademoiselle
Begon, Marquise de, 48
Rochechouart, Aimery Louis
Roger, Comte de, 36
Rohan, Louis René Édouard,
Cardinal, Prince de, 110–11
Rousseau, Jean Jacques, 8, 83,
132
Ruault, Nicolas, 193

Sabathier de Cabre, Abbé, 118, 120, 121
Saint-Fargeau, Louis Michel, Marquis de, 213, 235
Saint-Georges, Joseph Boulogne, Chevalier de, 9, 113
Saint-Just, Louis Antoine, 223, 224, 226, 233
Sand, George, 26
Sartine, Antoine Raymond Jean Gabriel de, 71, 73
Schomberg, Henri de, Comte de, 48, 81
Séchelles, Marie Jean Hérault de, 61
Seguin, M, 78
Segur, Philippe Henri, Marquis de, 129, 181
Sercey, Henriette de, 84
Sèze, Romain de, 227
Shée, Henri, 112, 163
Sieyès, Emmanuel Joseph, 127, 130, 131, 142
Sillery, see Genlis
Stael, Germaine Necker, Baronne de, 83
Stanislaus Leszcynski, King of Poland, 39

Tallard, Marie Isabelle de Rohan, Duchesse de, 21
Talleyrand, Charles Maurice de Talleyrand Perigord, Prince de, 59, 112, 116, 174, 181
Tessé, Françoise Gabrielle de, Comtesse de, 142

Thiard, Henri Charles de Bissy, Comte de, 81
Thouret, Jacques Guillaume, 183
Treilhard, Jean Baptiste, 227, 231
Tronchin, Théodore, 28-9, 81
Turgot, Anne Robert Jacques, 68

van der Noot, Henri 175
Vauban, Sébastien le Prestre, Maréchal de, 129
Voltaire, François-Marie Arouet, known as, 8, 55, 58, 72

Wharton, Philip, Duke of, 55

Young, Arthur, 148